GETTING STARTED IN BACKYARD FLYING

From the publishers of

PRINTED IN THE USA

 ISBN: 0-911295-55-0

Published by Air Age Inc., 100 East Ridge, Ridgefield, CT 06877-4606 USA
(203) 431-9000; fax (203) 431-3000; www.airage.com.

www.backyardflyer.com

ON THE COVER: The WattAge Cub 180 (27.3-inch span) is an example of the new generation of ready-to-fly park and backyard flyers.

ABOUT THE AUTHOR

Bob Aberle is a retired aerospace engineering manager who has been involved in the model aviation hobby since 1951. He began his interest in model planes with free-flight models. Bob transitioned into RC during his high school years. After school, he began a 30-year professional career with the Grumman Corporation at Bethpage, Long Island, NY, from which he retired in 1994.

While employed in the aerospace industry, Bob began writing for various hobby publications. He worked for *Flying Models* magazine for almost 25 years, first as contributing editor and later as technical editor. Recently, Bob has been associated with Air Age Publishing and is currently a contributing editor for *Model Airplane News* and *Backyard Flyer*, and editor-at-large for *RC MicroFlight*.

In the early '80s, Bob chaired the prestigious AMA RC Frequency Committee as it successfully negotiated with the FCC to obtain 80 new RC channels for model aircraft and surface vehicle use. These are the same channels as we all enjoy using today. For his efforts, Bob has earned numerous awards, including the Howard McEntee Memorial Award (1982), AMA Fellow (1983), Vintage RC Society Hall of Fame (1993) and, the most cherished, the AMA Hall of Fame (1998).

Bob flew his first electric-powered model in 1979. As the years progressed, he began to favor electric flight over fueled models, and today he flies electric-powered models exclusively. As a regular competitor at the annual AMA Electric Nationals (E-Nats) in Muncie, IN, Bob finally managed a first-, a second- and two third-place awards in 1996. As he points out, it took him almost 50 years of modeling to accomplish that feat, but the fun made it all worthwhile.

ACKNOWLEDGMENTS

A book is always the product of many people. This book is no exception, and so it is my pleasure to thank the many people who made this final product possible. First on my list, and so important to me, is my "bride" of 39 years, Irene, who painstakingly went through the complete draft of the text several times to do a truly professional editing job. That effort made it easier for everyone who joined in later in the process.

The Air Age staff, with particular thanks to Tom Atwood, Debra Sharp, Corey Smith and Caroline LaFleur, did a fantastic job of editing and coordinating all the photos, the diagrams and everything necessary to assemble the finished product. My thanks also to Gerry Yarrish, Rick Bell, Matt Boyd and Jaime Lagor for their contributions.

I was also lucky to have a group of close friends who were willing to share their technical knowledge of micro flight with me. First and foremost, a big thanks to my close friend and flying partner for many years, Tom Hunt. This book would not have happened without Tom's patient inputs and encouragement. Many others answered my questions and concerns so that the final product would be as technically accurate as possible. Those friends include John Worth, Bob Wilder, Dave Robelen, Dick Miller, Carl Martin, Don Srull, Phil Smith, George Steiner and Jack Albrecht. My thanks to all of these folks, and more, for all of their help.

Last, but certainly not least, is the guy who "launched" me into a model aviation writing career more than 30 years ago: fellow AMA Hall of Famer Nick Ziroli Sr. My sincere thanks to you, Nick, for your friendship, patience and guidance over all these years.

CONTENTS

INTRODUCTION

The terms "micro flight," "indoor RC," "parking lot," "backyard," "slow flyers" and "schoolyard flyers" all pertain to a new and rapidly growing portion of the radio controlled (RC) model aircraft hobby. They represent a portion of model aviation that includes some of the smallest models intended for very close-in flying, in places such as indoor facilities, parking lots and schoolyards.

Most regular RC flying is done at large remote sites requiring some travel time, while micro flying can literally be done in your own backyard. The fact is, indoor RC flying in facilities such as school gymnasiums, field houses, sports arenas and the like can provide considerable fun during the winter months, when many hobbyists are forced to be content with just model building.

In addition to being flown indoors, these same small model airplanes can be flown in parking lots, making it possible for young modelers to fly locally without the need for a long family trip to a regional flying field. The key element here is local flying, close to home.

Curiously, over the years, quite a few small model designs have been featured in various hobby magazines. Most of these models required special homebuilt RC equipment, and it took considerable skill and patience to obtain marginal results. So why micro RC at this time? Recent advances in RC equipment design and manufacturing have produced miniature RC systems and components that have become quite reliable and, best of all, comparatively inexpensive. Along with the development of micro RC equipment, we have also seen the rise in miniature power systems. The most important new items are small lightweight electric motors, as well as lightweight battery packs, which are easily rechargeable.

The terms "micro flyer" (micro indoor RC flyer) and "parking lot flyer" are broad descriptions of new RC categories. Since this book will specialize in both areas, I felt it was important to define basic categories for these small RC model aircraft. I have provided a list of micro flyer definitions that cover five separate categories. These categories are merely supplied as a guideline. It is important to note that the smallest models are intended for indoor-only flying. These models, if flown outdoors, could be destroyed by excessive winds. When you get to the sub-micro category, you might consider flying outdoors in early morning or evening, during very calm weather. Parking-lot and Speed 400 models should be considered for outdoor flying only, based on

ULTRA MICRO

- Total model weight, from the smallest up to 2 ounces.
- Intended for indoor flying only!

For use with the smallest RC system components, magnetic actuators, possibly super regen micro receivers, and infrared (IR) control systems; might include CO_2 and rubber power, in addition to electric motor.

One of the best examples of an ultra-micro category model (less than 2 ounces) is Don Srull's Blu-Bug. It weighs 1.23 ounces and includes a 3-channel RC system, KP00 electric motor geared 2.75:1 and a Union 3.15-inch diameter prop running on three 120mAh NiMH battery cells. This little plane uses a Sky Hooks & Rigging receiver, a Dynamic Unlimited pulse decoder and ESC, as well as two Fritz Mueller BIRD magnetic actuators that provide full proportional control of the rudder and elevator.

This ultra-micro model, kitted by IMA of Belgium, was flown at the May 2001 Southwestern Aeromodeling Conference (SWAC) in Arlington, TX. The pilot was Bob Selman of Carthage, MO. This 3-channel model (rudder, elevator and motor control) weighs just 1.41 ounces (44 grams) ready to fly. It is powered by a Kenway KR-1 4.2:1 geared motor and uses a Kenway 120mm (4.7-inch) prop running on only three 120mAh NiMH batteries. Its radio system is the MicroMag, by Rick Ruijsink of the Netherlands. This system is carried by Bob Selman and David Lewis in the U.S. It operates on 27MHz FM frequency. As we went to press, FMA Direct was planning to manufacture a 72MHz version under license in the U.S.

SUB MICRO

- Total model weight, 2 to 3 ounces
- Intended for indoor and/or absolutely calm weather outdoor flying!

For use with the smallest proportional-control servos, like the WES-Technik linear output variety.

Dave Robelen of Farmville, VA, a retired NASA Langley engineer, has been designing and building tiny "several-ounce" models for the last 30 years. With modern, lightweight RC equipment and motors, Dave produces one innovative design after another. Here he holds two sub-micro (2- to 3-ounce) models. The semi-scale P-51 (left) weighs just 2.32 ounces, ready to fly. On the right is Dave's 2.64-ounce Pepper, a low-wing sport design. Both planes use WES-Technik L-24 linear servos and the DC 5-2.4 motor with 4.2:1 gearing.

DJ Aerotech (Don Stackhouse and Joe Hahn) offer the Roadkill Series of 3-channel profile models. These resemble WW II aircraft and are made entirely of laser-cut balsa sheet, with a few plywood parts. All of these models are provided with an N-20 electric motor, 4.2:1 gear drive and a Gunther 5x4 prop. The twin motor P-38 weighs 4.5 ounces. The single motor models, BF-109, F4U Corsair, P-51 Mustang, Spitfire and Zero all weigh between 2.8 and 3.0 ounces ready to fly. The recommended battery pack is a 6 to 7 cell 120mAh NiMH. Motor current is 900mA maximum, providing 8- to 10-minute flight times.

MICRO

- Total model weight, 3 to 8 ounces.
- Intended for indoor and relatively calm weather outdoor flying!

For use with more conventional micro RC equipment, with selective and sensitive RC receivers and more standard, but still miniature, proportional-control servos.

Tom Herr's Starlite weighs 3.5 ounces ready to fly. This model was featured as a construction article with a free downloadable plan on page 12 of the November 1999 issue of RC MicroFlight.

While still in the micro category, the WattAge Lite Stik (also marketed as the GWS Pico Stick) almost qualifies for the parking lot category (8 to 14 ounces)—depending on the final weight. The Lite Stik comes almost ready to fly and weighs between 6 and 10 ounces, depending on the equipment and batteries used. It can be assembled in a couple of hours. The kit has been selling for as little as $30, and that includes the GWS-IPS 5.87:1 geared motor and a 10x4.7 GWS prop.

PARKING-LOT/ SLOW FLYERS

- Total model weight, 8 to 14 ounces.
- Intended for outdoor flying only, but still requiring light winds!

For use with more conventional size and weight RC system components and power systems; includes a large number of available almost-ready-to-fly (ARF) and ready-to-fly (RTF) model aircraft. Generally, these models will employ motors typical of 280/300 motor power levels.

More on the upper end of the parking-lot category is this nearly 14-ounce Hobby Lobby Miss Bohemia. The construction and flying of this model will be discussed further in Chapter 12 (Putting it all Together). This model is powered by a geared RE-280 motor running on a 7-cell, 270mAh NiMH battery.

Noted giant-scale designer, Nick Ziroli, Sr., with his Aeronca Champion 7AC semi-scale electric model. Total weight is 11 ounces, so it fits in the parking lot category of 8 to 14 ounces. It has a 170-square-inch wing and wing loading of 9 ounces per square foot. An RE-280 geared 3:1 (Titanic Airlines motor) running on a 7-cell, 270mAh Ni-Cd battery powers the plane. This design was featured as a construction article on page 74 of the November 2000 Model Airplane News. A full-size plan is available from Model Airplane News, along with a molded cowl and windshield provided by Nick.

SPEED 400

- Total model weight, 14 ounces and up.
- Intended strictly for outdoor flying, no exceptions!

For use with regular RC systems, Speed 400 typical motors and models that are capable of flying as fast as fuel-powered types.

The WattAge Impress from Global Hobby Distributors represents a typical Speed 400 (geared) powered model. It weighs 26 ounces, has a wing area of 310 square inches and a wing loading of 12 ounces per square foot. This model is flown on an 8-cell, 800mAh NiMH battery. It can be flown "full house" with aileron, elevator, rudder and throttle control.

On the upper end, at 29 ounces total weight, the Hobby Lobby Miss-2 has 390 square inches of wing area and a wing loading of 10.8 ounces per square foot. The geared Speed 400 motor is powered by an 8-cell, 1100mAh NiMH battery.

common sense safety considerations. These models are heavier and are capable of flying at very fast speeds.

At this writing, a "gentlemen's agreement" among micro fliers has established 8 ounces as the maximum recommended weight for indoor models. This may change over time, and it may be necessary to add a wing-loading requirement (i.e. weight in ounces per square foot carried by the wing) as well. Why? Because a model with very small wing area but a high wing loading, and still within 8 ounces, could perform like a rocket indoors, making it dangerous.

Several basic assumptions are incorporated in this book. To make it truly of value for everyone, I have tried to address the beginner with an interest in micro flying. This could be a person with no previous model airplane experience, or it could be a modeler with some glow- or even gas-powered-model experience who wishes to pursue micro flight. I also hope to address the needs of more experienced micro fliers, as well. I may jump around somewhat throughout this book, but please be a little patient because my goal is to get as many people as possible involved in this wonderful new world of small RC model aircraft.

Also note that I did not supply address, phone number, or website information for manufacturers and suppliers on a chapter-by-chapter basis. This reference information is supplied at the end of the book in the Source Guide.

1

Overview

Successful piloting of small RC airplanes is based on familiarity with several components—the airframe, power system and radio control (RC) system. This overview briefly identifies the several elements that will be explained in depth in following chapters.

Several elements of micro radio control (RC) model aircraft flying must be learned before taking that first flight. You will, of course, need the model airplane itself. You will also need a power system or conveyance to get the plane into the air. Equally important, you will need an RC system to guide your aircraft in flight. Chapter by chapter, I will detail all of these elements and lead you up to that first flight.

ELECTRIC POWER

At this time, the best way to sustain the flight of small indoor or larger parking-lot model aircraft is to use a small electric motor of appropriate size. These miniature motors can be purchased for use in model aircraft of no more than an ounce or so (total flying weight) on up. They can be operated by small rechargeable battery packs, which can provide minutes, or in some cases, hours of flying time, and there is no messy fuel residue to contend with. Probably the best feature of electric motors is the fact that they make virtually no noise. The best way to describe electric power is to say that it is both "clean and quiet." Throughout this book, the primary source of power primarily discussed will be electric, as it is presently the most advanced.

How about a six-motor scale electric project weighing only 12.7 ounces? This B-36 was constructed by Gary Jones and flown at the Southwestern Aeromodeling Conference (SWAC) in Arlington, TX, in May 2001. It is powered by six WattAge B-2 motors (Mabuchi N-20 direct) with U-80 props running on 6, 350mAh Ni-Cd batteries.

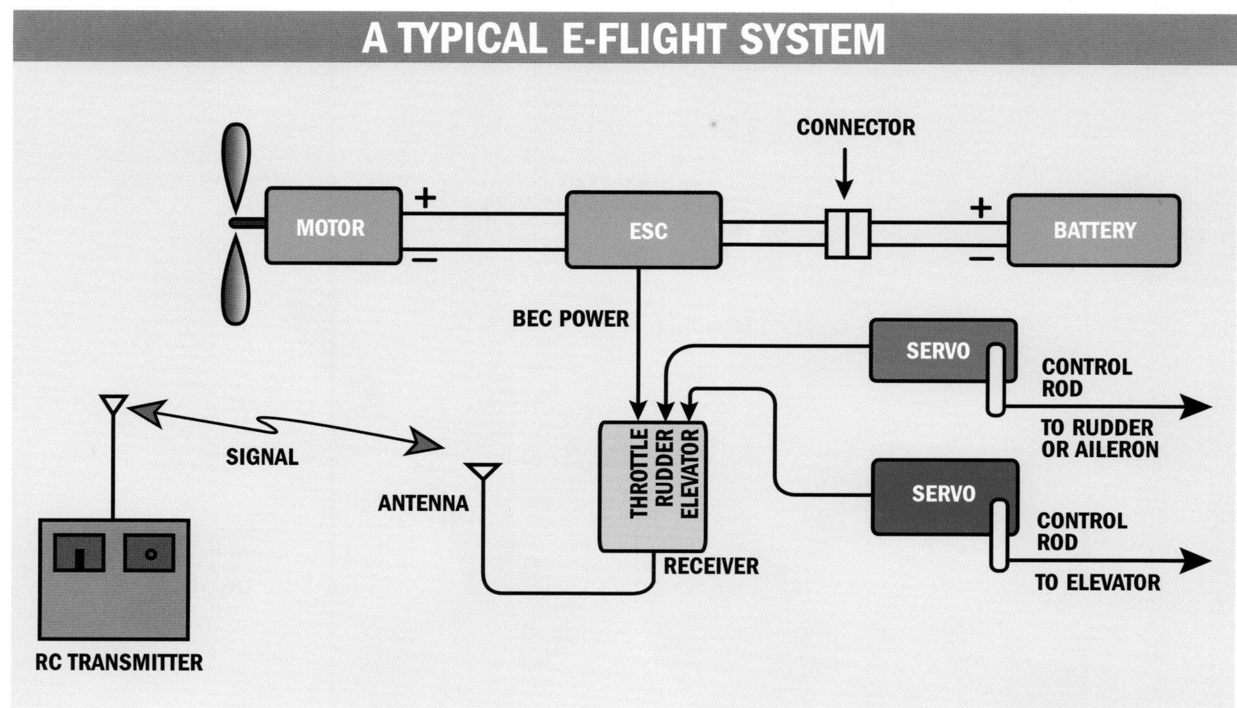

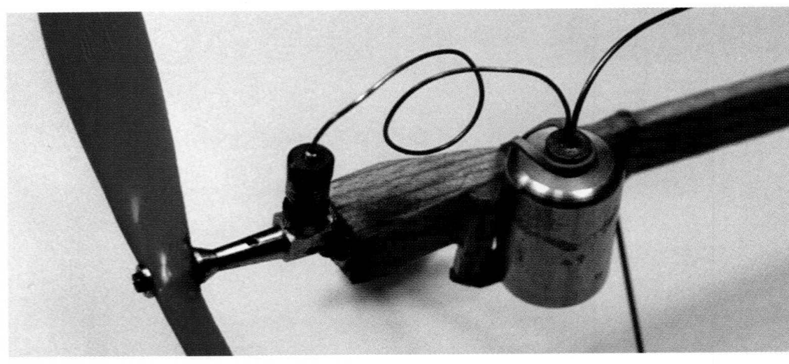

An alternative to electric power is CO_2, or pressurized carbon-dioxide gas. CO_2 motors are popular for some of the lightest indoor models. A CO_2 motor and tank weigh less than an electric power system, but run times are also shorter. You can refill the gas tank in seconds instead of the usual 20- to 30-minute battery-recharge time. Throttling a CO_2 remains a technical challenge, although some progress is being made. Right: Bob Aberle with his Hobby Lobby Bebe Jodel semi-scale parking-lot flyer with an RE-280 direct motor.

CO_2 POWER

In addition to electric power, there are a few more possibilities to consider. One is CO_2 power, in which pressurized carbon dioxide gas provides the fuel. CO_2 motors can be obtained in sizes small enough to fly model aircraft that are as little as ½-ounce total weight. There are certain advantages to using CO_2 motors. For example, they are quiet, certainly as quiet as electric power. They also produce little, if any, residue. They are lighter in overall weight, since the CO_2 gas tank weighs less than a comparable battery pack, and they can also be "fueled" (gassed-up!) in a matter of seconds. Compare this to battery charging, which can sometimes take 15 to 30 minutes.

On the other hand, there are several drawbacks: CO_2 motors are generally much more expensive than electric motors. At the present time, they are not readily throttleable; it is difficult to reduce power in flight. You cannot stop a CO_2 motor in flight and then restart it, as you can with an electric motor.

Rubber-powered indoor RC is yet another possibility. This little model weighs just 14 grams (less than ½ ounce) with rudder-only control. Wingspan is just 19.7 inches.

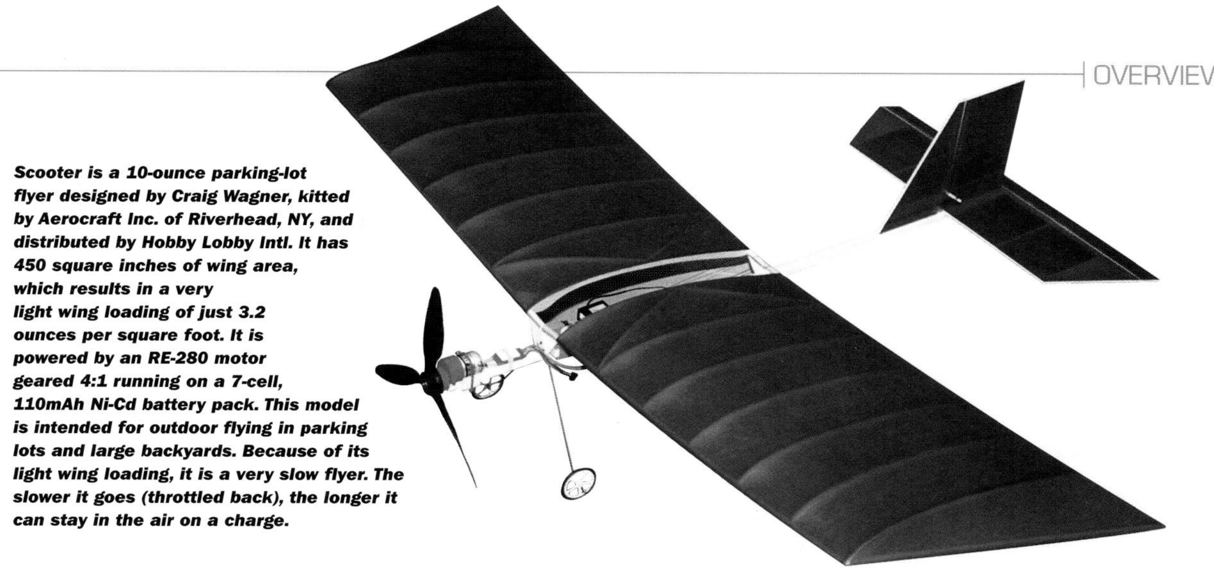

Scooter is a 10-ounce parking-lot flyer designed by Craig Wagner, kitted by Aerocraft Inc. of Riverhead, NY, and distributed by Hobby Lobby Intl. It has 450 square inches of wing area, which results in a very light wing loading of just 3.2 ounces per square foot. It is powered by an RE-280 motor geared 4:1 running on a 7-cell, 110mAh Ni-Cd battery pack. This model is intended for outdoor flying in parking lots and large backyards. Because of its light wing loading, it is a very slow flyer. The slower it goes (throttled back), the longer it can stay in the air on a charge.

Also, gas leaks and certain ambient temperatures can affect the overall performance; but this is, nonetheless, a source of power that will grow in the future. As we go to press, we have just learned of a new experimental CO_2 motor capable of being throttled, stopped and restarted by RC while in flight.

RUBBER POWER

Another source of power is twisted rubber (known simply as rubber power). You wind up the stranded rubber in one direction and then let it unwind, causing the prop to turn. If the model is light enough, and the rubber motor and prop size are selected properly, you can expect some flights of reasonable duration under some very slow flying conditions. This would be perfect for indoor flying, especially in very small facilities. But again, the motor cannot be throttled or turned off during the flight.

The RE-280 motor with a 3:1 gear reduction by Titantic Airlines. The prop is plastic with a 7-inch diameter. A motor such as this can power models that weigh 10 to 15 ounces.

Dr. Keith Shaw designed this scale Flapjack. It is reminiscent of the Chance Vought V-173 Skimmer. It has a 16-inch span, 200 square inches of area and a total weight of 8.5 ounces. It's powered by two AstroFlight Firefly motors geared 16:1 on 8, 250mAh NiMH battery cells.

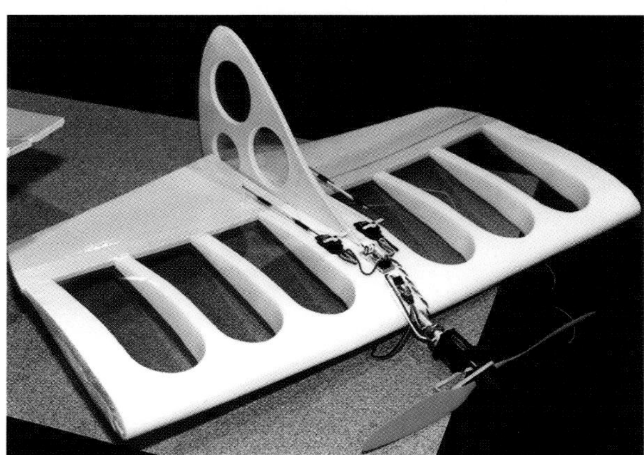

Greg Sutter of Madison, WI, designed this little Flitter B flying wing for micro and indoor flying. It has a 22-inch span and is powered by a GWS-A geared motor running on 3, 800mAh (4.2 volts per cell) lithium-ion batteries. Total model weight is 6 ounces.

A typical RC transmitter that's held by the pilot and transmits control input to the model aircraft. This single-stick, 2-axis control SS3 transmitter by Futaba is capable of 3-channel control (rudder or aileron, elevator and motor control).

GLIDERS

In larger indoor facilities or parking lots, one might try hand-launched RC gliders. In this application, the modeler's throwing arm essentially becomes the motor. This technique has been very popular over the years and has prompted many forms of flying competitions. For our micro applications, the gliders would have to be greatly scaled down in size.

For gliders or sailplanes, another possibility is towing by another equally small powered model. In this case, there would be a tow plane and a glider, with two RC systems and two pilots. You would tow the glider up to altitude and then release it via radio control. I recently heard about a variation of this scheme in Texas where an RC micro glider was towed to altitude using an RC racing car vehicle on the ground. The car has only the straight distance of the indoor facility or parking lot to loft the glider into the air. It might appear far-fetched, but it is still a possibility.

THE RC SYSTEM

Last, but not least, one might also consider helium-filled RC blimps for indoor flying fun. A variety of blimps are available in many sizes. Several sources for these are listed at the end of this book.

To make these power sources work (make the models fly) you need an RC system. Since we are dealing with small or micro models, this RC equipment must also be miniature and extremely light in weight. Components developed for cell-phone technology have obviously helped to reduce the size and weight of micro RC equipment. In this book, you will learn about these specialized new RC systems, how they work, how they are installed in the micro models, and how you will use them to control your model in flight.

Let's now proceed, chapter by chapter, item by item, until we launch our first flight.

This GWS "flight pack" includes two microservos, a micro receiver (lower left) a battery and an electronic speed control (ESC).

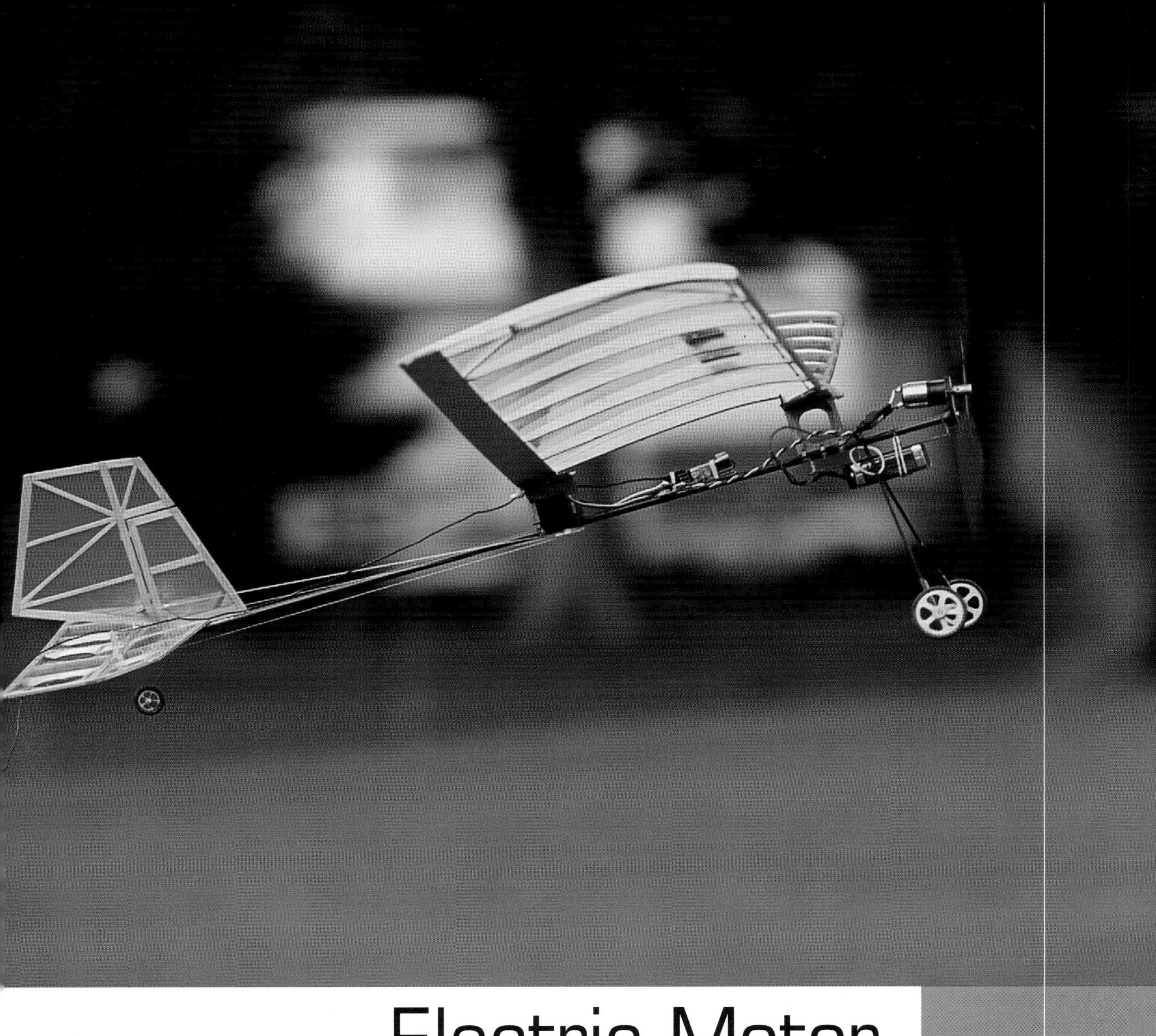

Electric Motor Systems

2

Many types of miniature electric motors have successfully powered park, backyard and indoor flyers. In this chapter, the author provides an overview of basic motor power systems and gives tips on direct-drive and geared systems as well as motor winding and polarity. See also tips on mounting your motor in your aircraft.

One of the biggest challenges is to make certain that your model's motor is properly matched to its size and weight. If the model is too heavy, or the motor underpowers it, your model will never get off the ground. On the other hand, installing a motor that is too powerful can result in excessive speed, higher motor current and very short flight times between charges.

Miniature electric motors come in many sizes and types. The most commonly seen, mass-produced motor is the ferrite "can" motor. These motors are sealed in metal cans; hence, the name. If they fail, they are simply discarded and replaced by new ones, as they are usually very reasonably priced. They are generally made in the Far East by big motor manufacturers such as Mabuchi and Johnson. Millions of these motors are made every year, probably selling for a few cents each as they leave their point of manufacture. By the time they reach the hobby distribution process, they will have changed their original identity to some new name or style number. Identifying these little ferrite motors has been a constant challenge over the years. The same basic motor can easily show up in the hobby market under various brand names. Unlike glow (methanol-burning) engines, in which the cubic-inch (ci) displacement has a specific meaning, electric motor identification has become more of a guarded secret. We hope that this problem will be solved in the future.

It would be nice to have an instruction sheet supplied with a particular motor stating the recommended number of battery cells to operate, the size of the prop, the expected motor current, expected prop rpm, the expected running time on a charge using a particular capacity of battery cell, an estimate of how much thrust can be expected, and last, an idea of the size and total weight of a model aircraft that this motor is capable of flying. Some manufacturers/distributors are now providing such information. We hope that more will follow.

The Kenway KR-2 is a dual motor unit that also uses a specially designed Gary Jones motor mount. The motors are the Mabuchi N-20s. The assembly weighs only 15 grams (0.52 ounce).

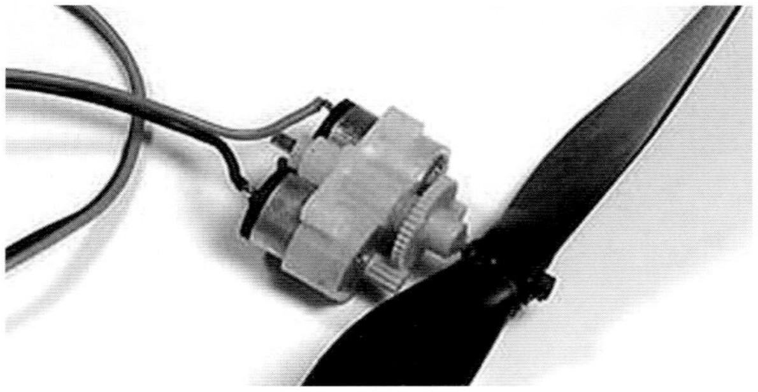

The "coreless" motor is a step up in quality from the ferrite class. These motors are generally more expensive, more efficient, lighter in weight for a given output and very smooth running during regular operation. Several manufacturers produce speed controls expressly designed for use with coreless motors.

The MYSYS-1524 motor as supplied by Tom McCann of Sky Hooks & Rigging in Canada. They're available in 11.8:1 and 6.3:1 reduction ratios. Full data on these motors can be found in the November 2000 issue of RC MicroFlight.

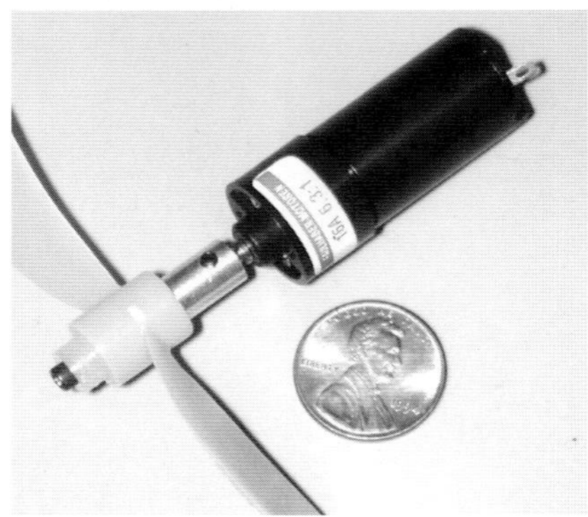

Both ferrite can and coreless motors use "brushes" to provide the electrical contacts within the motor as it rotates. The least expensive motors use a copper or steel wiper brush. These wipers wear out quickly, cause a lot of electrical noise and can be easily burned out if too much current is applied. Higher-quality motors use carbon brushes, which usually tolerate more current, produce less noise and generally last a lot longer. Some of the better motors can be opened for periodic maintenance and replacement of the carbon brushes.

BRUSHLESS MOTORS

At the top end of the motor scale are the newer "brushless" motors, pioneered in the model aircraft industry by the Aveox company approximately 10 years ago. These highly efficient motors have grown in popularity in the electric-powered hobby. Until recently, brushless motors were only available to power larger model aircraft (from 5 to 15 pounds total weight). However, AstroFlight has produced a new 010-class of brushless motors that are capable of flying models of from 7 to 10 ounces total weight. At the top end of the scale for indoor flying, the Astro 010 is just about perfect for parking-lot flyers.

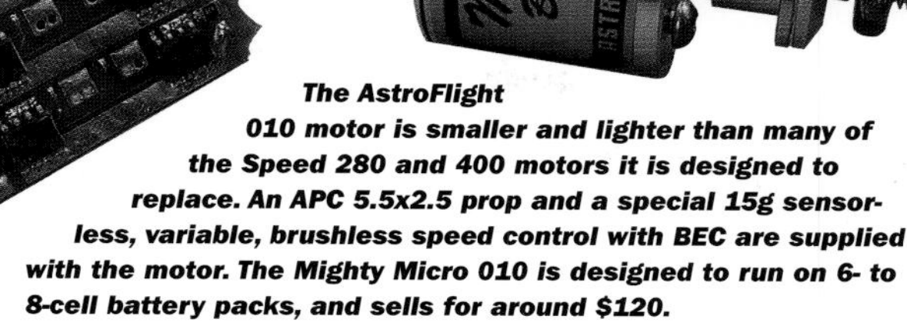

The AstroFlight 010 motor is smaller and lighter than many of the Speed 280 and 400 motors it is designed to replace. An APC 5.5x2.5 prop and a special 15g sensorless, variable, brushless speed control with BEC are supplied with the motor. The Mighty Micro 010 is designed to run on 6- to 8-cell battery packs, and sells for around $120.

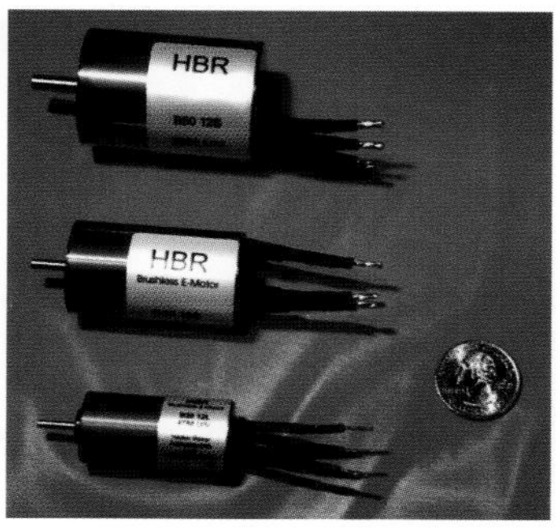

The Hacker Co., a German manufacturer, produces a series of small brushless motors. The smallest is equivalent to a 280-size motor and would be perfect for a parking-lot flyer. Hacker series motors are available in the U.S. from Electric Jet Factory and Aero-Model Inc.

Additional small brushless motors are being manufactured in Germany, e.g., the new Hacker motors available from both the Electric Jet Factory and Aero-Model Inc. At press time, other new brushless motors were also expected from Castle Creations, MTM Intl. (a German company) and others. The MTM motor will have a diameter of about 1 inch and is only ½ inch long. It will weigh approximately 40 grams and is primarily designed to run direct (i.e., without a gearbox). An APC 10x4.7 prop is expected to turn at 6,000rpm.

Since there are no brushes to contend with, the brushless motor has the advantage of providing a very long service life (possibly years). The drawbacks are the need for a specialized speed controller and the fact that, at this time, these motors and their speed controllers are quite expensive. Development work is proceeding with the goal of producing smaller and smaller brushless motors in the near future. It is conceivable that the next few years will see the development of a new breed of reduced size brushless motors capable of flying indoor RC models at well under the 8-ounce maximum weight guideline.

The S-240 SloFly motor from MTM Intl. is excellent for parking-lot and slow flyers. It can fly 8- to 12-ounce models on 7 or 8 cells with currents approaching 2.5 to 3 amps. It is a little smaller and lighter than a standard RE-280 motor.

DRIVE SYSTEMS

Now that we have categorized the basic motors, let us talk about how they drive a propeller. There are two choices. One is direct drive, in which the propeller is simply attached to the motor shaft. With this type of setup, the prop and motor turn at the same speed. Generally, this results in very high motor/prop rpm. To keep the motor current down to an acceptable level, the props will generally be smaller. Models flown with direct drive—such as pylon racers and aerobatic models—often fall into the "sprint" category.

GEARED SYSTEMS

More common than direct drive are gear-drive assemblies. These assemblies are attached to the motor shaft (which turns at high revs). Then, through a series of two or more gears, the output shaft speed is considerably reduced. By using the right gear reduction ratio, you enjoy the benefit of lower motor current, and that equates to longer flights. Moreover, geared systems have the ability to swing a larger diameter/higher-pitched prop, thereby producing more thrust. The gearbox does add weight, and it also adds mechanical complexity, which usually costs more than just a plain direct-drive motor, but

TECH TIP

MULTI-MOTOR POWER SYSTEMS

Recently, we have seen some of our smallest electric motors used with very small props (2½ to 3 inches in diameter) on direct drive. Placing two, three, four and more of these motor/prop assemblies in series can provide an excellent power source for multi-motor scale aircraft projects, which is definitely something to think about!

This is the Dymond Modelsports Max-001 (M-1) ferrite motor with a simple pinion spur gear. The motor is a geared 6:1 spinning a 7-inch prop at 1.3 amps on 8, 120mAh NiMH cells. This will power models of 4½ to 7 ounces. Note the easy-mounting flange on the front of the motor.

the advantages make it all worthwhile.

Gearboxes (or drives) come in several varieties. The most basic is a common pinion and spur gear. Typically, the smaller pinion gear is pressed onto the motor-output shaft. A secondary shaft is then added for a much larger diameter gear, which is known as the spur gear. The prop is then attached to this additional (output) shaft. Many modelers have had considerable success making up their own simple gear drives using separately purchased pinion and spur gears. The gears, shafts and prop adapters are now readily available from many suppliers.

EPICYCLE GEARING

A variation of the basic pinion and spur gear drive involves the use of an enclosed spur gear (with internal gears) known as epicyclical gearing. This arrangement has become more popular in recent times. The gearing itself weighs a little more than the common pinion/spur gear, but by nature of design, the offset between the prop shaft and the motor shaft is less, so it's easier to mount in most models. Also, the "covered" spur gear offers a degree of protection against dirt getting into the gear train. Again, it is easy to count the teeth on the pinion and spur gears to determine the reduction ratio.

PLANETARY GEARING

The final gear train is known as the planetary type. It is the heaviest and most expensive in the group. It has been known to load down the motor if improperly adjusted, but the advantage is that it operates along the same axis as the motor shaft. Stated another way, there is no offset from motor to prop shaft. This allows very streamlined installation in models. Planetary gear drives are usually sealed units, and that helps keep out dirt. Unless you take the gear drive apart, you won't be able to count the gear teeth to determine the reduction ratio, so in this case, you must depend on the manufacturer's supplied data.

BELT DRIVES

Beyond gear drives, there are also belt drives such as those pioneered by Tom Hunt of Modelair-Tech. Belt drives provide the same function as gear drives

This HiLine Ltd. Gremlin dual motor system combines two Hiline Mini-6 motors with a 4.5:1 gear-reduction ratio. It is rated at 12 watts. On 5 to 6 cells, the Gremlin spins a 6-inch prop at 4,500rpm while pulling 2 amps. It is capable of flying models with 150 to 225 square inches of wing area and 5 to 7 ounces total weight.

and operate very quietly, but the belt-drive assembly is much heavier. From a practical standpoint, Tom has made belt drives down to only Speed 400 motors (the Modelair-Tech H-100 belt drive).

MOTOR WINDING

Many motors are available with various windings. Each winding is meant for a specific voltage level of operation. Speed 400 motors, for example, are available in 4.8, 6 and 7.2V windings. Each voltage level is suited to a different purpose. Obviously, this further complicates modelers' choices. Fortunately

TECH TIP
CALCULATING GEAR REDUCTION RATIOS

It is useful to be able to calculate your gearbox's reduction ratio, so let's discuss that for a moment. First, count the number of teeth on the smaller pinion gear that's attached to the motor shaft. It may have something like 10 teeth. In turn, this pinion gear will mesh to a much larger spur gear, which might have, for example, 50 teeth. If you divide the spur-gear teeth (50) by the pinion-gear teeth (10; 50 ÷ 10 = 5), the resulting number is referred to as a 5:1 (five-to-one) reduction ratio. Using this ratio, a motor might turn at 10,000rpm while the prop turns at just 2,000rpm (⅕ the motor speed). It's that simple!

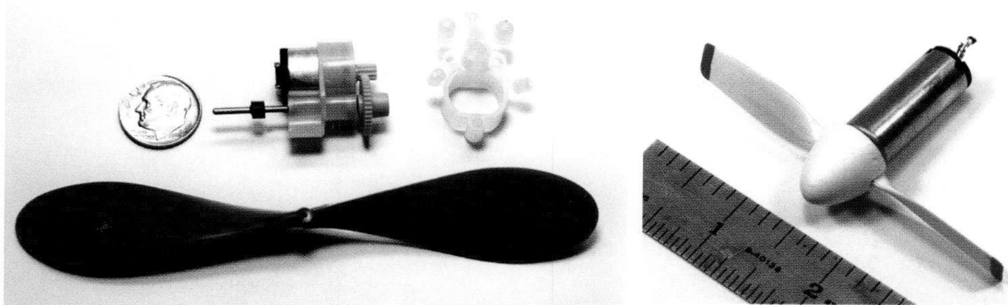

A Cloud 9 Firecracker direct-drive motor with a 3¼-inch-diameter prop. This motor is similar to the basic GWS motor. It will run at 1.4 amps on a 4-cell, 120mAh NiMH battery pack. At this power level, this motor should be able to support a 4-ounce model.

This Kenway KR-1 motor with a 4.2:1 gear-reduction drive is intended for the ultra-micro class—models weighing less than 2 ounces. The molded motor/gear drive mount (at right) was designed by Gary Jones.

MTM's Hummingbird S-100 is a ferrite motor with a ball-bearing-supported pinion and spur gear. Its reduction ratio is 5:1. It is intended for 8 Ni-Cd cell operation at motor currents of 1 to 1.4 amps (10 to 12 watts). Best model weights: 6 to 9 ounces.

for our micro-flying efforts, most motors that are smaller than Speed 400s are discrete types with only a single winding available. However, that could change as new micro-size motors enter service.

POLARITY

Something else to be aware of is the polarity of the motor leads, or terminals. The two motor terminals are usually marked + (positive) or – (negative). Some have just a red dot marking the positive terminal. If the electric current flowing through the motor leads has reversed polarity (i.e., the positive lead is connected to the negative terminal), the motor will run backward. In turn, the airstream (prop wash) will be directed forward rather than aft, and the model will not fly. The first time you run up an electric motor, verify the direction of the prop wash.

A typical Speed 400 motor—in this case, direct drive. These very popular motors for models of 14 to 30 ounces are available in 4.8, 6 and 7.2V windings, depending on the application. The 6V motor is generally used for direct drive, typically with a 6-inch-diameter prop on 7 cells.

Everything just said applies to a direct-drive motor. When you attach certain gear drives to a motor, the polarity may have to be reversed because the drive may cause the prop shaft to spin in the wrong direction. If you purchase a motor with a gear drive already attached, it will most likely be marked with the proper polarity. A belt drive will not prompt reversed polarity, but you won't see many of these used on tiny models.

MOTOR NOISE

As already pointed out, electric motors can cause interference that might affect the radio's operation. The noisier the motor, the more likely it is to cause radio interference. To help eliminate this problem, modelers are advised to install three bypass, or interference, capacitors on each motor. The common technique is to place one capacitor directly across the motor terminals and then place one from each terminal directly to the motor case (a ground connection). Many types of capacitors are acceptable for this purpose, and many are provided by the motor supplier. I generally purchase .01-microfarad 50V polyester film capacitors from RadioShack (part no. 272-1065). These capacitors must be soldered into place. Also be advised that some small electric motors come with the capacitors already installed inside the metal case. Since this isn't always obvious, it is still best to install your own interference capacitors on the outside, just to be safe.

On the subject of soldering: it is generally acceptable for the wires going to the motor terminals to be soldered into place. You could use a small connector set, which makes it easier to swap motors. The connector will, however, add weight, so it is advisable to make solder connections. See Chapter 6 (Connectors, Wires and Soldering) for tips on soldering.

TIMING

You can often improve the performance of Speed 400 and larger motors by "timing" the motor for the specific direction of rotation. Timing involves rotating the endbell of the motor using a special tool. This endbell is rotated very slightly, and the direction depends on which way your motor will be spinning.

J.C. Smith of Delta, OH, makes a neat retiming tool designed especially for Speed 400 motors; you might want consider buying one for this application.

MOTOR BREAK-IN

Motor break-in allows the brushes to wear in a way that creates an optimal electrical contact within the motor. Break-in generally involves running a

Mounting the Motor

If you are an experienced glow-power modeler, you will need to learn an entirely new way to mount motors. There are generally no mounting lugs or brackets supplied with the smallest electric motors because electric motors cause very little vibration; therefore, the mounting techniques employed can be quite simple. One of the best mounting techniques is to have one or two wooden dowels protruded from the plywood firewall. The motor can be held in place with a couple of small rubber bands, or you can use some double-sided tape with a small nylon tie to anchor everything in place. Look at several of the photos and illustrations provided. I suspect as the micro industry grows, accessory suppliers will begin to design all kinds of motor-mounting aids. Until then, you will have to use your own initiative.

My Hobby Lobby Bebe Jodel. The direct-drive Speed 280 motor is placed between two lengths of ⅛-inch wooden dowels that protrude from the firewall. The motor is held in position by a couple of small rubber bands.

Mounting a Dymond M-1 motor on my 80-square-inch Cessna Skyhawk. A 3/16-inch wooden dowel protrudes from the firewall. A piece of double-sided tape is placed on top of the dowel, and then the motor is pressed to the tape. A nylon tie around the motor and dowel holds everything in place.

This single-beam mount for GWS A through F motors is simple and quick to make. The motor is secured to the beam with a dowel that's held in place by a rubber band. Pull the dowel, and the motor slides off the beam. It's recommended that you mount the hardwood beam on bulkheads behind the motor.

new motor without a propeller attached on a battery pack containing about half the cells the motor was designed to use. If you plan to fly with an 8-cell pack, your break-in battery needs to have only 4 cells. Charge up this pack and run the propless motor until the charge runs out. The brushes should then be seated properly. With respect to the smallest motors used in micro flying, you need not be particularly concerned about motor break-in.

MOTOR RUNNING TIPS

Another important point to consider when using any electric motor is that they do get warm during normal operation. If you completely seal the front end of your model, the motor will surely get hot. To prevent this from happening, you should provide airflow in the front, passing over the motor and exiting out the rear.

If you are new to the electric-powered aircraft hobby or have converted from fuel to electric flying, please note the following safety precautions. With electric power, you just connect a battery to the motor terminals, and you are running at full power. If something blocks the propeller, the motor

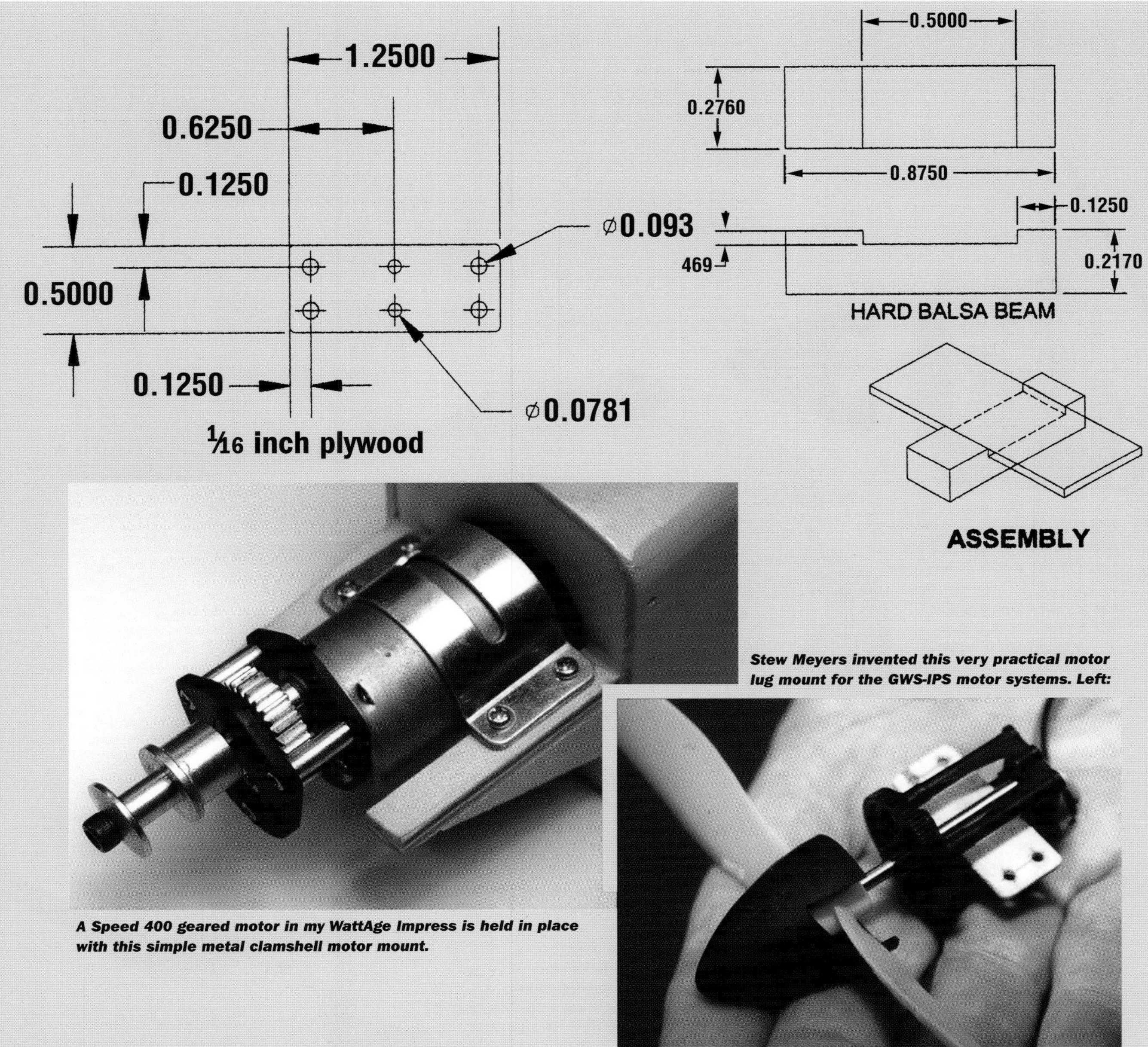

A Speed 400 geared motor in my WattAge Impress is held in place with this simple metal clamshell motor mount.

Stew Meyers invented this very practical motor lug mount for the GWS-IPS motor systems. Left:

ELECTRIC MOTORS FOR USE WITH PARKING LOT/INDOOR FLYERS

ULTRA MICRO 2 OZ. OR LESS	SUB MICRO 2-3 OZ.	MICRO 3-8 OZ.
INDOORS		
KP-00 (Knight & Pridham)	WES-Technik DC 5-2.4 (geared)	WES-Technik D1717 (coreless, geared)
KR-1 (single, Kenway)	GWS-IPS (direct, 180 size)	AstroFlight Firefly-800 (coreless, direct and geared)
HiLine Micro-4	HiLine Mini-6	Cloud 9 Take Off 2000
Mabuchi N-20 (geared, lower voltage wind)	Cloud 9 Take Off 2000 (Firecracker, direct)	HY-50F Firecracker (geared)
	Mabuchi N-20 (geared, higher voltage wind)	MTM Hummingbird S-100 (geared)
	MSYS-524-2 (Sky Hooks & Rigging)	GWS IPS (geared, standard and deluxe, 180 size)
	KR-2 (dual motor, Kenway)	HiLine Gremlin GR01 (dual Mini-6 geared)
	PU-02 (RCS-Technik)	MTM Colobri S-050 (DC5-2.4 geared)
		DC1524 coreless
		VL Products HY-50B
		Potensky POT-1 & POT-2
		Hobby Club PUMA-05
		MPS/Penn Hobbies MG-1

The Grand Wing Servo GWS-IPS STD geared motor at right is a 180-size basic ferrite motor. At left is the new GWS-EPS series geared motor with a 370 designation motor (which is actually comparable to a Speed 300 motor).

GWS motors come in many variations, all of which are very affordable. Both of these motors are suitable for parking-lot models.

The motor above right can easily fly 5- to 8-ounce models indoors if the wing loading does not exceed 5 ounces per square foot. It is one of a series of approximately half a dozen motors in this size category, all with various gear-reduction ratios.

The MTM Intl. Lil Bee S-200 motor with a Maxon planetary gearbox. A 7.5x4 cam folder prop running on 8, 250mAh Ni-Cd cells generates about 2.5A motor current. This system can fly 9- to 14-ounce models.

will draw more current and the applied torque will increase. If you are planning to run an electric motor in your shop, properly anchor the motor to a test stand. Avoid installing the prop on the motor until you are ready to fly.

By using electric motors, you gain a powerful advantage with respect to multi-engine models. With traditional glow-powered models, you have to separately start up and control each engine, and there is always the possibility that one engine will quit before the other in flight. With electric power, each motor can be hooked up in a series loop with a common battery supplying all the power. One switch turns all the motors on or off at the same time. There can't be a "motor out" situation.

Now that you have a basic understanding of electric motors, let's move on to the subject of propellers.

OUTDOORS

PARKING-LOT/ BACKYARD FLYER 8-14 OZ.	SPEED 400 14+ OZ.
Graupner RC-280 (direct Speed 280)	Graupner Speed 400 (4.8, 6, 7.2V, geared and direct) — Maxx Products Intl. — Dymond Modelsports — Northeast Sailplane — Hobby Lobby Intl.
Dymond Max-250 & 025	MTM WASP-380 (geared)
MP Jet Geared 280 (Hobby Lobby)	MFA Rocket-400 (Hobby Lobby)
GWS-EPS A-F Carbon brushed (Speed 280 size)	Speed 400 Variants (geared)
GWS-EPS A-F Carbon brushed (Speed 370 size)	AstroFlight brushless 020
MTM Little Bee S-200	Hacker brushless (400 size)
Titanic Airlines (geared 280)	
MTM-SLO FLY S-240	
Airplane Planet TS-389	
AstroFlight 010 (brushless)	
MTM Brushless (new)	
Hobby People/Global 280 geared	
Great Planes 280 geared	
Horizon 280 geared	
Hacker brushless (280 size)	

Above: I built this 4.8-ounce all-foam Micro Cessna Skyhawk from an old Union Model Co. free-flight kit. It's powered by a Dymond M-1 motor geared at 6:1 with a 7-inch prop on eight 120mAh NiMH cells. Motor current is 1.3 amp. A fast and snappy performer, it's capable of 6- to 8-minute flights. I feel this plane should be put back in production as a micro RC model.

Left: the KP-00 (KP stands for "Knight & Pridham") is another tiny motor for indoor models that weigh less than 2 ounces. This motor, shown with a KP 3-inch-diameter folding prop, operates on 3, 120mAh NiMH cells and provides about 5-minute flights.

3

Propellers

Although most kits and ready-to-fly micro flyers come with recommended propellers, you will benefit by knowing how to choose propellers that best match your airplane. The author explains how propeller size and pitch influence performance, he summarizes the range of available propellers and offers tips on how to mount a propeller on the prop shaft.

Since we are dealing with aircraft, it is obvious that the next subject to discuss after motors must be the propellers (props) that are mounted on the motors. This chapter is most important for beginners, but is also very important for glow pilots who are just getting into micro flight. Props meant for glow engines have been around for a long time. Popular brands such as Top Flight, APC, Rev Up, Master Airscrew and many others are well known. Equally well known is that these props are identified by both diameter (size in inches) as well as pitch (the angle of the prop blades, also measured in inches). Charts are readily available to help select basic prop sizes for every displacement engine.

Our electric-powered hobby is new and growing but, unfortunately, to date we have not been as well organized as our fueled engine counterparts when it comes to propeller identification. A few lists are available that might recommend prop types and sizes for specific micro-electric motor applications. Noted electric power modeler, Dick Miller, provides motor data on his personal website (http://home.ptd.net/~rcm65/). Included in that data are propeller size recommendations for various model sizes and weights. He obviously can't cover every single motor on the market, but it is a most helpful listing. I'll talk more about this later in Chapter 8 (Sizing Motor Systems to Your Aircraft).

Many of the props intended for indoor and parking-lot flying have non-standard markings or, in some cases, no markings at all. Even the manufacturers' names don't appear on many of these props. So what is the micro flier to do?

WES-Technik CFP-23 carbon-fiber prop, 23cm in diameter with 12cm pitch (9x4.7 inches).

GLOW VS. ELECTRIC PROPS

The first and most important thing to learn concerning props for electric power is that they should

TECH TIP

UNDERSTANDING PROP PITCH AND DIAMETER

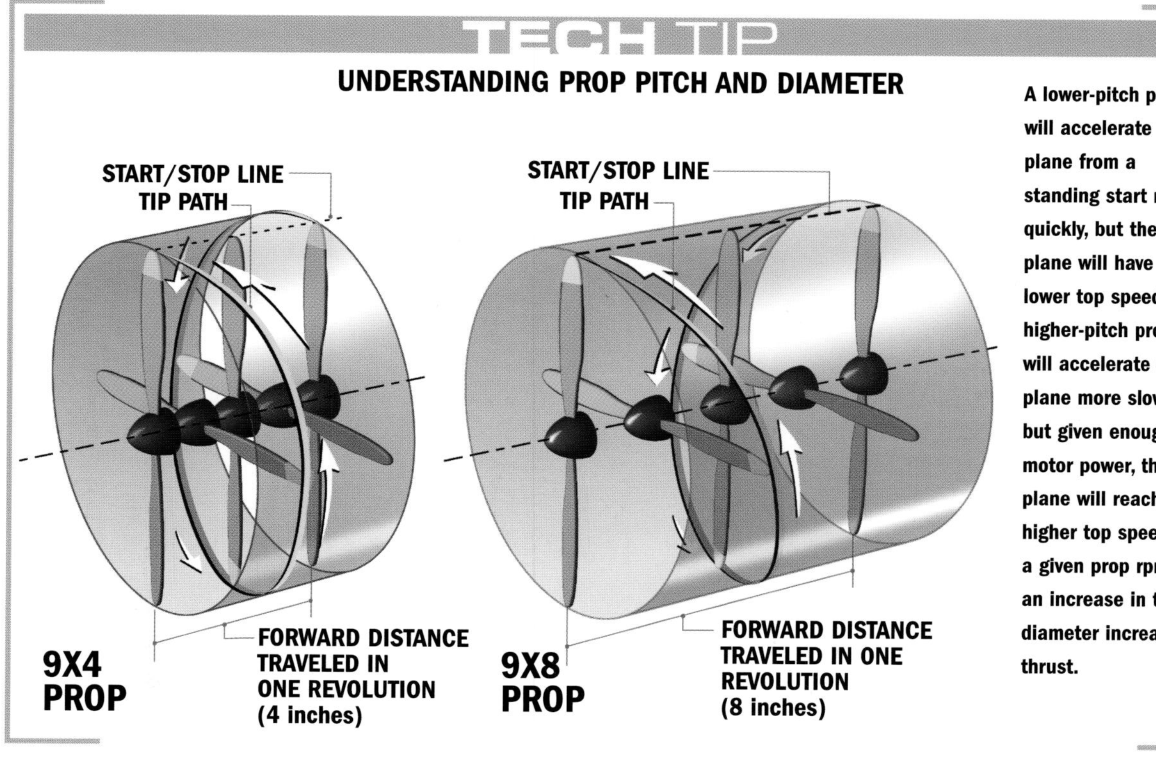

A lower-pitch prop will accelerate the plane from a standing start more quickly, but the plane will have a lower top speed. A higher-pitch prop will accelerate the plane more slowly, but given enough motor power, the plane will reach a higher top speed. At a given prop rpm, an increase in the diameter increases thrust.

never be used on a fueled engine. Props intended for use with electric motors are typically much lighter in weight and use less material; as such, they should not be considered for use on glow engines. This is especially true of electric folding props. The blade attachment pins are not intended for the high revs and vibration levels of fueled engines. In the same regard, props intended for fueled engines are usually too heavy to be used with electric motors.

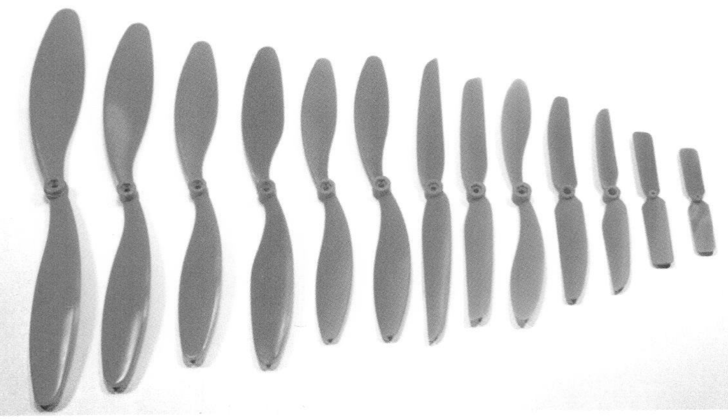

The new line of Grand Wing Servo (GWS) orange plastic props intended for both parking-lot and indoor RC flight. These props are available from 2½ inches in diameter to 14 inches in diameter. They are available from Global, Horizon Hobby Inc., Balsa Products, Maxx Products Intl. and Cloud 9 RC.

CHOOSING A PROP

Your prop choices are as follows: fixed 2-blade, which is the most common; folding 2-blade; and, to a lesser degree, fixed 3- and 4-blade props for certain scale applications. Most distributors of micro-flight models and equipment can supply the proper propeller for your motor . When shopping for that correct prop size, always be ready to tell your supplier the type of motor you use, your gear-reduction ratio, if any, and the model's estimated wing area and total weight. With this information, a vendor can usually recommend a prop to start with. After that, you can experiment with slightly different sizes and pitches to optimize performance (see Chapter 12 for examples of how to optimize performance).

Keep in mind that the correct prop choice can make the difference between having a model that flies great and a model that either sits on the ground or barely supports flight. And, as you will learn later on, the motor current and the number of battery cells used also enter this equation.

TECH TIP

PROPS AND PERFORMANCE

The GWS Tiger Moth comes with a 9x7 propeller. How would the Tiger Moth's flight performance be affected if alternative props were used? Bob Wilder tested a range of GWS props with the standard GWS DX2BB-AX "A" motor (gear ratio of 5.86:1) that comes with the Tiger Moth. He tested the amp draw on both the motor and the thrust at 7 volts. When fully charged, the 6-cell Ni-Cd pack used in the Tiger Moth can provide a nominal 7.2 volts. But under load and as the battery becomes depleted (as in flight) voltage declines.

Prop	Current (amps)	Thrust (grams)	Thrust per watt
8x6	1.24	91	10.5
9x4.7	1.41	113	11.4
9x7	1.78	118	9.5
10x4.7	1.81	138	10.9
10x8	2.27	134	8.4

- **Although the 10x8 draws more than 2 amps at 7 volts, it could be used because current draw decreases in flight.**
- **The 10x4.7's current draw is only slightly greater than that of the stock 9x7 prop, but it produces more static thrust than the 10x8.**
- **The 9x4.7 prop provides almost as much thrust as the stock prop but at a lower current draw, which suggests longer flights at cruising speed but a lower top-end speed.**

Additional props intended for parking-lot and indoor flying. They include brands such as APC, Peck-Polymers, Union, Gunther, Sig Mfg. and many more. The hardest part is identifying some of these props, especially the ones with no imprinted markings.

GWS PROPS

One Far East manufacturer, Grand Wing Servo (GWS), recently introduced an entire line of molded-plastic props specially designed for the electric-power modeler interested in indoor and parking-lot flying. These props are easily identified because they are all molded of a bright orange color. They are currently available from Global, Horizon Hobby Inc, Maxx Products Intl. and Balsa Products, but I'm sure other distributors will soon be added to the list. Sizes are now available from 2½ inches in diameter up to 12 inches in diameter.

To identify the manufacturer, each prop has GWS molded into the plastic. Also molded into the plastic blades is the size, written as EP-1080. This identifies an electric prop, 10 inches in diameter, with an 8-inch pitch. The two smallest sizes as we went to print were the EP-2510 (2½-inch diameter, 1-inch pitch) and the 3.2-inch diameter, 2-inch pitch prop. Both of these extremely tiny blades are best suited to direct drive with both the Mabuchi N-20 motor and the GWS carbon-brushed motor (without gear train). Generally, GWS offers even sizes from 4 through 12 inches in diameter. Some will have a 4.7-, 6- and 8-inch pitch, with the same diameter. When using a geared motor that turns a prop at lower rpm, it is more common to see higher pitched props in use.

The Union U-180 prop, which is 7 inches in diameter. This prop was originally designed for rubber-powered models but now finds favor with the electric fliers.

ADDITIONAL SOURCES OF PROPS

Some other excellent fixed-blade props intended for electric power are made by companies such as: APC; Gunther and Graupner (Slim and Cam Props), available from Hobby Lobby Intl. in the U.S.; Peck-Polymers; Sig Mfg. Co.; K&P Props (Great Britain), distributed by David Lewis in the U.S.; Union Model Co., distributed by Peck-Polymers; MTM Intl. (Germany); WES-Technik (Germany), distributed by David Lewis in the U.S.; Braun (Germany); and John Worth at Cloud 9 RC. In addition to the ones on this list, I have also come upon small props identified as IGRA and TERN. They are available from HiLine Inc., Kenway Micro Flight, VL Products and Penn Valley Hobby Center.

To obtain the best props for indoor and parking-lot flying you must be willing to do some research. I advise you to obtain catalogs from as many of these prop suppliers as possible; then, when a particular prop is recommended for use with a micro-electric motor, you will know where to purchase it.

FOLDING PROPS

While fixed-blade props are the most common and least expensive, they are also the most likely to break, especially on models with short length or no landing gear at all. To solve that problem, folding prop blades are becoming more popular. They usually consist of a metal or molded-plastic hub to which two separate prop blades are attached. The hub tends to act as a yoke. A hole is drilled through the blade end and a metal pin is passed through the blade and into the yoke. When the prop is rotating, the blades will fully extend and perform much the same as a rigid prop blade. But when the motor stops, these blades tend to fold back (with the help of the airstream) along the fuselage sides. Restarting the motor in flight will cause the blades to extend. Be careful when experimenting with longer blades, as their tips can accidentally hit the leading edge of the wing as they extend.

Excellent folding prop-blade assemblies can be

Above: some typical folding props for electric motor use. From top to bottom: Sonic-Tronics (largest prop), RASA (from MTM Intl.), Graupner Cam folder, Graupner standard folder with spinner and the Robbe folder with spinner.

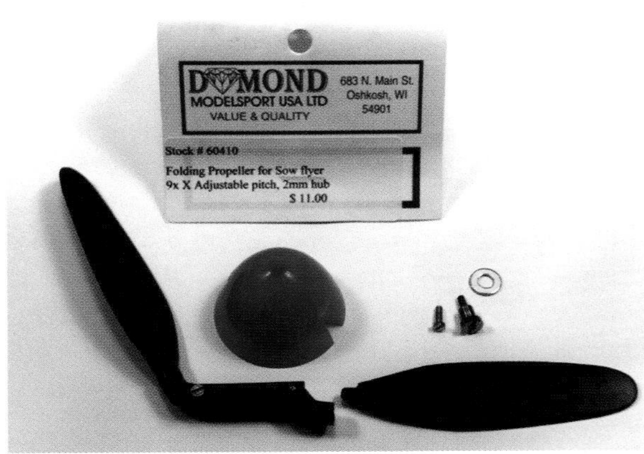

New and very interesting, the Dymond Modelsports folding/variable pitch prop. This prop not only folds back when the motor stops, but the pitch angle of both blades is adjustable. This is a 9-inch diameter prop with a 2mm hub.

obtained from Graupner, MTM Intl., Sonic-Tronics and K&P Props. Additionally, new APC folders have just been introduced. Traditionally, folding blades were associated with large-diameter props, but recently I have seen folders fewer than 5 inches in diameter.

VARIABLE-PITCH PROPS

Another interesting innovation in prop design is the variable-pitch prop. These props cannot yet change pitch in flight, but several props allow you to literally dial in the desired pitch angle within reason. K&P Props of Great Britain has 2-, 3- and 4-blade props available with adjustable pitch. Another possible source is Hobby Lobby Intl., which sells a 6.7-inch-diameter prop with adjustable pitch (catalog no. POT1AP).

CARL MARTIN'S ARC PROP LINE

In addition to adjustable-pitch props, you can also assemble your own propeller using a technique developed by Carl Martin (cmartin@nidlink.com). Carl's ARC-1 and ARC-2 props can be set up in 8- to 10-inch diameter sizes. You purchase the prop hub along with carbon-fiber laser-cut blade paddles. Separately, he offers a universal propeller assembly fixture that allows you to set the prop pitch over a wide variety of angles. You set the hub and blades into the fixture and then cement them in place. These prop assemblies are not expensive, and the fixture is a one-time tooling expense. Carl sells these props through Chris Hansen at Anything RC (www.anything-rc.com). An interesting article on this concept, written by Carl Martin, appears in the December 2000 issue of *RC MicroFlight* on pages 8 and 9.

While putting the finishing touches on this book, I corresponded with Carl Martin and asked if his prop-assembly fixture might also be used to help us identify the exact pitch of "unknown" props. The surprising answer was that Carl had recently developed a new and very simple prop-pitch gauge, which can be easily assembled by any modeler from a few parts. I'm hoping Carl can be encouraged to produce kits of this gauge. See the

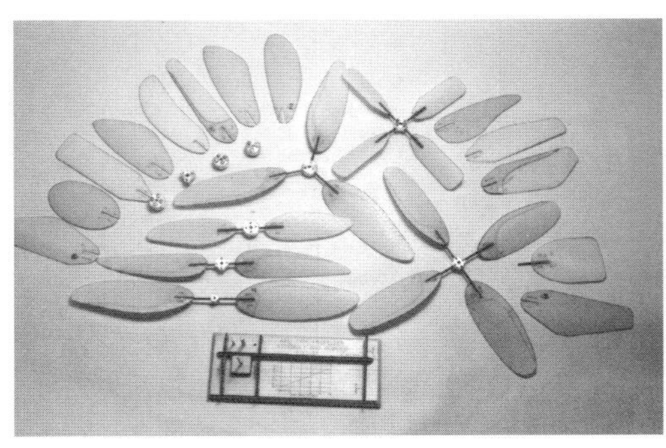

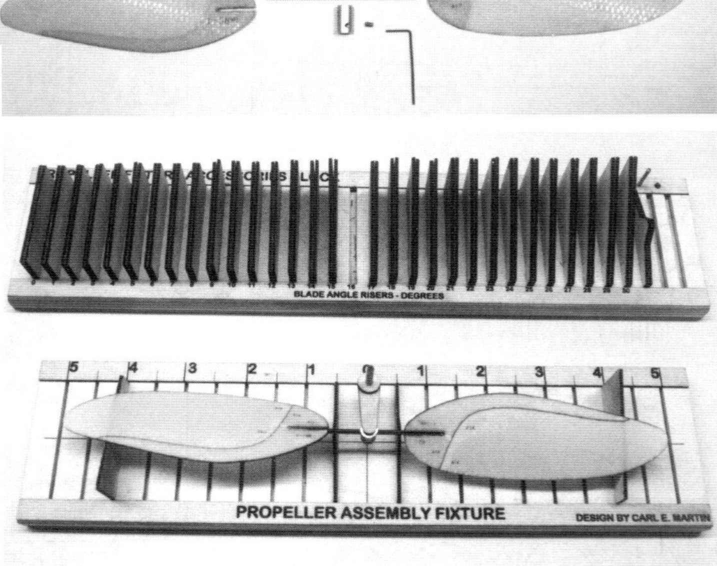

Just to give you an idea of the potential for the Carl Martin ARC prop system. Literally any prop configuration can be built, including 2-, 3- and 4-blade. Right: you can make your own custom props using the ARC system designed by Carl Martin. Carl sells blade paddles and prop hubs along with an assembly jig that allows you to make props up to 12 inches in diameter with pitch angles from 0 to 22 degrees.

CARL MARTIN'S PITCH GAUGE

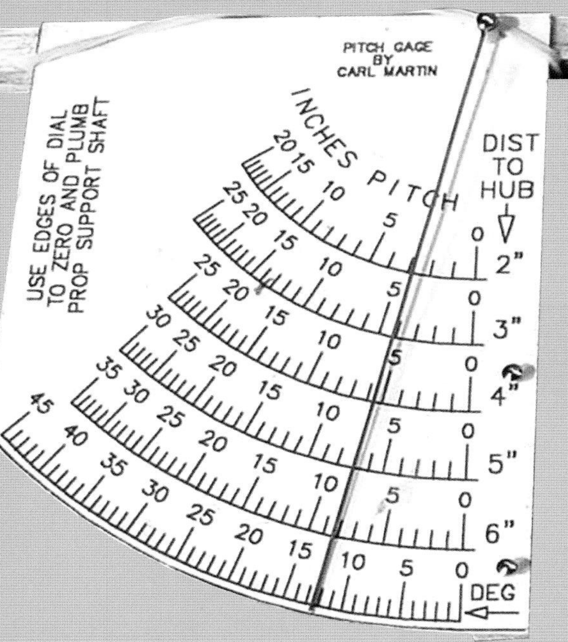

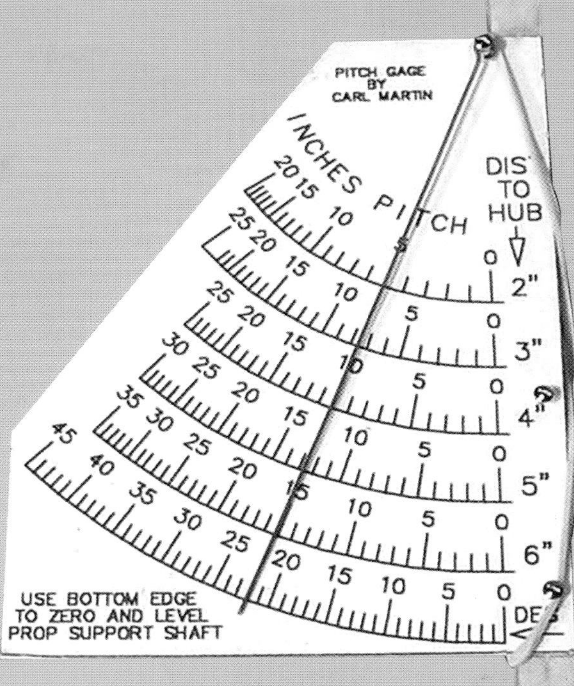

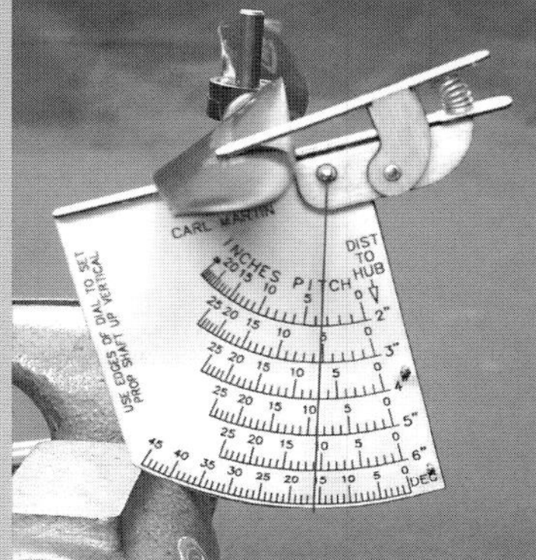

This ingenious pitch gauge was designed by Carl Martin and was first published in the November 2001 issue of *RC MicroFlight*. One version uses a vertical prop-shaft support, and one uses a horizontal prop shaft. It is a real help in determining the pitch of propellers that do not have an indicated pitch, and you can determine the pitch at the base, center, or tip of the blade. For further information on how to build and use either version of this gauge, go to www.rcmicroflight.com and click on the "Free Library" link in the navigation bar on the left side of the home page. Look for the article: "Measuring Prop Pitch—Homemade Gauges speed the Process." The smaller photos show earlier prototypes in use.

Interesting 3-blade prop offered by Dymond Modelsports for use with their Max 250 motor (item number 22954). The motor is a geared Speed 280. This particular motor/prop combination is intended for the Chubby Lady ARF model. Right: the little KP-00 (Knight & Pridham) motor comes with two adjustable-pitch props.

photos of this gauge above.

MOUNTING YOUR PROP

Now that you know a little more about what's available for indoor and parking-lot flyer props, you need to know how to mount them on the motor shaft. The most common way is to purchase a suitable prop adapter. This is usually a machined part that slips over the motor shaft or gear-train shaft and is held in place with one or two setscrews. It is advisable to file a small flat on the motor shaft to prevent the prop adapter from later shifting position and pos-

Left: this tiny prop adapter by Tom Notti of Cloverdale, CA, demonstrates his skills as a machinist. The 3/8-inch-long adapter is secured to the 1mm shaft of a Takeoff 2000 motor using two 0-80 machine screws. The 3 1/8-inch diameter prop is held into the adapter with a longer 0-80 machine screw. Tom might be persuaded to make special prop adapters on a custom-order basis.

Below: a variation of the Dymond Modelsports Max-1 motor is their P/N 22904 with an enclosed epicyclical gear box. Note that the prop is held in place by a small O-ring. In the case of a crash, the prop can easily pop loose with less chance of breaking.

Below: a close-up of the MP JET prop adapter. The collet is at the top mount on the motor gearbox shaft. The prop, in turn, goes on the threaded shaft and is held in place with the hex nut and washer.

sibly rotating off the motor. On the opposite end of the adapter will be another shaft, usually with a threaded end. You slip the prop on this shaft, then add a drive washer and finally a hex type nut, or possibly, a spinner.

There are variations on prop mounts. Some motors have tapped shaft ends that accept a small screw, which holds the prop in place. Another recent innovation, seen on the Airplane Planet TR-389 motor, is a prop-holder bracket that employs a rubber band instead of a screw or bolt. During a rough landing, the rubber band will give slightly or allow the prop to dismount, which effectively protects the prop and shaft.

Many popular motors come with the necessary prop adapters. A variety of adapters that fit many shaft sizes can be obtained from Hobby Lobby Intl. Another new source for prop adapters, especially for very tiny motors, is Tom Notti of Cloverdale, CA. Still another excellent source of precision-machined adapters is BMC Model Products (this series of adapters is also available from Cloud 9 RC).

ELECTRIC DUCTED FANS

Electric ducted fans that simulate jet power also fit into the prop category. The fan blades are usually small in diameter, and the fan units can include 4 to 6 blades or more. They turn at very high speeds and are semi-enclosed in a small duct or tube, hence the name "ducted fan." Very scale-like jet power can be obtained from these fan units. Ducted-fan assemblies are available from such suppliers as GWS, HiLine Inc., Kenway and Electric Jet Factory. You could contact either of these companies to get more information on ducted-fan assemblies.

The GWS ducted fan unit.

Electronic Speed Controls

4

Recent advances in electronics have led to the development of a variety of sophisticated, miniature speed controls for small electric airplanes. This chapter introduces basic speed-control functions and provides the background you'll need to choose and operate these miniature electronic throttles.

Electronic speed controls (ESCs) allow you to turn an electric motor on or off and to vary the speed from low to high. The ESC is operated by the radio-control unit while the model is in flight. With an engine-powered model, you must use a separate throttle servo, which is mechanically connected to the carburetor on the engine. This usually involves control wires or rods, which must, in turn, be properly adjusted to obtain the full range of engine speeds. Using an ESC to control an electric motor is much easier, since it is purely an electrical connection; no mechanics are involved. Everything is handled by electrical wiring.

WHAT TO LOOK FOR

ESCs come in a variety of sizes to suit most motors. Several specifications are important when you select your ESC. Most important is the maximum operating current of the ESC. If you know your motor current will be around 4 amps, you should have an ESC capable of at least 5 amps continuous current, to be on the safe side.

The next important parameter is the number of battery cells the ESC can handle. Most of the ESCs we use for indoor and parking-lot flyers should be capable of handling from 5 to 10 battery cells. As the micro hobby progresses, we are beginning to see motors working on only 2 or 3 cells. Be advised, when we get to that point, you must consider your selection of an ESC accordingly.

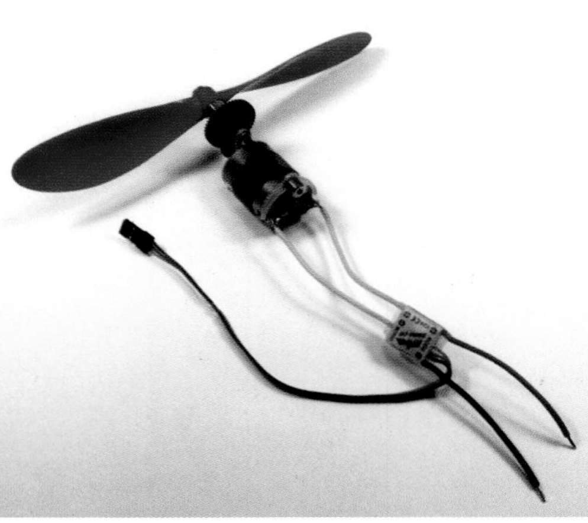

Here is a basic RE-280 geared motor (Titanic Airlines) with an Airwise Intl. SMM-08 ESC attached. In this case, the two leads have been soldered to the motor terminals. The cable with the RC system connector plugs into the throttle port on the RC receiver. The remaining two wires both will have connectors attached. They will then connect to the battery pack.

There are other ESC features that are also worth looking into. For example, you will probably want one of the more modern ESCs that employs a microprocessor. The microprocessor can be programmed for slow start-ups so that the gear train doesn't get damaged. A brake might be included to stop the prop from free-wheeling in flight once the motor is shut off. This can be especially handy when using a folding-prop assembly, since the prop must first stop rotating before it can fold. Other ESCs will prevent the motor from starting if the RC transmitter has accidentally been left on at any position other than dead idle. Still others will shut down the motor in flight should the radio receive any electrical interference. Many of these features are very worthwhile to have and are becoming quite common in modern ESCs.

BATTERY ELIMINATOR CIRCUIT—BEC

One of the most important features offered by an ESC is a battery eliminator circuit (BEC). With a BEC, you can operate your RC airborne system (receiver and servos) from the same battery pack that powers your electric flight motor. This is done with a regulator circuit that is capable of reducing something as high as 10 to 12 volts down to a fixed 5V level. A servo-type cable going from the ESC into the throttle port (connector plug-in) on your RC receiver carries the 5V operating voltage with it. Obviously, with this type of setup, it is possible to run the single battery pack down to a point where it is no longer capable of operating the radio system. Should that happen, the model could easily crash. To prevent that from happening, a voltage cutoff point is set into most ESCs. Usually this level is around 4.0 to 4.5 volts.

When the cutoff is reached, it will shut down the electric motor, but the RC system will still continue to work. As a safety measure, you are sometimes offered the chance to turn the motor back on for a short period, e.g., 30 seconds. You do this by bringing the throttle-control stick first back to full idle and then advancing it once again. Sometimes that extra 30 seconds can help you position your model aircraft for a better or more controllable landing.

HOW MANY CELLS?

When you use a regular BEC circuit as part of your ESC, if you attempt to use a 4-cell battery pack, you must realize that you will be very close to the

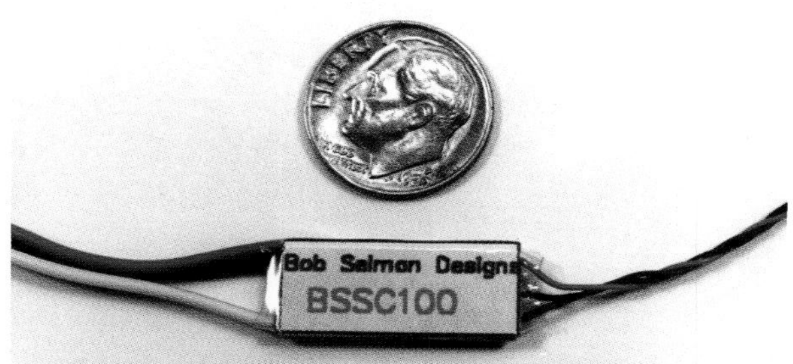

Bob Selman Designs' new BSSC100 ESC. This ESC is rated at 4A motor current, weighs 0.6 grams without wires and 1.7 grams with wires (cables), operates at 2kHz and, most interestingly, operates on only 3 or 4 Ni-Cd or NiMH cells with a BEC.

voltage cutoff point, which might be reached shortly into the start of your flight. For this reason, it has been generally advised not to go below 5 cells when using a standard BEC. But we are now seeing very small models, flying at under 2 ounces total weight, that operate from only 1 or 2 battery cells. For these particular models, you will likely have to choose a very special ESC with either no voltage cutoff or a very low cutoff. One company, FMA Direct, is now making available a voltage "step-up" circuit. This will boost the operating voltage (from 1 or 2 cells) up to a more useable level to operate the RC system. Keep in mind that this is all very experimental at this time, but new developments occur daily in the world of micro flight.

BEC CURRENT REQUIREMENTS

When discussing BEC operation, it's important to note that the regulator device has a definite current limitation. Some provide .5 amps and some 1 amp. Usually the ESC specification sheet will inform you of this. Typically, an RC micro receiver might need about 10mA to operate. Each servo might idle at 10 or 20mA, but that current could easily reach a range of 200 to 300mA when the servos are moving. You must determine that a particular BEC circuit is capable of driving your RC equipment. Otherwise, you'll either fail to have sufficient power to drive multiple servos or you'll burn out the regulator device in the ESC.

THE PROGRAMMABLE PIXIE-7P

A new approach to ESC design is the Castle Creations Pixie-7P ESC. It has most of the features just discussed, but it allows the modeler to select any one of four voltage cutoff points or to have no cutoff at all. The four cutoffs are as follows: 3.5, 4.7, 6.0 and 8.0 volts. There are also other programmable options associated with this fine controller. You can select to have the motor stop fully, or to just slow down when the cutoff point is reached. You can also choose auto throttle calibration (in which the ESC automatically sets the throttle response to match your transmitter), or you can set it for a fixed throttle range of your own choice. With a 7A current rating and a weight of only 3 grams (0.1 ounce), the Pixie-7P is becoming very popular for the smallest indoor models up through parking-lot flyers using RS-280 size motors or equivalent. When you reach Speed 400 motor power, you will need ESC current ratings of 12 to 15 amps and heavier gauge wire.

BEC WIRING TIPS

When you purchase your ESC, three sets of cables will, most likely, be included. One cable will have three wires and will usually be terminated in a standard servo connector. In most cases, this connector can be made to plug into just about any micro RC receiver on the market. But even knowing this, you best check the polarity of the three wires before plugging in and attempting to operate the system.

A second cable consisting of two wires will be marked "BATTERY." It should be marked with polarity (+ and -), which is very important. If you hook up this cable backwards you could possibly burn out the ESC. Generally, this cable will not come with a connector, so that will become your responsibility. As the micro RC hobby grows, we hope that more and more manufacturers will supply their various components with connectors already installed. This will allow the modeler to "plug and fly" without the need to solder.

A third cable, also consisting of two wires, will be marked "MOTOR." It, too, will have a polarity marking (+ and -). These wires will go to the two terminals on your motor. A connector set can be used, but as already noted, it is generally acceptable to solder these wires to the motor terminals. Unlike with the battery side, if you get the motor connection wrong, the only problem will be the motor turning backwards, and the solution is to just reverse the connections.

The lower the current rating of an ESC, the smaller the size of the cables (wires) employed. Obviously lower currents allow for the use of lighter wiring. ESCs intended for micro indoor flying can now be purchased weighing only a gram or two. Despite the low current levels, these ESCs can still get warm to hot during operation. Therefore, it is advisable to keep them clear of warm motors or battery packs. Some airflow over the ESC—as is the case with the motor and battery—is a good idea, but common sense should prevail as well. If nothing is very hot to the touch after a full flight, you are doing fine.

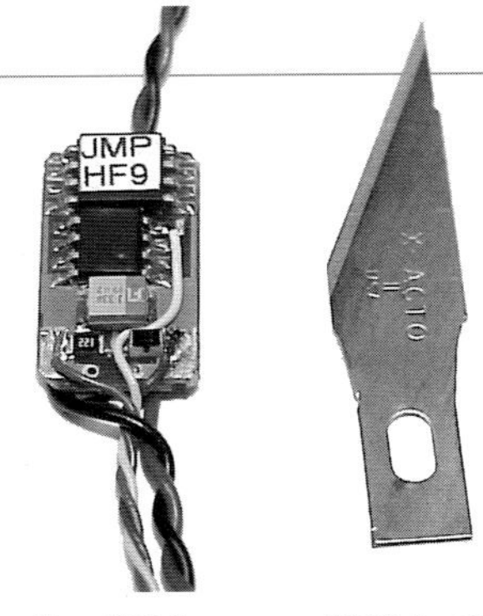

Another high-frequency ESC intended for coreless motor operation is the JMP-HF9 designed by Jean-Marie Piednoir of France. Current rating is only 1.5 amps continuous. Weight is 1.9 grams with wires. Operating frequency is 60kHz.

BEC OPERATING FREQUENCY

Another parameter of an ESC that you should be concerned with is its operating frequency. This is usually expressed in the term "cycles" with the symbol Hz (for hertz). It might also be expressed in kilohertz (kHz). A typical ESC may have an operating frequency of 1000 to 3000Hz or 1 to 3kHz. At full power, an ESC is generally quite efficient in operation. That means it is not imposing any real losses in the electric power system. At half-throttle settings, that efficiency level can be reduced. In many cases this need not be a concern. But it has been noted that when using coreless motors, it appears to be advisable to employ special ESCs that have a considerably higher operating frequency.

Two such controllers come to mind: one is the

REPRESENTATIVE ESCS FOR MICRO RC AIRPLANES

This compilation of electronic speed controls is not exhaustive, yet it reflects the wide variety that are available for use in small electric airplanes. Some weigh less than a gram and many are feature-rich with automated functionality. Check out the brief descriptions.

AIRWISE INTERNATIONAL
SMM-08

SMM-08 ESC with an 8A motor current rating. Perfect for parking-lot flyers with up to Speed 280-300 power. A larger version of this unit is available with an 18A rating for Speed 400/480 applications.

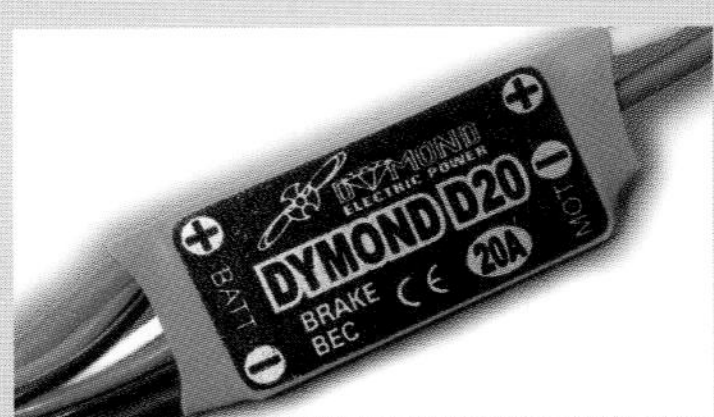

DYMOND MODELSPORTS
D20

Intended mainly for use with larger park flyers, the micro-size D20 is highly efficient and just right for Speed 400 motors. It's equipped with a digital microprocessor and comes factory set. It weighs 11 grams and can handle up to 20 amps. It is designed for use with 5 to 10 cells.

GREAT PLANES
ELECTRIFLY C-10

Best for Speed 400 motors, the C-10 can take up to 12 amps of continuous current and can run on 5 to 8 cells. The Electrifly is light and compact and has a low-voltage cutoff at 3.7 volts.

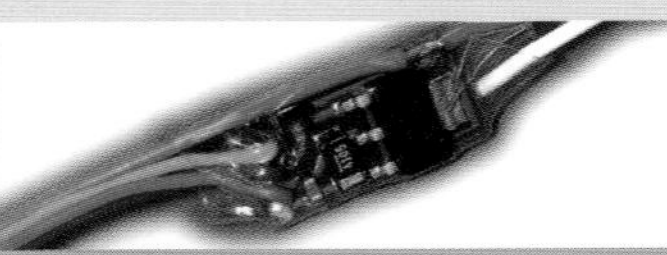

CASTLE CREATIONS
PIXIE-7P

The only one of its kind, the Pixie-7P permits you to program cutoff voltage, motor cutoffs and throttle range. It can handle up to 7 amps of continuous current and is designed for 3 to 8 cells with BEC and 3 to 18 cells without. The Pixie is microprocessor controlled and shuts off automatically when the signal is lost. It weighs 3 grams.

FMA
MINI 5A

Designed specifically for backyard flyers, the Mini 5A is one of the smallest speed controls currently available. Featuring high-frequency operation, the Mini 5 is microprocessor controlled and can handle up to 5 amps of continuous current. It runs on 5 to 8 cells and weighs only 2.5 grams.

GWS
ICS-50

Weighing only 1 gram, the ICS-50 is one of the lightest speed controls available. It features automatic low-voltage cutoff and self-resetting. It can handle up to 2 amps and is designed to run on 4 to 8 cells. The GWS ICS-50E is the recommended controller for all GWS IPS power systems.

This is a special 125kHz operating frequency ESC developed by MTM Intl. (Germany) for use specifically with the small coreless motors. It is rated at 4 amps and will work on 6 to 9 cells. A BEC is included. Weight is 3.5 grams with wires. Note the toroidal core filter on the one end of the unit.

JMP HF9 (made in France and sold by David Lewis and Cloud 9 RC in the U.S.) with an operating frequency of 60,000Hz; the other is a 125,000Hz ESC available from MTM Intl. (in Germany). These specialty controllers are about the same size and weight as regular ESCs, but they do cost considerably more (approximately $60 as opposed to $30).

AstroFlight Inc. recently introduced a companion ESC for its little Firefly-800 micro coreless motor. The new ESC is designated as its Model 200 and weighs about 2 grams. AstroFlight claims this controller has been designed to provide a smooth variable DC voltage to the motor.

BRUSHLESS MOTOR ESCS

Although still much in the minority, brushless motor technology is beginning to show up in the world of micro flight. As already mentioned, both AstroFlight and Hacker are offering small brushless motors. Brushless motors require a special ESC that is totally different from those used with "brushed" motors. They are also considerably more expensive. So, for now, be advised that if you choose a brushless motor you must follow the manufacturer's recommendation for a companion ESC.

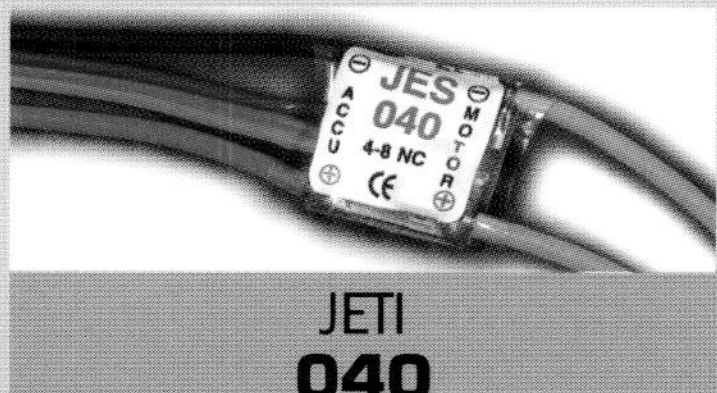

JETI
040

The Jeti 040 can handle up to 4 amps of continuous current and 10 amps of maximum current. It is designed specifically for Speed 280 and smaller motors powered by 4 to 8 cells. The 040 features automatic setup, temperature-overload protection, automatic low-voltage cutoff and a switching frequency. It weighs 1.2 grams.

KONTRONIK
MICRO-10

Kontronik Micro-10 ESC. It has a 5A current rating and will operate on 4 to 10 volts. Weight is 0.9 grams without wires. Operates at 2kHz. Unit is available in the USA from Northeast Sailplanes, Inc.

MAXX PRODUCTS
MX-9104 PICO

Along with its light design, the MX-9104 Pico ESC is a high-frequency controller that has soft start and automatic low-voltage cutoff. It weighs 1 gram and can take up to 4 amps of continuous current or 5.5 amps of instantaneous current. The MX-9104 is designed for 5 to 8 cells.

SIRIUS ELECTRONICS
GFS

Sirius Electronics GFS ESC. Available in a 10A version weighing 4 grams with wires or 1 gram without wires. A larger version with a 20A current rating is also available.

SKY HOOKS & RIGGING
SCSH-7A-LITH

Skyhooks & Rigging's SCSH-7A-LITH ESC. Rated at 7 amps, it weighs 1 gram with cables. The unit was designed specifically to be used with three Tadiran lithium metal batteries. Voltage cutoff is set for 7.2 volts. Operating frequency is 4kHz.

SKY HOOKS & RIGGING
RX72-N HYBRID

The RX72-N is unique in that it's actually a receiver with a speed controller built into it. The speed-control feature has selectable throttle cutoff points and can handle up to 7 amps of continuous current. The unit weighs 5.5 grams.

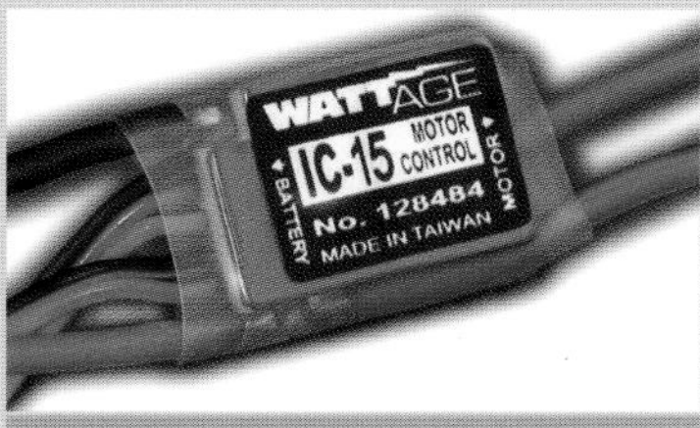

WATTAGE
IC-15

The high-frequency IC-15 can handle up to 15 amps and is designed to run on 6 to 10 cells. It features brake, a reset capability and automatic low-voltage cutoff. It weighs only 2.4 grams.

Just to give you an idea of what a digital pulse-width meter looks like. This particular unit was designed by Mike Dorffler years ago and marketed at the time by Estes, the rocket people. Recently Mike introduced an upgraded version of his Electronic Digital Pulse Meter, which he is now offering fully assembled for just $39.95.

TRANSMITTER TIPS

There is one other operational aspect of an ESC that you might want to consider. Your basic RC system produces a string of pulses that repeat themselves at a fast and regular rate. Within each "word" of information are individual channels for the rudder, elevator, throttle, etc. Each channel may typically be at a neutral pulse position of 1.5 milliseconds. Going to one extreme of control (like full throttle) might bring the pulse up to 2 milliseconds (I'm guessing, using these figures merely as examples). Going to low throttle might send the pulse down to 1.0 milliseconds. This, therefore, would be the normal span of your throttle control.

But let's say your transmitter has what is known as endpoint adjustment (EPA) capability. You may have set your throttle channel for use on another aircraft to a high throttle position of only 1.8 milliseconds—not quite the full range. Not knowing this, you might obtain something less than full power when using this ESC to operate your new model. The less than normal power might not be readily detectable by the sound of the prop. The problem, as you can see, is not the fault of your ESC, but is, in fact, the fault of the setting on your transmitter.

How can you avoid such a problem? Fortunately, our ESC circuit designers are getting smarter, and they are developing new microprocessor chips that are capable of reading the pulse signal from the transmitter and adjusting it automatically, so you will always have the full command of the ESC and obtain a full range of power settings. If you are curious about the pulse-width position, there are devices available on the RC market called digital pulse-width meters. Some RC systems are known to have lower pulse widths than others. This situation can also tend to reduce certain power settings. Again, modern ESC design will help eliminate any problems, but a digital pulse-width meter can help to at least satisfy your curiosity. At this book's press time, a new Electronic Digital Pulse Meter was introduced by Colorado modeler, Mike Dorffler. Mike's meter will sell fully assembled for just $39.95. For his address, please refer to the Source Guide at the end of this book.

MEASURING ESC EFFICIENCY

As already mentioned, some ESCs can introduce a loss into your electric motor power system. By just studying the advertised specifications, you can't always determine the overall efficiency of the particular ESC. You can, however, run your own experiment to satisfy yourself. Mount your electric motor to a test stand, attach a suitable prop, then power up the motor directly from your battery. Measure your motor current and prop rpm (see Chapter 7, Measuring Motor Parameters). Once you have these readings, insert your ESC into this loop. You will need to temporarily hook up an RC system as well. Run up the motor using the ESC and take the same current and rpm readings again. If all is well, both sets of readings should be about the same. Of course, you must recognize that this type of test is only good for full power checks, which is when ESCs are most efficient, but it is still a good guide.

NON-LINEAR ESC THROTTLES

You should know that some ESCs offer a more linear control of the motor speed than others. If you tend to fly most of the time at full power, this non-linear control might never bother you; however, there are some ESCs that will go to full throttle long before your transmitter control stick gets to the half-way mark. When this happens, you may end up with full power most of the time and only a small portion of the throttle usable for reduced- speed flying. Happily, these non-linear type ESCs are disappearing quickly from the hobby market and are being replaced by more linear types that provide a more realistic motor speed control.

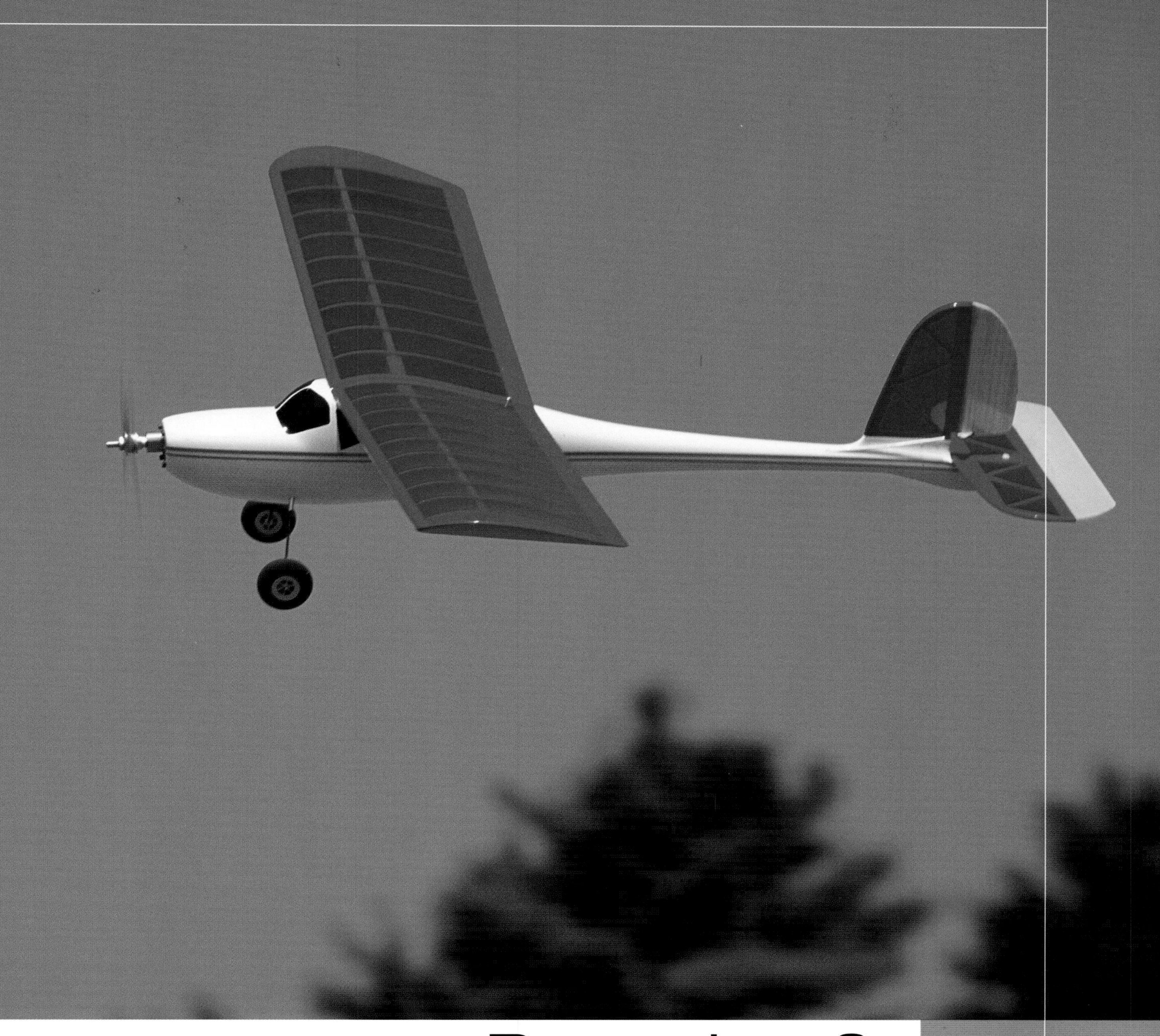

Batteries & Chargers

5

To obtain the best performance from your small electric aircraft, you'll need to know how to choose batteries and how to get the best performance out of the battery packs you use. In this chapter, you'll learn how to charge and maintain nickel cadmium (Ni-Cd) and nickel-metal-hydride (NiMH) packs in a variety of capacity sizes. The author also offers valuable advice that will help you choose the charger best suited to your needs.

As you can see, nickel-cadmium (Ni-Cd) and nickel-metal-hydride (NiMH) batteries come in a wide variety of sizes and shapes.

Batteries provide the "fuel" for electric-powered flight. To obtain enjoyable, long duration e-power flights you must understand how to select the right capacity battery cell for each specific application. You must also know how many cells are required to make up a battery pack. Finally, you must be able to charge these battery packs.

I wrote a comprehensive article called "Battery Basics," which was published in the April 2001 issue of *Model Airplane News*, pages 78 to 80. If you are familiar with that article, you will recognize that it was a reference source for this chapter. The original article was geared to electric power in general, while this chapter provides information on the specific application of batteries for indoor and parking-lot RC model aircraft. Please keep in mind that this entire chapter is concerned primarily with the batteries used to power your electric motor and, through a BEC circuit in your ESC, the airborne RC equipment (receiver and servos).

BATTERY CHARGING DEFINITIONS

The three basic types of battery charging rates are defined as fast, overnight and trickle. The fast charge rate can usually bring a battery up to full charge in fewer than 30 minutes. This fast rate can be used at indoor flying facilities or at parking-lot locations and will allow you to make many flights during the course of a single flying session. Batteries used for fast charging are so specified by their manufacturers/distributors.

The overnight charge rate (also referred to as a slow charge rate) is calculated by taking the battery capacity (in milliampere hours or mAh) and dividing by 10. This amount of charge can remain on the battery for periods of 10 to 24 hours. It helps condition or equalize the various cells that make up a battery pack. This is the preferred rate for some of the very small size (low capacity) cells used for micro flying. It is also the charge rate of choice when using standard or regular battery cells.

It is important to remember that in micro RC electric-powered flying we are using batteries with capacities as low as 50mAh. If you take 50mAh divided by 10, you obtain an overnight charge rate of only 5mA, which is an extremely small current. As such, it can often be difficult to set a charge current as low as 5mA.

Trickle charge rate is a very low or maintenance level, defined as capacity (in mAh) divided by 50. This type of charge rate can be left on the battery indefinitely. Trickle charging is usually not done with electric power packs, but it tends to be more common with regard to RC transmitter batteries.

BATTERIES

To get the most enjoyment out of electric-powered flight, you will need to use batteries intended for fast charging. The optimum situation is to obtain approximately an 8- to 10-minute flight on a charge and then be able "fast" recharge the batteries within 20 to 30 minutes. Using more than one battery pack, it is possible to fly almost continuously. In other words, while flying on one pack, have another connected to the charger.

Batteries suitable for fast charging are available from companies such as Batteries America (also known as E. H. Yost & Co.), B & T Racing Products, FMA Direct, Maxx Products Intl., New Creations R/C, SR Batteries, TNR and others. The capacity of these cells is generally stated in terms of milliampere hours, or simply mAh. A battery rated at 270mAh is capable of supplying 270mA current (the same as 0.275 amps) for a period of one hour, after which it is fully depleted and must be recharged.

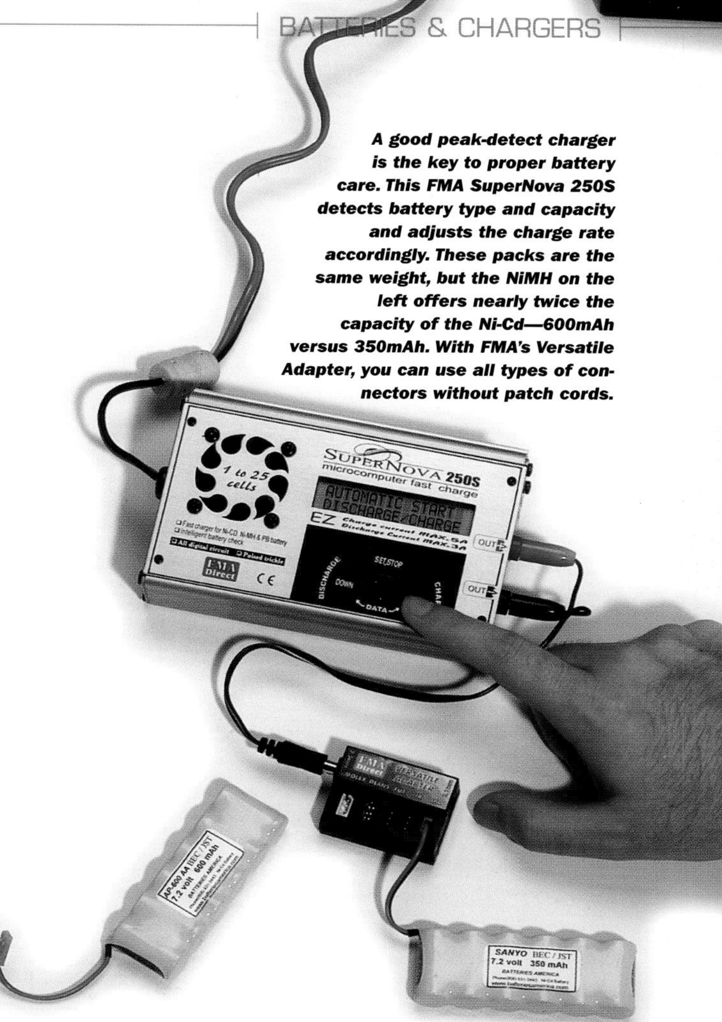

A good peak-detect charger is the key to proper battery care. This FMA SuperNova 250S detects battery type and capacity and adjusts the charge rate accordingly. These packs are the same weight, but the NiMH on the left offers nearly twice the capacity of the Ni-Cd—600mAh versus 350mAh. With FMA's Versatile Adapter, you can use all types of connectors without patch cords.

NICKEL-CADMIUM—NI-CD—BATTERIES

The most common batteries used today in electric-powered flight are the nickel-cadmium (Ni-Cd) type. They are available in fast and overnight charge cells. The fast charge is the most popular for powering electric-powered aircraft, while the slow charge or overnight charge cells are more commonly used for RC systems (receivers and servos). Keep in mind that many low capacity, overnight charge capable cells work quite well with micro flyers. Capacities intended for indoor and parking-lot flyer models can range from as little as 50mAh to as much as 1200mAh (1.2 amp hours) and even more. The indoor flyers will be better suited for the 50 to 175mAh capacity cells, while parking-lot flyers will use the 275 to 600mAh capacity cells. From 600mAh on up you are into Speed 400 type flyers.

The actual capacity of a cell or pack is usually stamped right on the product. If you can't find a marking, ask the manufacturer or distributor. You need to know the capacity to be able to determine the proper charge current.

NiMH cells (green) have a size/weight-to-capacity advantage over Ni-Cds (yellow). The large cells on the left are the same size, but the NiMH has nearly twice the capacity—9000mAh versus 5000mAh. The small cells are both 600mAh, but the smaller diameter of the NiMH saves weight.

Of course, the higher the capacity of the battery the more it will weigh. Everything in electric-powered flight is a careful balance between motor power (wattage), battery capacity and battery voltage (determined by the number of cells in the pack). Get the correct balance and you will obtain the longest flights, with maneuverability that can rival glow-fuel-powered models

NICKEL-METAL HYDRIDE—NIMH—BATTERIES

A newer type of battery now becoming very popular, especially for the small flyers, is the nickel-metal hydride (or NiMH). These batteries are somewhat lighter than comparable capacity Ni-Cd cells. The fast charge current has to be somewhat limited (as compared to Ni-Cd cells). They also exhibit more of a voltage drop (offer a lower voltage per cell when under load) than Ni-Cd cells. As such, it is often necessary to add one more cell to a pack when going from Ni-Cd to NiMH cells. These limitations must be observed carefully to obtain the very best advantages of NiMH cells, but the bottom line is that you can end up with much more capacity in a battery that weighs roughly the same as a Ni-Cd.

Also understand that not all sizes (or brands) of NiMH batteries will suit micro-flying needs. Some particular cells just can't meet load demands. You will only find this out by experimenting or asking the advice of other modelers. Be very alert to the fact that, when using NiMH cells, the capacity is directly related to the load placed on the battery. You could have 270mAh capacity at a 500mA load, but by the time you've reached a 1A load, that capacity might only be 200mAh. Take it up to an even higher load, e.g., 1.5 amps, and that capacity might drop even further to 150mAh. This is why experimentation is necessary to get the optimum results.

The CR-2 lithium (non-rechargeable) 3V battery and a set of 3, 50mAh Sanyo Ni-Cd cells (3.6 volts) weigh about the same, but the CR-2 is rated at 750mAh. The CR-2 will provide many more flights before it dies, whereas the Ni-Cds can be recharged. Initial cost is about the same.

LITHIUM BATTERIES

An even newer type of battery is the lithium metal battery, which is becoming popular with micro RC flyers. These cells can only be charged with specialized chargers intended specifically for that application. With the proper number of these cells (usually 2 or 3), it is possible to obtain flight durations in excess of one hour on a single charge.

Beyond lithium metal cells are even newer variation, known as lithium ion and lithium polymer batteries. They were developed for the laptop computer and cell phone market. Now these same cells are appearing in some experimental micro-electric power systems. It is only a matter of time before larger quantities will be available for modeler applications. There are also non-rechargeable lithium cells that can power micro flyers. These cells include the CR2 developed for the camera market.

BATTERY CHARGERS

To fully appreciate electric-powered flight you will need what we call a "peak detect" battery charger. Basic chargers that operate simply from a timing

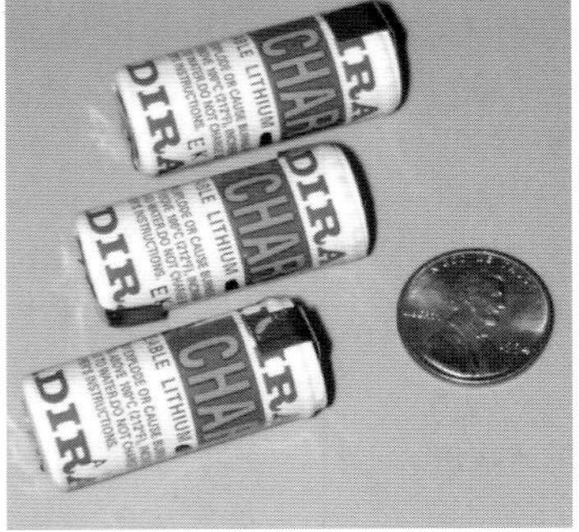

Special lithium metal batteries made by the Tadiran Co. of Israel. These are available in a basic 800mAh capacity cell that is about the same size as an AA battery. They have a higher characteristic voltage, 3.4 volts per cell at full charge, so it is easy to power up a model using just two of these cells. If your total current drain is 800mA, you can achieve one-hour-duration flights. But lithium metal batteries require the use of special chargers. NEVER ATTEMPT TO USE A STANDARD PEAK CHARGER ON THEM!

Lithium-polymer cells are one of the newest battery types to be used to power miniature electrics. These photos show one method of ganging two cells into a 7.4V battery with a capacity of 1250mAh.

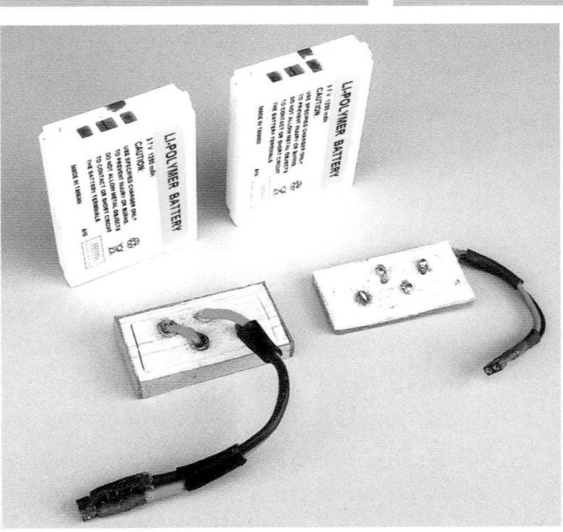

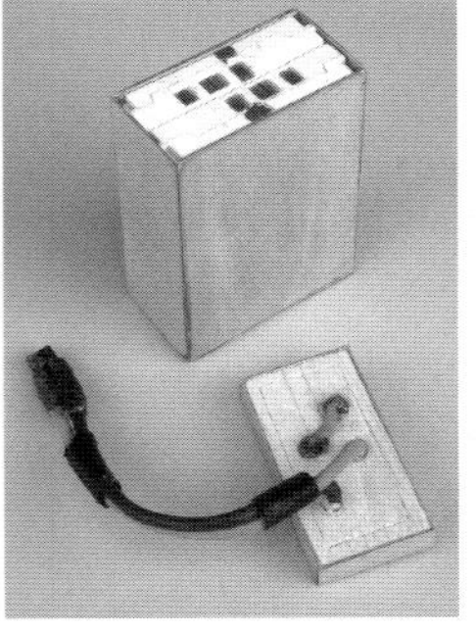

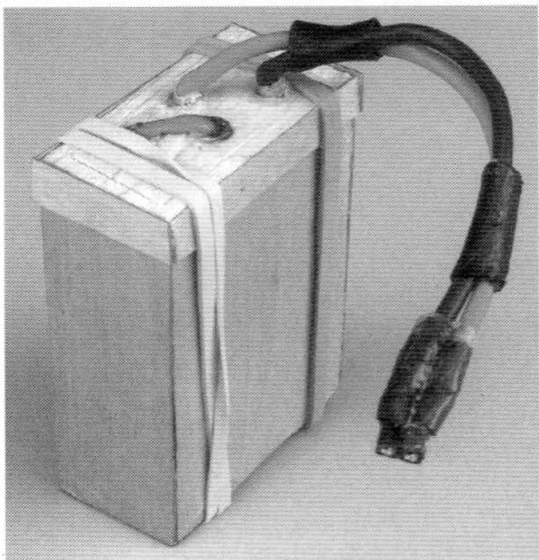

Above middle: the lithium packs fit securely into a 1/64-inch-ply box to form the completed pack. Right: a fully assembled battery. Rubber bands hold the cap securely over the battery. (See the January 2002 issue of RC MicroFlight for construction details; these cells are for the Nokia 3390 cell phone; NK33 Polymerbatt).

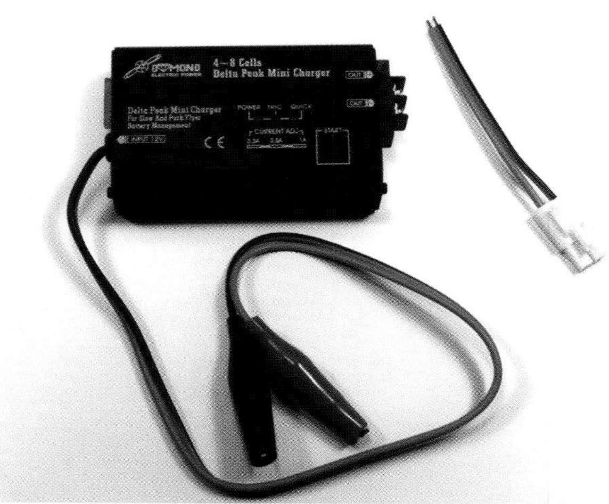

A peak detect charger from Dymond Modelsports intended for the smaller or lower capacity cells with a very affordable price. It can charge 4 to 8 cells at selectable current levels of 300mA, 500mA and 1 amp. In a practical sense, it can charge Ni-Cd batteries up to about 350mAh capacity and NiMH cells up to about 600mAh. Higher capacity cells could also be charged, but the time needed to reach full charge increases.

device can easily cause over- or under-charging. The peak-detect charger senses when the battery pack is at full charge (full capacity) and shuts itself off automatically (some revert to a trickle or sustaining charge level). It would be wise to invest a little more than a $100 in a peak detect charger right from the start.

My favorite, because it is inexpensive, easy to operate and reliable, is the AstroFlight 110D. It can handle up to 18 Ni-Cd or NiMH cells at up to 5.0 amps charge current. But it is on the lower end that this charger really excels. The AstroFlight 110D can fast or slow charge. In either mode the peak detect circuit operates. When in the slow charge mode, it is possible to set charge currents to as low as 100mA; anything less and you wouldn't be able to read it on the LCD display. This is just about perfect for the lowest capacity cells, like the 50 to 100mAh variety.

The AstroFlight 110D charger operates from a 12V car battery or a comparable battery (at least the size of a regular car battery). Just as a tip, DO NOT ATTEMPT TO USE a 12V field kit (motorcycle type) battery left over from your fueled-engine days. It has only a fraction of the current capacity of a car battery and the charge will quickly be depleted long before the flying session is over. This can be very frustrating, because with diminishing capacity the fast-charge period will take longer and longer.

A good overnight charger is the Ace Hobby Distributors' Digital Dual Vari-Charger (DDVC), which has two adjustable outputs from 0 to 500mA and operates from either a 12V DC source or from 115V AC household power. For more details on this DDVC, please look up my review, which appeared

The ever-popular AstroFlight 110D charger. This peak detect charger only charges, it does not discharge. It operates from a 12V battery (such as a car battery). It can charge from 100mA up to about 5 amps and up to 18 battery cells. It works equally well with both Ni-Cd and NiMH cells. It is also one of the easiest chargers to learn to use.

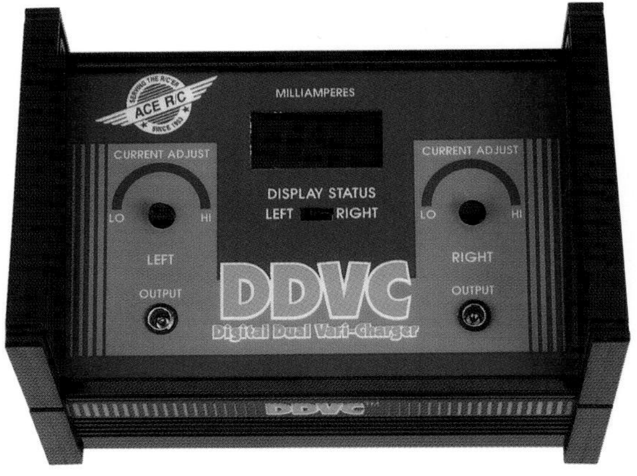

For an overnight charger, I recommend the Ace Hobby Distributors' DDVC (Digital Dual Vari-Charger). It has two separate outputs, each of which can be adjusted from zero up to about 300mA charge current and up to about 10 cells. Most serious e-power modelers own several of these units, which sell for about $85.

TECH TIP

INITIAL CHARGE

All new Ni-Cd or NiMH batteries should be initially charged at the overnight rate, which is determined by taking the capacity of the batteries (in milliampere hours or mAh) and dividing that by 10. In other words, a 275mAh-rated capacity battery pack will need 275 divided by 10 or 27.5 (28 is fine!) milliamperes (mA) of charge current.

on page 108 of the May 2000 issue of *Model Airplane News*. An overnight period is defined as anything more than 10 hours, up to as long as 24 hours.

To recap, for indoor and parking-lot flying you will need a peak detect battery charger, like the AstroFlight 110D and an overnight charger, like the Ace DDVC.

CHARGING ROUTINE

I generally charge my battery packs overnight at the C/10 rate, i.e., 1⁄10 nominal capacity, a day or two before I plan to go flying. When I get to the gym, auditorium or parking lot, I make my first flight of the day on that overnight charge. It usually will not be a strong flight, but it does help to condition the battery. For all my remaining flights of the day, I fast charge the batteries using the peak detect charger. These flights will always be stronger than the first flight. When I return home from flying, I charge overnight once again and then store the batteries. Some modelers leave their packs discharged. Either way will not harm the batteries. Personally, I never maintain my flight packs on any sort of trickle charger.

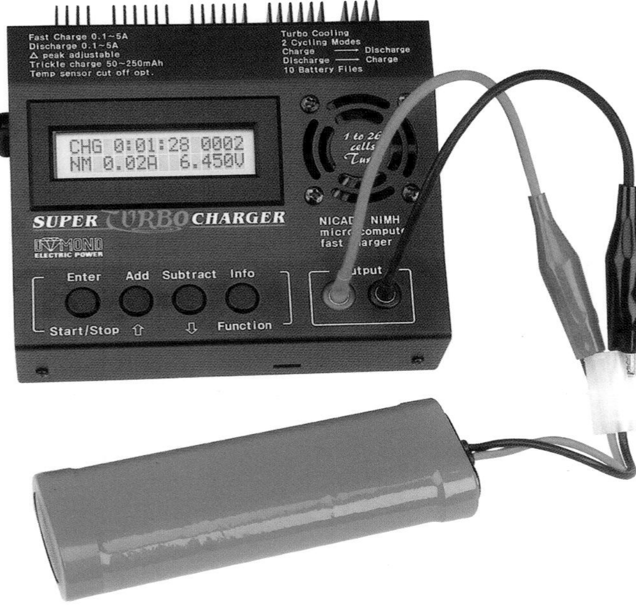

The Dymond Modelsports Super Turbo Charger is a recent addition to the available units. It can charge 1 to 26 Ni-Cd or NiMH cells with capacities ranging from 50mAh to 3000mAh.

SELECTING FAST-CHARGE CURRENT

For Ni-Cd batteries, the fast-charge current should be determined by taking the rated capacity (in mAh or amp hours) and multiplying that by a factor of three. This 3C rate is probably the best all-around fast charge rate for the EP beginner.

MAXIMUM FAST-CHARGE CURRENT

Cell capacity	Ni-Cd 3x capacity in mA (amps)	NiMH 2x capacity in mA (amps)
50mAh	150	100
150mAh	450	300
300mAh	900 (0.9)	600 (0.6)
500mAh	1500 (1.5)	1000 (1.0)
600mAh	1800 (1.8)	1200 (1.2)
1000mAh	3000 (3.0)	2000 (2.0)
1300mAh	3900 (3.9)	2600 (2.6)
1600mAh	4800 (4.8)	3200 (3.2)

Again, let's take a battery rated at 275mAh (which is the same as saying 0.275 amp-hour), and take the 0.275 amp times three, which gives you 0.825 amps (825mA); then set your peak detect charger for 0.8 amps. If the pack was close to being fully depleted, it will take approximately 20 minutes to reach full charge. This is a very important step. Unless you own one of the very new, fully automatic battery chargers, the responsibility for setting the correct charge current will be up to you. Set it too low, and it will take too long to charge; set it too high, and you will overheat your batteries and possibly ruin them. As you become more experienced, you will find that higher-capacity Ni-Cd batteries can take more than the 3C fast-charge rate.

Just about the smallest battery you will have to fast charge is the 50mAh Ni-Cd battery. The 3C

Another peak-detect charger intended for small- and low-capacity batteries, the Sirius Charge 100 operates from a 12V battery. It can charge 4 to 8 cells with capacities ranging from 50 to 200mAh using a fixed charge rate of 100mA. A 50mAh battery will therefore reach full charge in about 30 minutes.

charge rate for this battery works out to 150mA (0.15 amps). The AstroFlight 110D charger can be set to this rate with a little care. With a 3C charge rate, these little cells can be fully charged in 20 minutes.

As a point of information, several specialty peak detect chargers have recently come on the market. One that comes to mind is the Sirius Charge100 charger. This unit is 12V DC powered and is capable of charging from 4 to 8 Ni-Cd or NiMH cells (50 to 200mAh capacity) at a fixed 100mA current level. A 50mAh pack could reach full charge in 30 minutes. Higher capacity batteries will take longer to recharge. This charger works well and is extremely simple to use.

Another new small battery charger is now available from Bob Selman Designs. His model BSPC1 Peak Charger handles 2 to 7 Ni-Cd cells at a fixed 200mA charge rate (suitable for 50 to 180mAh capacity cells). A second model BSPC2 Peak Charger also works on 2 to 7 cells but at a higher fixed-charge current of 300mA (for battery capacities ranging from 110 to 270mAh). These are specialized units that have been tailored expressly for the charging of low-capacity battery cells.

The newer NiMH batteries must be treated a little more conservatively. For these cells, you should use the capacity of the battery multiplied by two. So a 120mAh NiMH battery would be charged at 0.12 times 2 or 0.24 amps (240mA). To reach a full charge will take approximately 30 minutes. Some chargers have problems peak detecting NiMH cells. The AstroFlight 110D just recommended has no problem doing this.

LITHIUM BATTERY CHARGERS

Lithium metal batteries are usually rated at 800mAh. Chargers for this type of cell are set at

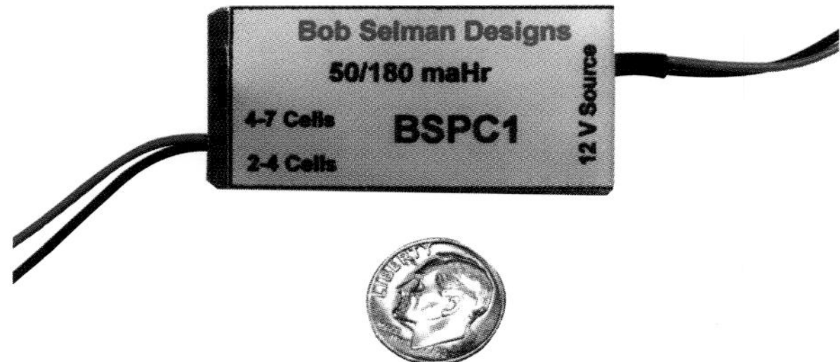

Bob Selman Designs has developed this peak detect charger for very low capacity batteries. This BSPC1 charger can charge 2 to 4 or 4 to 7 Ni-Cd or NiMH cells. Charge current is preset at 200mA, which is a 4C rate for 50mAh cells. At that rate they would reach full charge in approximately 15 minutes. 110mAh cells would take 33 minutes for a full charge, and 180mAh cells would take almost an hour.

The Magellan lithium-metal charger is 2½ inches square and 1 inch thick. Note the single output cable consisting of two wires; you must attach the connector of your choice.

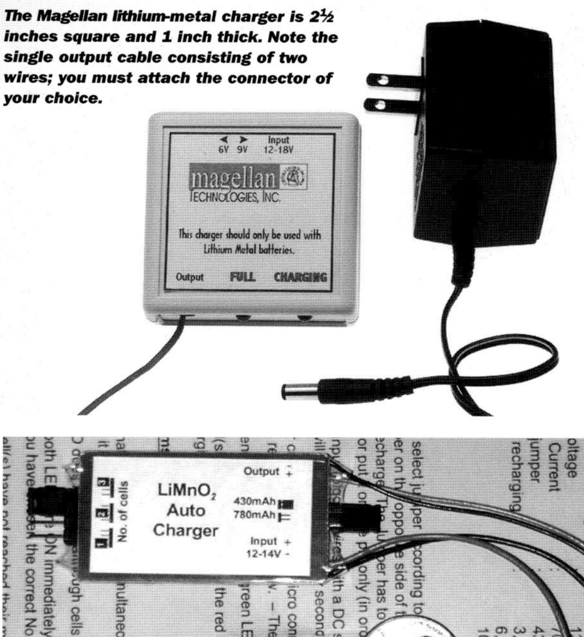

Another lithium metal battery charger, this from JMP in France. This charger is unique in that it can charge 1, 2, or 3 lithium metal cells. It can also charge the regular Tadiran 800mAh cell or the special smaller capacity cell (400mAh).

about 80mA current, although several use a higher rate and will automatically cut off when the voltage under charge reaches 3.4 volts per cell. Generally, these specialty chargers can be set to charge one, two, or three lithium metal cells. A good charger for this purpose, the Magellan Lithium metal charger, manufactured by Magellan Technologies, Inc. is reviewed in depth on page 13 in the January 2000 issue of *RC MicroFlight*. Another excellent charger is the JMP designed by Jean Marie Piednoir of France and sold by various European distributors, including Chris Stewart of RCS Technik in Great Britain. I have mentioned only a few of the specialty chargers now available, but this should give you a good start in choosing the charger that will best meet your needs.

NEVER CHARGE A HOT BATTERY PACK

If a battery is fast charged at the proper current level on a peak detect charger, it is likely that it will not heat up beyond the point of being slightly or moderately warm. However, at a 2C or 3C charge rate that is to be expected. On the other hand, when powering a model in flight, current levels can typically average up to 2 amps for indoor flyers, up to 5 amps with parking-lot flyers and 8 to 12 amps for Speed 400 aircraft. At these high currents, the battery may return after a flight in a very warm, sometimes "hot" state. Sometimes it might even be too hot to handle! BEFORE CHARGING A HOT BATTERY PACK YOU MUST FIRST COOL IT DOWN to avoid damage. Some modelers have resorted to using ice or dry-ice in a cooler to quickly reduce battery temperature. This technique, unfortunately, can cause very uneven temperatures throughout the pack and possibly result in one side staying hot and the other side almost freezing.

My solution, thanks to United Airlines Captain. Ric Vaughn, (an AMA Electric Nationals First Place Winner in 1999), is to use a RadioShack 12V electric fan (catalog no. 273-243), which is inserted into one end of a piece of 3-inch diameter PVC tube (about 12 inches in length). This fan draws only about 100mA of power and so can be connected all day to your car battery without a problem. You insert the hot battery pack into the open end of this tube and simply let the air from the fan flow over it. In about 5 minutes the battery pack will be cool enough to charge. If you do this every time, before you recharge your battery packs, they should last a long time.

REGULAR FLIGHT USE CYCLES BATTERIES

When discussing RC system batteries, you often hear the expression "cycling." This is the technique of taking a battery pack all the way down to minimum charge (usually 1 volt per cell) and then recharging. Battery capacity can be measured (in mAh) during this type of discharge. Cycling is said to eliminate the "memory" effect, in which the battery "gets used to" providing only a certain amount of its total capacity after being charged.

Keep in mind that with batteries used for electric-powered flight, each and every time the model is flown the battery is taken down practically to minimum capacity. As such, you are essentially cycling these batteries with every flight, and nothing else need be done to them. You can, of course, discharge them once in a while to measure the effective capacity of a pack, but generally speaking, you will easily recognize when a battery pack is going bad because your flight time will be noticeably less.

ASSEMBLING BATTERY PACKS

For our flying purposes, individual battery cells must be assembled into "packs" or groups of cells.

TECH TIP

NEVER PARTIALLY CHARGE YOUR BATTERY

When you fast charge a battery pack on a peak detect charger, it will be done automatically. Full charge is sensed and the charger cuts itself off. For overnight charging, the charger should be left on for 10 hours or more. Some modelers are of the belief that if only a small amount of charge is used up, only a short recharge is necessary. That is definitely not the case. The battery chemistry always expects a full charge. NEVER PARTIALLY CHARGE A BATTERY. This is especially true for RC system batteries.

Many of the battery cell suppliers already mentioned offer battery pack assembly services. You select the capacity (type) of cell and tell them how many cells you want in the pack. You can also decide on a particular pack configuration (square, rectangular, etc.) that will best fit into your model. With that information, the supplier can weld or solder up a pack to meet your needs. The finished product is usually covered with a heat-shrink tubing wrap. You might even specify a connector of your choice or add a connector yourself later on.

I personally make up most of my own battery packs. This takes more time and effort, but I always have the assurance that when finished the pack will meet all my personal requirements. I would like to refer you to "Assemble Your Own Battery Packs," which appeared in the January 2000 issue of *Model Airplane News*, pages 148 to 150. For the smaller cells, such as 50 to 600mAh, I recommend the use of copper solder wick-type braid for the inter-cell connections. Actual pack wiring, connector wiring, choice of wire size and soldering techniques will be discussed in the next chapter.

MOUNTING A BATTERY IN YOUR AIRCRAFT

The easiest way to mount a battery pack in your model is with the help of hook-and-loop fastener tape. Over the years, I have standardized the use of this tape with my fellow club members. The hook part always goes on the battery, while the fuzzy or mating half of the tape is attached inside the model. By keeping this standard, I'm always free to swap packs with friends at the field, trusting that we use the same type and polarity connectors.

Another concern when placing a battery pack in a model is that certain installations may prompt radio interference. A motor turning on and off in flight without pilot commands can be an annoying form of interference. If you think you are getting interference somewhere in your power system, try to reposition the battery pack location. It is generally advisable to keep the battery away from the RC receiver.

Since most indoor and parking-lot flyers don't employ on/off switches, it is important to get into the habit of removing your battery pack from the model after every flight. Many of us have to remove the wing to access a battery pack, but despite that extra effort, you should disconnect the battery when not flying. Consider also that even when the motor is not operating, some ESCs will continue to draw small amounts of current even when in the "off" position. So, once again, when not flying, always disconnect your battery.

ESTIMATING FLIGHT TIME FOR A PARTICULAR BATTERY

The best battery for your model will always be a compromise between how much weight the model can handle and how long a flight you expect with an acceptable speed. One of the most important parameters is motor current. Later chapters discuss this, but for now, I'll share a basic formula that will prove helpful.

If you know your motor current and the capacity rating of your batteries, the formula to find estimated flight time involves multiplying the battery capacity expressed in amps by 60 and dividing that number by the motor current. The answer will be in minutes of flight time. Also, keep in mind that varying battery capacity also means you are varying the total weight of your model aircraft.

As an example, take a 120mAh capacity battery and a motor current of 1.3 amps. First take the 120mAh and express it in amps, which would be 0.120. Multiply that by 60, which equals 7.2. Divide that number by the motor current 1.3 amps and the answer is 5.5 minutes. You can take this same calculation and substitute higher-capacity cells to obtain longer flight times, but recognize that by doing so, you are increasing the total weight of your model. In the same regard, you might choose to lower your total weight by going down to 50mAh cells. The calculation then would be *50mAh or 0.050 amp x 60 = 3 ÷ by 1.3 amps motor current = 2.3 minutes flight time.* That would likely be too short and a poor choice.

One caution: never run an electric motor on the ground to determine how long it will run in actual flight. First of all, in-flight rpm readings will never be the same as those you obtain on the ground. All props tend to unload in flight. But more important, the motor and ESC can possibly overheat. Cooling air from the prop alone is insufficient to prevent damage to the motor and/or ESC.

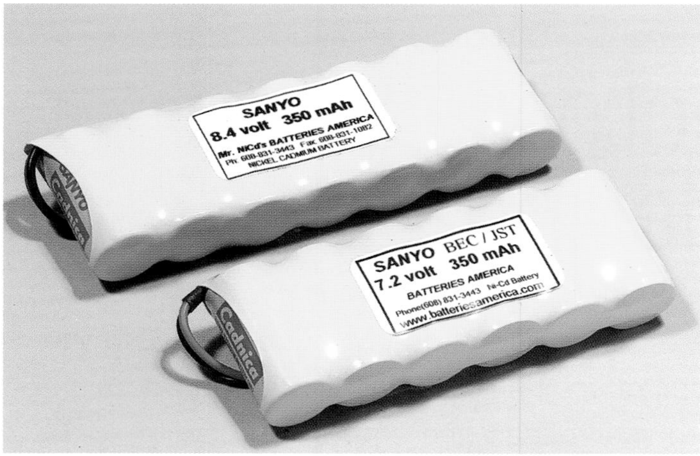

Here are two battery packs that use the exact same 350mAh cells. The upper pack has 7 cells; the one below has only 6. As you can plainly see from the markings, adding or subtracting a cell does not affect a pack's capacity—both are 350mAh. Adding a cell does, however, increase the voltage output from 7.2 to 8.4 volts.

RC SYSTEM BATTERIES

For our micro-flying purposes, just about everyone will be using a BEC circuit (as part of the ESC), which will allow you to share the motor battery power with the airborne RC system. This means no extra battery is required inside the model aircraft to operate the radio, but you will still have the RC transmitter power to contend with.

Certain basic RC transmitters may be intended for non-rechargeable alkaline battery cells. This is OK to start, although you will eventually want rechargeable batteries. Many of these inexpensive 3-channel RC transmitters can be retrofitted with Ni-Cd or NiMH battery packs. For charging, use a standard RC system charger, which will always be at the overnight charge rate. Most RC transmitters will operate for over 3 hours on a charge. That's a lot of flying time, so please, don't ever resort to field fast (peak) charging your RC transmitter battery. The extra charge current could easily damage certain components inside the transmitter case.

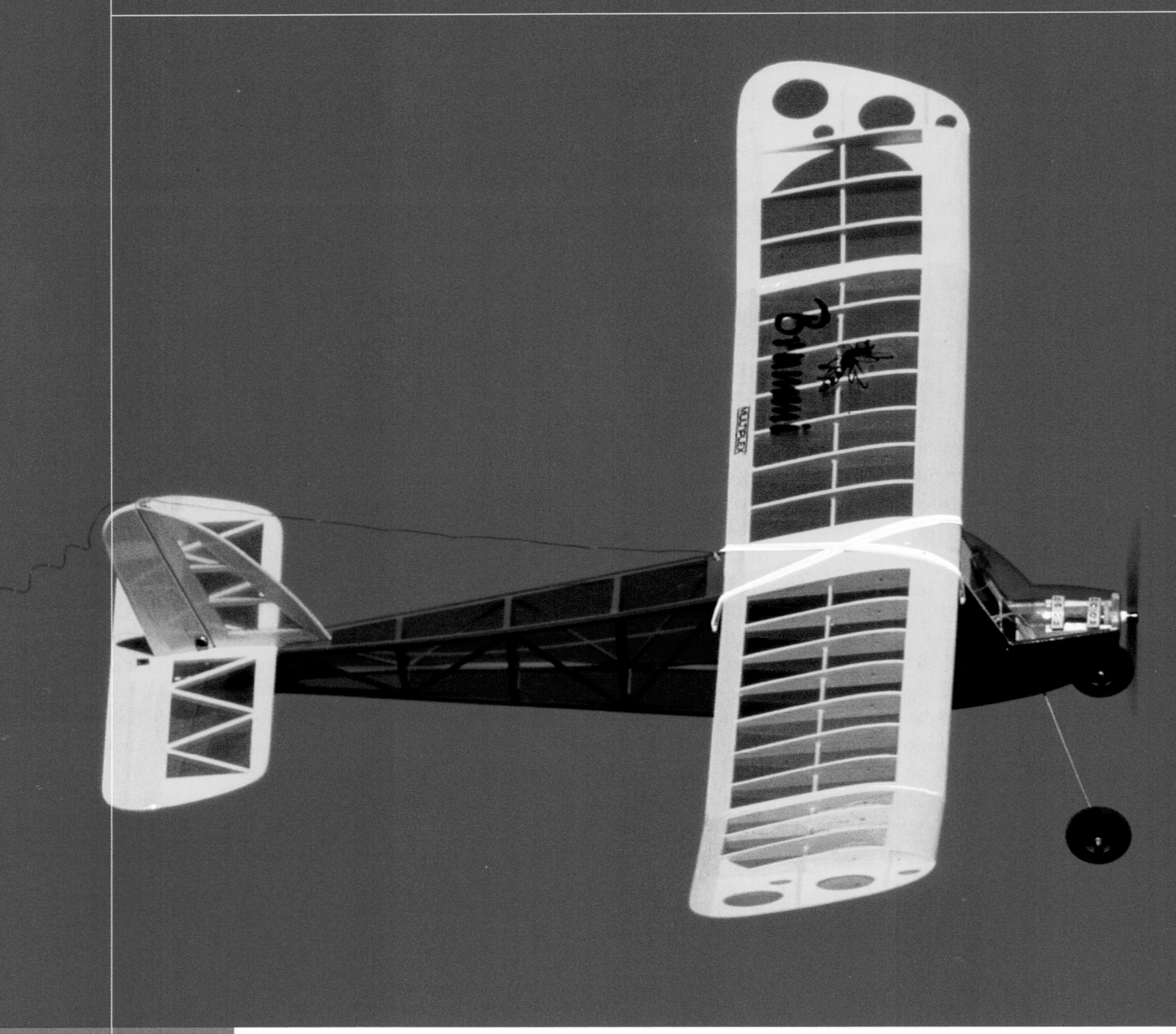

6

Connectors, Wire & Soldering

Standardizing the connectors used in your micro aircraft can offer advantages for "plug and play" ease of use. In this chapter, the author offers tips for choosing standard connectors best suited to your needs and shows you how to solder them. You will also learn about soldering electronic speed control (ESC) wires to a motor, soldering capacitors to a motor and more.

Up to this point, we have discussed in depth the various components of the electric-power system, including the motor, electronic speed control (ESC), prop and batteries. To hook up these components into a full working system requires additional knowledge on the use of connectors, wire, wiring and soldering techniques.

Connectors allow you to make or break wire connections within the power system. As a point of background information, with our larger electric-powered models (the ones ranging up to 15 to 20 pounds in total weight), it is common to see connector sets used both at the battery and at the motor. This can be a real convenience when swapping components, especially when at the flying field. In these same models it is also common to see charging jacks, which allow you to recharge the battery pack while the battery remains inside the aircraft. This can be a convenience, since in many cases the wing must be removed to gain access to the battery pack, but you still need to be careful not to charge a hot battery. In addition, you may see power on/off switches (or arming switches) and fuses used on the larger electric-powered model aircraft.

Experience has shown that weight is a critical issue when dealing with micro-size parking-lot and indoor flyers. Adding extra connectors, switches, wiring and fuses will add additional weight that cannot be tolerated in such small models. Remember, some of these models weigh less than 2 ounces total weight. Therefore, for our micro-flying applications, it is safe to say we want the least number of connectors and the lightest wire size that can still safely carry the electrical current, and we certainly don't want to consider switches and fuses. It all boils down to this: for micro flying, you plug in the battery, the system is armed, and you are ready to fly. When you unplug the battery the system is turned off. To recharge, it may be necessary to remove the wing to gain access to the battery. Charging is then accomplished through that single connector on the battery.

CHOOSING CONNECTORS

For micro flying, we must consider one connector set for the battery; then, the two wires going to the motor are soldered in place. For the parking-lot, Speed 400 (4 to 5A current, on up) and larger electric-powered models, the choice of connector is the Anderson Power Pole or the Sermos connector (which is the Anderson with a heavier silver plating on the pins). This connector type has proven reliable over the years; it is relatively easy to attach to wire ends, and even easier to attach with a mechanical crimping tool (see the Tech Tip at the end of this chapter).

As an alternate to the Anderson/Sermos connector you might consider the Deans 4-pin connector (usually a red color), which is quite acceptable in the motor current range of roughly 3 to 6 amps and is easy to solder. To make these 4-pin connectors even better suited for that current range, I usually solder a single wire to two of the four pins. By "ganging up" the pins this way, you achieve a higher current acceptance and the pins won't get hot. Again, the technique is to solder one wire to two pins and the other wire to the two remaining pins.

Some of the basic connectors used for indoor and parking-lot flyers. At left is the Deans 3-pin, which is suitable for everything up through the micro category (8 ounces total weight). In the center is the Deans 4-pin connector. I usually gang up the pins on this with one wire going to two pins. This would be OK for micros and up through the parking-lot category (models weighing 6 to 10 ounces). At the right are the Sermos connectors and the silver-plated pins that go inside the plastic housings. Use the Sermos on all models that weigh more than 10 ounces. That includes the heavier parking-lot models and certainly all of the Speed 400 models.

For the very tiny models (mainly the indoor flyers) we are talking about 2 amps motor current down to as low as ½ amp (500mA). For this kind of current, the Deans 3-pin (black) connector is popular, again because it is easy to obtain, inexpensive and very easy to solder. The 3-pin

Dymond Modelsports offers this connector assembly kit that enables you to make up your own lightweight connectors using these gold-plated pins and heat-shrink tubing.

configuration makes it simple to maintain the proper polarity because if you accidentally reverse the connector halves, the circuit is simply open—nothing will be shorted out.

Another lightweight connector that has gained some popularity with the micro fliers is the JST type. It comes with pigtail leads already attached to the pins. These connectors are polarized for proper connection, but you can't solder directly to the pins; you must use the pigtail leads as they come.

Several articles recently have described the use of computer-system-type cable connectors. The suggestion has been to "cannibalize" these connectors, using the male and female pins to make up your own connectors (see page 7 of the April 2000 issue of *RC MicroFlight*). These connectors can be lightweight, but be careful of the polarity.

The JST connector set. These connectors come preassembled with pig-tail leads already attached. You can't solder the pins on a JST. Current rating is up to about 2 amps. This is a nice light connector, especially good for indoor flyers.

One application of a reverse polarity battery could easily wipe out a receiver, the servos and/or the ESC.

CHOOSING WIRE

Now that I have identified the connectors, let's talk about the wire that must be used throughout the electric power system. The diameter of the wire is referred to as "gauge." Any wire for our

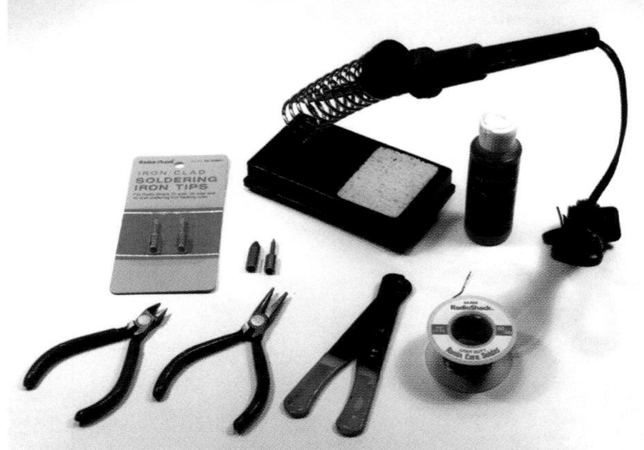

The items you will need to do a good soldering job. Most of these items came from RadioShack. At the top is a soldering iron handle with a 35W heating element screwed into the handle (they are available separately). The soldering unit is nested in its stand (note the cleaning pad). At left are two choices of soldering iron tips: one set is copper, while the other is iron clad, which does not require any tinning (solder coating). At the top right center is liquid rosin flux from Sears. In the foreground are small needle-nose pliers and wire cutters (which always prove helpful) along with the wire stripper and the .032-inch diameter RadioShack rosin-core solder.

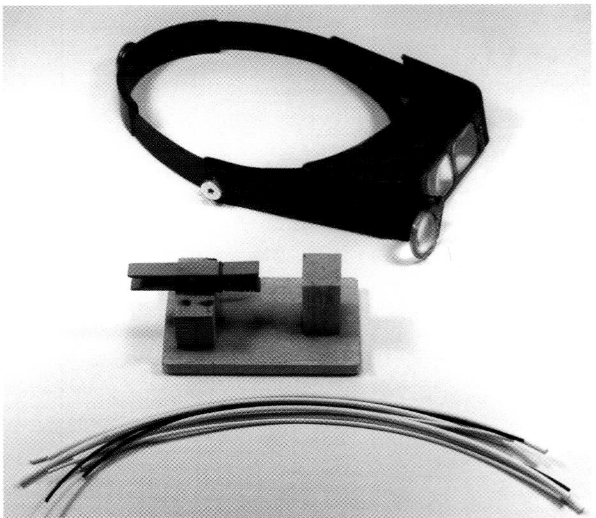

Some helpful soldering accessories. A magnifier that allows you to keep your hands free is a valuable item, especially when soldering small Deans connector pins. In the center, a simple clothespin acts as a vise to grip the Deans connector during the soldering process. At the bottom is an assortment of heat-shrink tubing used to cover connector solder joints.

flying purposes must be of the multi-stranded variety; never use solid wire (which could break far too easily). The larger the diameter or gauge of the wire, the more current it can handle; but you must also consider that the heavier the gauge, the heavier the wire itself. To keep the weight down on tiny models, you should try to select the minimum acceptable wire gauge.

On the Speed 400 powered models (roughly 8 to 12 amps), I use no. 16 gauge wire. For polarity identification purposes, always try to use the red wire for positive (+) and the black for negative (-). Parking-lot flyers with Speed 280 motors (3 to 7A current) can use no. 20 gauge wire. The micro flyers drawing current from about 2 amps on down should use no. 24 gauge wire. You will note that I am somewhat conservative with these recommendations, but better to be on the safe side. Many of the popular battery-cell suppliers also carry a full line of connectors, as well as wire in a variety of gauges and colors.

As we discuss soldering techniques, I would once again like to be able to tell you that all connectors come pre-wired, so that all you have to do is plug everything together as you would with an RC system and you're ready to fly. Unfortunately, that hasn't happened universally with regard to electric power systems, so you will have to face up to some soldering whether you like it or not.

TIPS ON USING DEANS CONNECTORS

Since I did recommend the Deans connectors, I thought a few words and photos might

SOLDERING DEANS CONNECTORS

1

Copper soldering iron tips must be pre-tinned. Plug in the iron and, as it begins to warm up, introduce generous amounts of solder. Add some liquid rosin flux as you continue. Keep applying the solder all over the tip until the iron reaches full operating temperature, usually in about 5 minutes. Wipe off the excess solder with a rag or paper towel (quickly so it doesn't catch fire). You are ready. Thereafter, you need to pre-tin the soldering iron tip only on occasion.

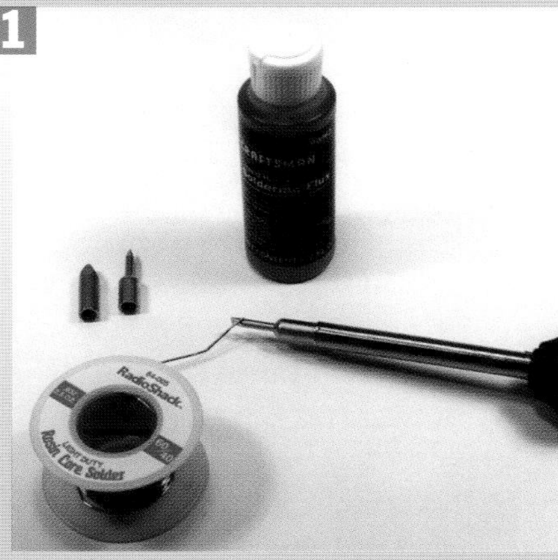

2

Prepare a piece of wire by first stripping off about ¼ inch of insulation.

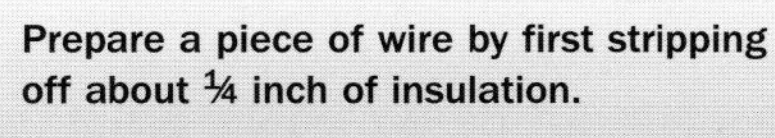

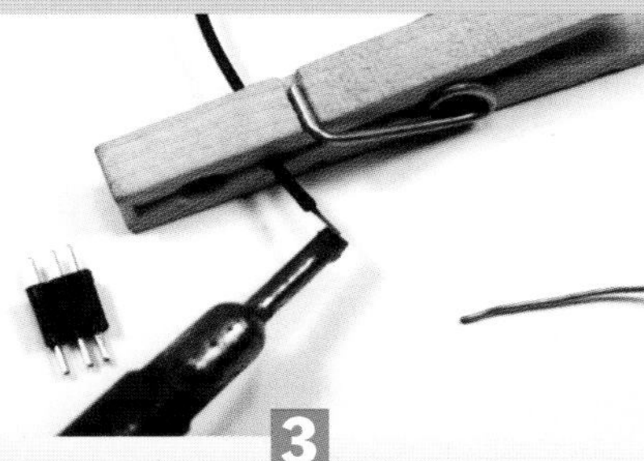

3

Using a clothespin to hold the wire, pre-tin the wire end with solder. The Deans connector will be next.

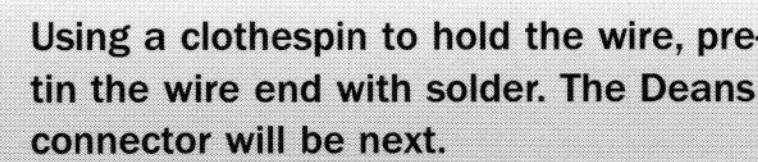

4

Hold the Deans connector with a clothespin as shown. Pre-tin the connector pins with solder.

5

Now touch the wire to the connector pin and let the soldering iron melt the solder to form a perfect connection.

help with the soldering of these particular connectors. First, you need the right soldering equipment, which can be found at any RadioShack store. I prefer a small pencil-type soldering iron, rather than the larger gun-type iron. You will need to purchase an iron handle (RadioShack no. 64-2110), a 35W heating element—about the best for most of our applications (RadioShack no. 64-2112), an assortment of soldering iron tips (three in all: Radio Shack no. 64-2084), rosin-core solder (Radio Shack no. 64-009) and a small metal stand to hold the hot iron when not in use.

In addition to these items, I like to use a liquid rosin flux sold at Sears (item no. 80063). I use this liquid flux for most soldering work, with one exception: when soldering the wires into the Anderson/Sermos pins I refrain from using the liquid flux because the flux allows the solder to "wick" up inside the wire insulation, making the wire stiff and brittle. For all other applications, the liquid flux is a great help, but always make sure it is a rosin flux. If you accidentally used acid flux (as in plumbing work) your wiring wouldn't last very long.

To solder wires to the Deans connectors, I made up a simple holding fixture from a block of wood and added a clothespin to grip the connector. This leaves my hands free to hold the soldering iron and the solder. I also use heat-shrink tubing on all of my connector-pin wiring. This acts as a strain relief. Don't use the tubing supplied with the Deans connectors—it is too stiff. Buy a separate package of heat-shrink tubing (various sizes) from RadioShack. Cut pieces of this tubing and slip them back up the wires to keep them away from the iron heat.

Before your first attempt at soldering, you must pre-tin the heating element tip. Use a smaller diameter tip for the Deans pins, and as the iron heats up, apply some of the liquid flux and solder to the tip. Keep doing this until the iron reaches close to full temperature. Then wipe the tip clean quickly (so the paper doesn't catch fire) with a folded piece of paper towel. Gripping the Deans connector with a clothespin, apply a few drops of the flux and then pre-tin the pins with solder. Apply the heated iron tip first to the connector pin, then introduce the solder. When you see a good shiny flow, remove the iron and let it cool.

Strip off a small amount of insulation from the wire ends, twist the wire to keep it neat and then also pre-tin these wire ends. The next step is easy: hold the wire to the pin with one hand while touching the pin with the tip of the iron. As soon as the solder melts, remove the heat and hold still for a few seconds until the solder connection cools. Try to use the recommended small-diameter solder since it tends to melt more quickly and makes a more "flowing" solder joint. Your final solder connection should always look shiny. If it looks dull or white, you might have what is known as a "cold solder joint," which can be brittle and which may be a poor connection. If in doubt, re-solder.

Next, slide the heat-shrink tubing up over each pin, then apply heat from a hot-air blower gun, which looks like a hair dryer. Never try to shrink up the tubing using the heat from your soldering iron, and keep in mind when attaching wires to connectors that the color-coded polarity is important. Be sure to connect the right wire to the right pin. These are just the basics, but everything is done the same way, whether you are soldering connector wiring or motor leads to the motor.

SOLDERING CAPACITORS

The last soldering step may involve soldering the all important interference capacitors across the motor terminals and from each terminal to the

Soldering an interference capacitor to the motor case (or ground). In this application you will need a lot of heat, so you might consider a larger diameter soldering iron tip.

Soldering interference capacitors onto your motor is one of the few soldering jobs an e-modeler is likely to face. All regular electric motors need interference capacitors placed on their terminals (some come with them pre-soldered, but not all). Typically, three capacitors are used on a motor. One goes across the two motor terminals; two others go from each terminal to ground (the motor case).

case or "ground," as it is referred to. The trick here is to get the solder joint to the motor case by first sanding the area of the motor case with light sandpaper where you expect to solder the capacitor lead; then wipe it clean with denatured alcohol, apply some flux and pre-tin the area with solder. The metal motor case will suck a lot of the heat away, so be prepared to go to a larger soldering-iron tip. As always, apply the heat first, then the solder. Later you will reheat this tinned area and then hold the capacitor wire in place with needle-nose pliers while applying the heat from the iron. Keep the iron on long enough to make a good connection, but not so long that you damage the motor wiring internally. We will conclude this chapter with three pictorial sidebars that explain additional important soldering techniques.

CUSTOM POLARIZED CONNECTORS

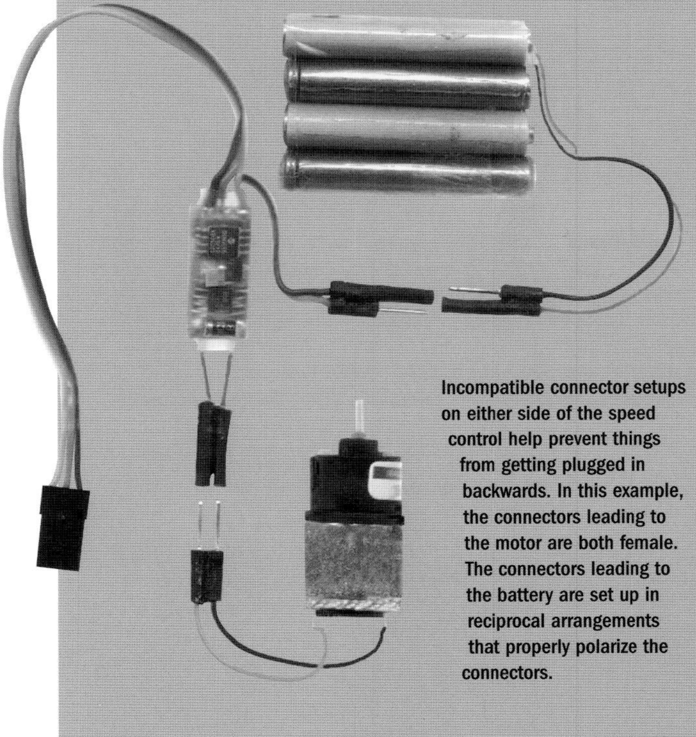

Incompatible connector setups on either side of the speed control help prevent things from getting plugged in backwards. In this example, the connectors leading to the motor are both female. The connectors leading to the battery are set up in reciprocal arrangements that properly polarize the connectors.

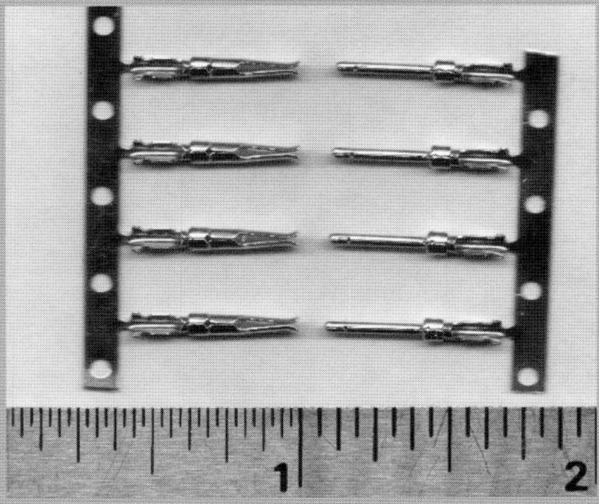

RadioShack connector pins are ready to use (item nos. 276-1430, female, and 276-1429, male).

Assembly is easy. After the wires have been soldered in place, you can squeeze the crimp connector down and then add some heat-shrink tubing over the base of the male connectors and the length of the female connectors to finish the job.

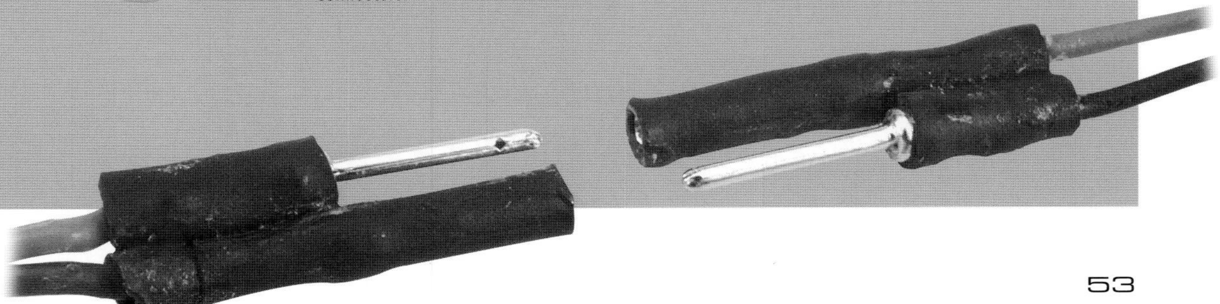

SOLDERING ESC WIRES TO MOTOR TERMINALS

1 This photo sequence shows how to solder speed control output wires to the motor terminals. Plug in the iron and, as it begins to warm up, place some liquid rosin flux on its tip. Hold a length of solder to the tip; as the solder melts, add more, then back off for several seconds while the iron heats to full temperature. Then wipe off excess solder.

2 Use a wire stripper to remove about ¼ inch of insulation from the wires you will solder to the motor. Twist the wire strands together to make them more compact. Now pre-tin each wire, one at a time. Hold the wire with a clothespin, apply a little flux and then touch the wire with the soldering iron tip while introducing the solder at the same time. The solder should melt quickly and leave a shiny quantity that coats the end of the wire. Be sure the wire polarity is correct, or the motor will turn in reverse.

3 If needed, pre-tin the motor terminals as well. Also, now is the time to slip small lengths of heat-shrink tubing over the wires if you want to relieve stress on the wires (slide the tubing away from the heat for the time being). Clamp the motor so it won't roll, and then touch the motor's positive terminal with the heated soldering iron and the tinned positive motor wire. When the solder appears to be melted well and is flowing, remove the iron (heat) and hold the wire in place for a few seconds while the joint cools.

4 You want to finish with a clean, shiny, soldered joint. If the solder joint has a dull or whitish surface, reheat the joint, remove the wire and repeat the process. Be sure to cut the previously soldered wire tip back, strip it again and start with a freshly tinned wire.

5 If you opted to use heat-shrink tubing, it's time to slide the tubing over the newly soldered connection. Apply heat from a hobby heat gun to shrink the tubing around the joint. Then repeat the steps for the negative wire.

HOW TO SOLDER UNIVERSAL CONNECTORS for Speed 400 Park Flyers

For several years, the Anderson PowerPole connector has been a favorite among modelers (it's also marketed, with additional plating and molded plastic housing options, as the Sermos connector). It consists of a silver-plated pin to which you solder the wire lead. The pin/wire assembly is then inserted into a molded-plastic housing until it snaps tightly into position. Two such connector assemblies can be inserted into each other to form an electrical connection, and the interlocking housings snap together to hold the connection securely.

Speed 400 powered park flyers typically draw around 10 amps of current and can easily use a lightweight, 16-gauge wire.

YOU'LL NEED

- soldering iron
- holding fixture
- wire stripper
- wire solder
- connectors

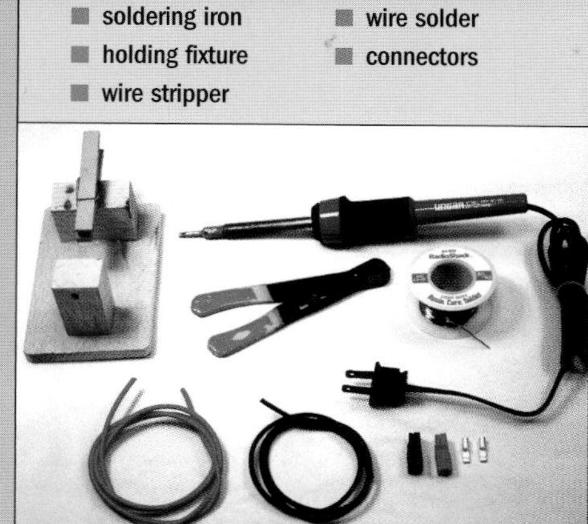

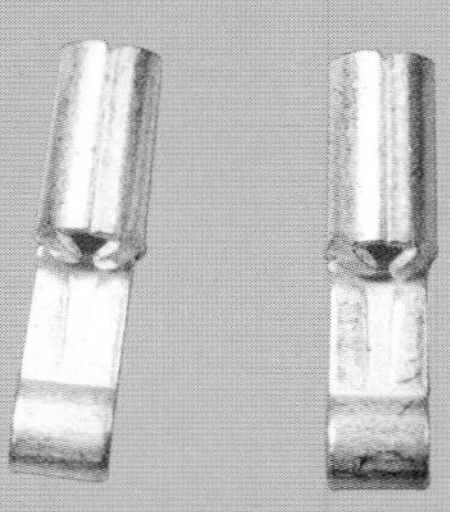

The plastic housings come in a variety of colors so that you can color code polarity (usually red for positive and black for negative). You can also color code specific devices; for example, use one pair of colors for the connection from the battery to the speed controller and another pair for the connection from the controller to the motor.

The standard connector housings are made of Lexan, which is quite strong but not impervious to many hydrocarbons. Contact with CA cement activator and contact cleaner can cause the housing to crumble in just a few days. Special hydrocarbon-resistant housings are available; if you require this type, be sure to specify them when purchasing.

1 I built a holding fixture out of scrap balsa blocks. One block has a hole drilled through it to accept up to 12-gauge wire, and the other has a clothespin glued to its top. First, strip about 1 inch of insulation off the end of the wire. Twist the strands of exposed wire together to prevent them from fraying. Insert the wire through the hole in the wood block and heat the stripped end for a few seconds with the soldering iron. Then apply the solder—just enough to make the wire end look shiny.

2 Clip the silver-plated connector pin in the clothespin. Insert a little solder into the pin's cup end, then heat the bottom of the connector pin with the iron until the solder starts to melt. As it melts, insert another inch or so of solder into the cup and then withdraw the heat. Do not apply so much solder that it runs out of the pin cup, or the connector won't snap into position later.

HOW TO SOLDERING UNIVERSAL CONNECTORS for Speed 400 Park Flyers

3

Turn the pin so that the cup faces the wire in the block and move the wire forward until it touches the pin. Heat the lower side of the pin with the iron until the solder softens, then feed the wire forward into the pin cup with your other hand. Remove the heat, let everything cool for 10 to 15 seconds, then examine the solder connection. If you did it correctly, you won't have burned the wire insulation.

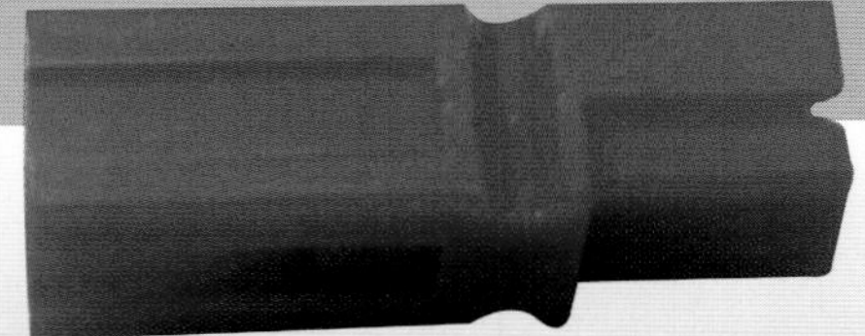

4

The final step is to insert the connector pin into the molded-plastic housing. The instructions will tell you the correct orientation for the pin, though you probably won't require directions (the lip of the pin snaps over a ridge in the housing). Push the wire into the housing. Thin wire may buckle before the pin is seated. If that happens, use a very narrow screwdriver blade to push the back of the pin until you hear it snap into place; if it doesn't snap, it isn't in yet.

To strengthen the solder joint, you may wish to cover it with heat-shrink tubing (put these on the wire, away from the heat, before soldering!). Shrink the tubing with a hair dryer set on maximum or with a hobby heat gun. Then insert the pin/wire assembly into the housing as noted. Once you have completely assembled a connector, mate it with another one. You should hear a positive snapping sound as the two seat firmly. It takes only a moment to make sure everything clicks together correctly, and it will save you frustration—and maybe a plane!—later on.

TECH TIP

CRIMPING OPTION

Be advised that there is an easier way to attach wires to the Anderson/Sermos connector pins. It involves the use of a mechanical crimping tool manufactured by Anderson expressly for this purpose. I have personally owned one for years and keep it in my tool kit; it makes for easy field repairs without the need for soldering. Some of the larger hobby shops have also purchased these crimpers, leaving them chained to the countertop for anyone to use (a great idea!). These tools can be obtained from either John Sermos at Sermos R/C Snap Connectors Co. or Azarr at Eclectic Electric Necessities for about $150.

Measuring Motor Parameters

7

To understand how your motor will perform with a given propeller and/or battery pack, you need to know how to measure voltage and current in your airplane's power system's circuit. With the tools available today, this is a very simple process that can yield helpful insights into how your aircraft will perform in flight. In this chapter, the author explains the basics.

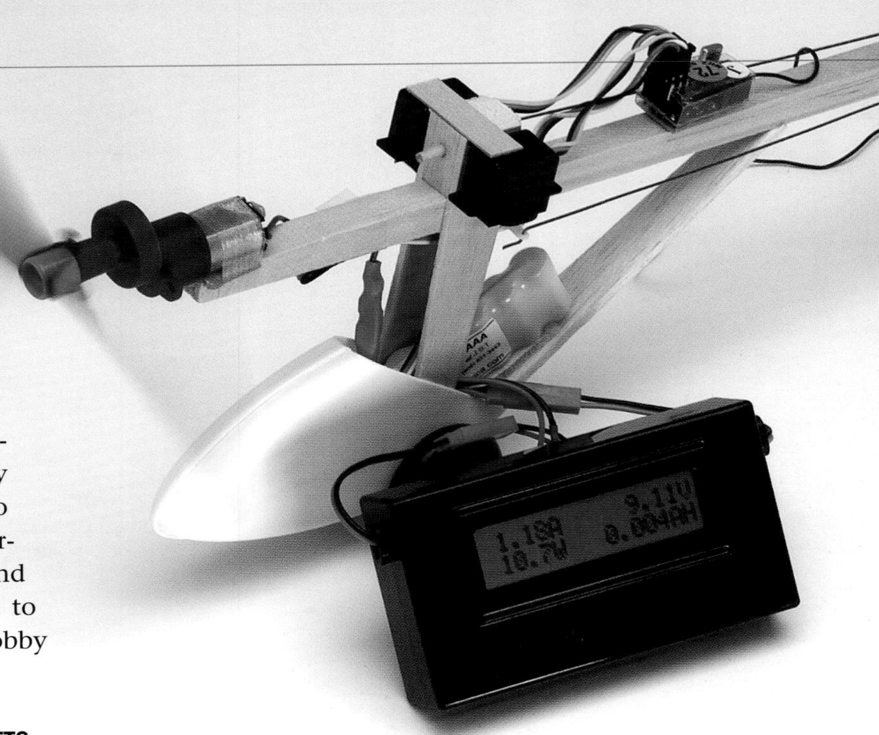

Here the AstroFlight model 100 Micro-Meter shows that the Dymond Modelsports Little Party pulls 1.18 amps at full throttle. Volts, watts and accumulated amps per hour are also indicated.

In the chapter on batteries, I provided a formula you can use to calculate the theoretical motor run time if you know the motor current and the capacity of your battery pack. Now I'm going tell you how to measure that all-important motor current. I try very hard to get all of my student pilots to buy an ammeter to measure motor current long before they buy their second model or RC system. You can't hope to advance in the electric-powered hobby unless you own and use an ammeter.

MEASURING AMPS, VOLTS AND WATTS

Because this is such an important function, AstroFlight Inc., one of the leaders in electric-powered flight for more than 30 years, developed a popular digital ammeter/voltmeter. Their first version required a flip of a switch to selectively read amps or volts. The second-generation meter, called the Astro Whatt Meter, displays amps, volts, total ampere hours that have flowed through the circuit and watts—all on the same LCD screen and at the same time. This second version is used today by most e-power fliers.

With the recent growth of micro flying, Bob Boucher of AstroFlight has produced a third micro meter expressly for the low current and voltage ranges typically experienced with parking -lot and indoor flying. The new digital meter (Astro Model 100 Micro-Meter) works from zero to 15 amps and reads to within 1⁄10 of an amp. Like its big brother, it also reads volts and watts at the same time. Because this meter comes with a rather lightweight wire terminating in JST connectors I have a suggestion that can make it even more versatile. The wiring can handle up to about 10 amps, and the JST connectors are good for only about 5 amps. So I cut off the JST connectors and substitute Deans 4-pin connectors with the two wires going to the four pins (two pins to a single wire). By doing this, I can get up to 7 amps, which would cover just about all parking-lot models with RS-280 or equivalent motors. For Speed 400 on up I use the larger meter, which has much heavier wiring and connectors.

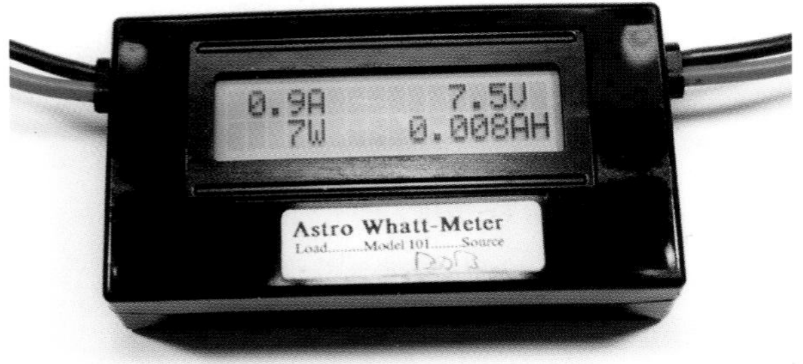

This is what a typical display screen looks like on the AstroFlight Whatt Meter. The current in amps is 0.9A, 7.5V is the voltage, 7W is the power or watts and 0.008AH is the ampere hours accumulating during the charge or discharge period.

Since I don't use Deans 4-pin connectors on all of my models, I made up a few adapters that convert to Deans 3-pin connectors and to the Anderson/Sermos connectors. Take note: on the AstroFlight meter, the right side is marked SOURCE, and it is for the battery connection; on the left side, the cable is marked LOAD, which means the motor. An important point when using either meter is to always connect the battery first and wait for the LCD screen to turn on. Then, and only then, can you attach the meter leads to the motor. When you complete this circuit, the motor will start and you can quickly observe your motor current in amps, the voltage under load and the product of the two (amps x volts), which is expressed in watts. Now you

know how to measure motor current, motor voltage and motor power (watts).

I might add that there are times that the ESC is also in use when measuring motor current. This would be the case when the electric power system is already installed in a model. When you do have the ESC in the loop, the meter must be placed in series between the battery and the ESC. A block diagram has been included to illustrate this meter connection.

MEASURING RPM

Another important measurement is prop speed or rpm (revolutions per minute). You measure this with a tachometer. For years, I have used the TNC digital tachometer manufactured by Tony Criscimagna of TNC Electronics. This device is very accurate and operates in a steady and reliable fashion. What I especially like is the ability

An interesting display test stand that was photographed at the MTM Intl. booth at the 2001 WRAM show in White Plains, NY. Here a battery, ESC and motor are all connected. A servo tester simulates an RC system and operates the motor over its full throttle range. This same type of setup could be used to take parameter measurements, such as motor current and prop rpm.

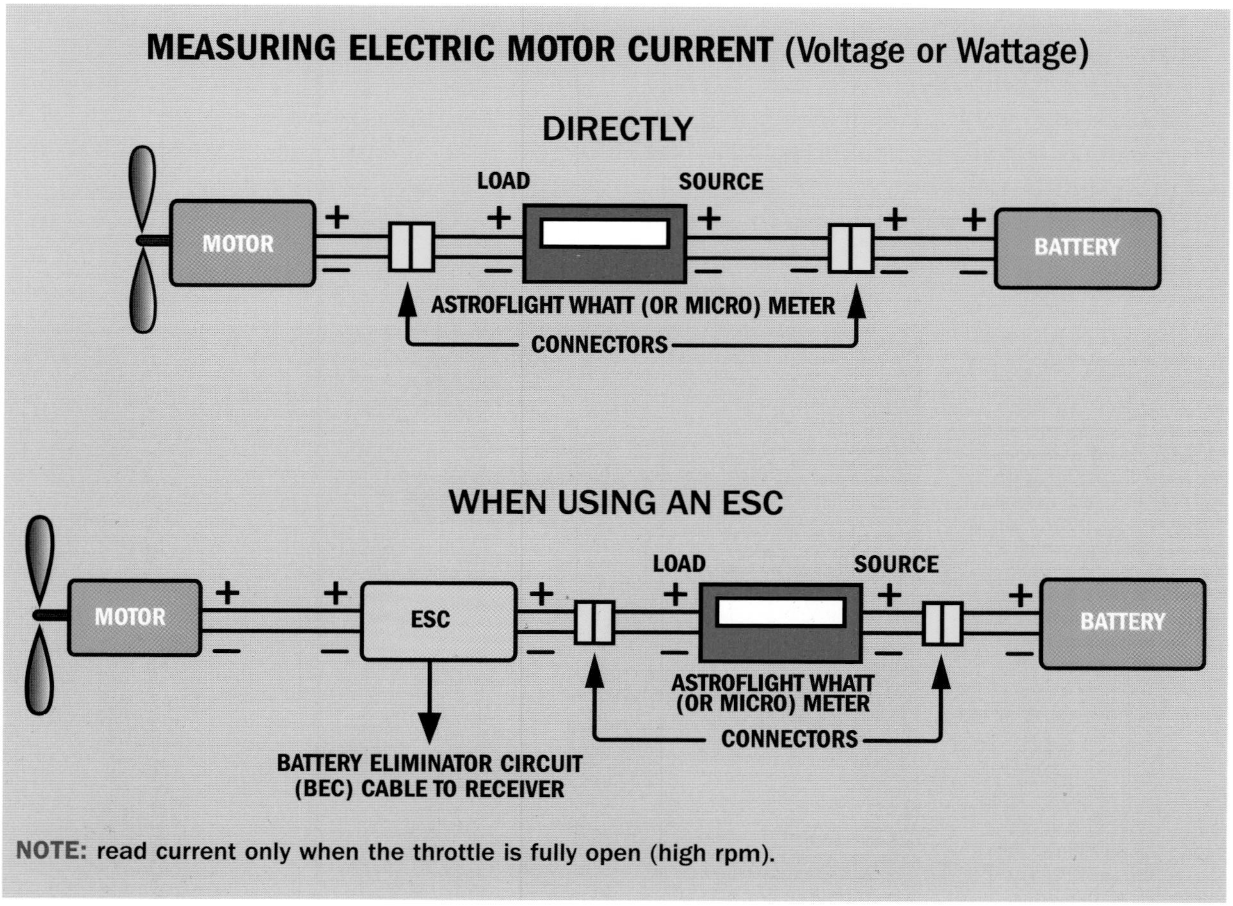

MEASURING ELECTRIC MOTOR CURRENT (Voltage or Wattage)

DIRECTLY

MOTOR + − | LOAD + − | SOURCE + − | + − | + − BATTERY

ASTROFLIGHT WHATT (OR MICRO) METER

CONNECTORS

WHEN USING AN ESC

MOTOR + − | + − ESC + − | LOAD + − | SOURCE + − | + − BATTERY

ASTROFLIGHT WHATT (OR MICRO) METER

CONNECTORS

BATTERY ELIMINATOR CIRCUIT (BEC) CABLE TO RECEIVER

NOTE: read current only when the throttle is fully open (high rpm).

of this tachometer to operate indoors. Since electric motors make little noise, it is easy to run them in a basement or garage, but be careful that the prop wash doesn't blow all the sawdust off your bench top.

To take indoor prop-speed measurements, you must mount the motor to a test stand or holding fixture. Then place the tachometer just behind the rotating prop and point the optical sensor forward toward the prop blades. Position a small halogen flashlight on the front side of the prop blades pointing back toward the tachometer. If you do this, the ambient room lighting (even my shop's fluorescent lamps) won't interfere with the reading. Just be careful not to get your fingers or hand in the prop blades (and stay away from the arc of the prop—the trajectory in which a blade would fly if one accidentally came loose).

The TNC digital tachometer.

With the motor current reading, you can use the formula in Chapter 5 (Batteries and Chargers) to calculate your motor running time per charge. With tachometer readings, you can help pick the right prop for the job. The pitch (or angle of the prop blade) can vary considerably on these small plastic props, which are supposedly of the same size. Try three props of the same brand and size and take individual rpm readings. I think you will be surprised by the variations.

MEASURING THRUST

Another parameter, which I feel is just a little too complicated for the beginner or sport flier, is thrust. We see this parameter in many of the published motor reviews. We also see it referenced in some, but not all, of the manufacturer motor specifications. I will try to explain in the next chapter what you can do with motor-thrust measurements. If you are interested, thrust readings can be taken with a motor set up on a moving test stand. The motor pulls one way, while you hold on with a small fish scale. Thrust in ounces can be measured in this way, but it is a rather crude test. More elaborate thrust testing can be done with a balance beam setup, in which the motor is mounted on one end of a pivoting beam, and the other end of the beam depresses a digital scale. This type of setup is rather complicated however, and beyond the scope of this book.

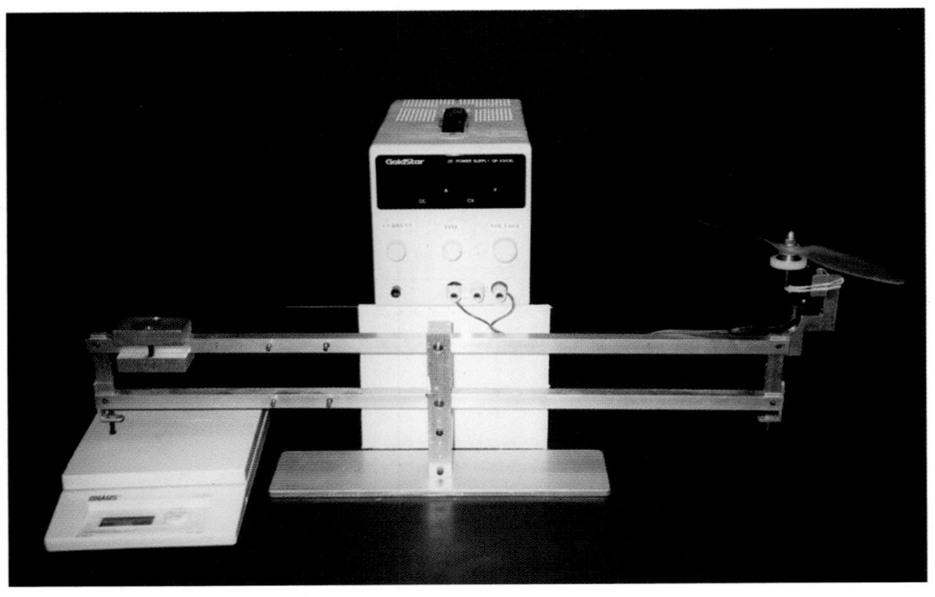

This elaborate piece of test equipment was designed and built by Bob Wilder, NIRAC President. This test stand allows you to measure motor thrust in grams or ounces. Basically, the motor at the right tends to lift the beam. The other end of the beam presses down on a digital scale, reading the thrust directly. In the center is a calibrated power supply used to run the motor. Bob's test reports on various motors appear regularly in and on its website (photo by Bob Wilder).

Sizing Motor Systems to Your Aircraft

8

If you are building your own aircraft from scratch or modifying an airplane to enhance performance, you will want to choose a motor by following the helpful rules of thumb explained in this chapter. The author explains the relationship between power, weight and performance and illustrates these relationships with specific examples in an overview chart. Software that can assist in motor sizing is also suggested.

Now we get to the most difficult aspect of electric-powered flight: how to select the proper motor system (motor, gear drive, prop, battery capacity and the number of cells) to get your model into the air and support flight. It can be difficult to select the right motor system for the job at hand, even for those of us who have been flying electric-powered model aircraft for many years. But this is especially true for the beginner in our hobby, or even for an experienced glow-engine pilot who is trying to learn and appreciate electric-powered flight. This chapter offers some ground rules that can help in the motor selection process.

Many of you will purchase complete aircraft kits or almost-ready-to build models with all of the "trimmings." In the best scenario, your supplier will be knowledgeable enough to select the correct components that make up the system and will save you from having to experiment.

There are several parameters you might find helpful to try out on your latest model if you are already flying an indoor or parking-lot model.

TECH TIP

KEEP A MODELING LOGBOOK

A good idea is to start your own engineering notebook. It is important that you keep accurate records on each model and detail all the important parameters. You would also be wise to record your model weight, the wing area and the resulting wing loading. Add your flying experiences to these records and you will have an excellent reference point for the future. Then, when you have a similar size and weight model in the future, you will be able to zero in on the appropriate electric-power system components. Even information provided in published product reviews or data obtained from one of the hobby nets on the Internet can be recorded in your book for future reference. This is a good way to learn and gather experience with electric-powered flight.

The first involves motor power input expressed in watts. It is possible to use a figure of so many watts per ounce (watts/oz.) to initially check to see if an electric motor can lift a model of a particular weight off the ground. The second involves the wing loading of the model expressed in ounces per square feet (oz./sq. ft.), which means that you take the physical size of the model into account along with its total weight. Another interesting parameter involves the motor thrust when a reliable thrust measurement can be obtained from a motor expert or author, or from the manufacturer.

FINDING WATTS PER OUNCE

As already outlined in Chapter 7, you can easily obtain the motor power (expressed in watts) by using an AstroFlight digital meter. If you take the motor power (watts) and divide it by the total weight of the model (ounces), you obtain a figure of watts per ounce. This guideline was recommended by Don Srull of Mc Lean, VA. Experience with these small electric-powered models has shown that the average sport aircraft, with average flying characteristics, does well with approximately 2.0 watts per ounce. If this figure increases to approximately 2.5 watts per ounce, you will have more of an aerobatic or sprint performer. Going in the opposite direction to 1.5 watts per ounce. will produce a more docile performance, as is the case with endurance or powered sailplane models.

DETERMINING WING LOADING

Next you want to take the aircraft size and weight into consideration by determining the wing loading of the model, which is usually expressed in ounces per square foot (oz./sq. ft.). This is calculated by taking the wing area in square inches (average span multiplied by chord) and dividing it by 144 to obtain square feet. Next take the total weight of the model in ounces and divide that by the area (square feet) to provide the wing loading (ounces per square foot). An average acceptable wing loading figure for ultra-micro, sub-micro and micro models is anything up to 5 ounces per square foot. Wing loading for parking-lot models can be up to 8 ounces per square foot. Speed 400 models will range between 8 and 10 ounces per square foot. By substituting these numbers, you

SOFTWARE TOOLS

Two very enterprising electric modelers, Stefan Vorkoetter and Sid Kauffman, have created two separate computer programs to assist in the electric motor selection process. These programs will allow you to play with various parameters to help optimize a theoretical e-powered system. Stefan's program is known as MotoCalc (www.motocalc.com/), while Sid's is known as ElectriCalc (www.slkelectronics.com/ecalc/). Both programs are sold as software discs intended for PC operation. A tremendous amount of reference data can be found in these programs. While they were originally conceived for the much larger electric-powered model aircraft, they will also be very useful for micro RC, as well.

The beauty of these motor programs is that you can perform "what-if" type calculations almost instantly. For example, you can change the gear-reduction ratio or prop size and immediately see how the motor current and prop rpm will be affected. You can add or subtract battery cells (raise or lower voltage) to also see the effects on the entire system. With some experience, either of these two programs can add considerably to the electric motor selection process. The price is right, so they're certainly worth a try!

MotoCalc Sample Screens

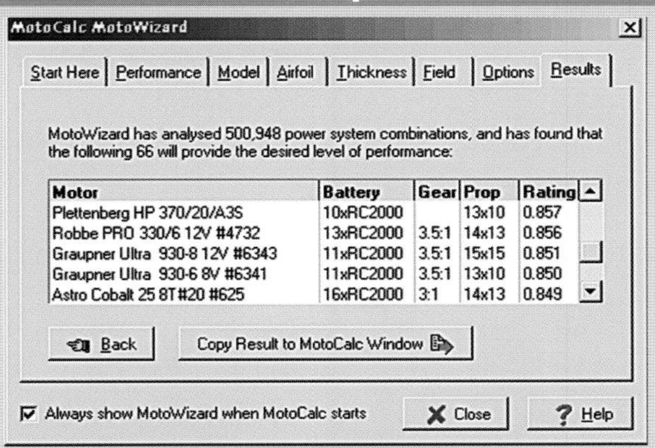

MotoCalc's MotoWizard feature quickly produces a list of suggested power systems for your model, based on some basic information you provide.

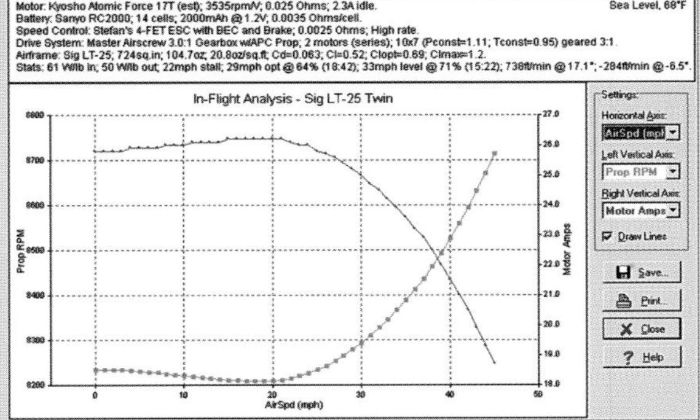

A picture is worth a thousand numbers. MotoCalc can produce graphs from any analysis, helping you visualize performance.

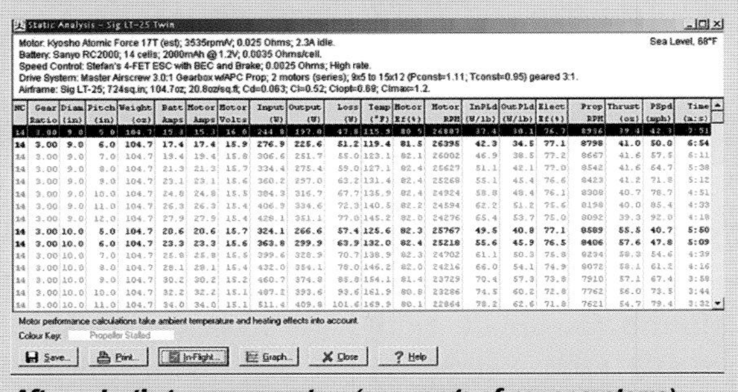

After selecting a power system (or a range of power systems), MotoCalc's static and in-flight analysis windows give you detailed predictions of amps, volts, efficiency, rpm, thrust and so on.

ElectriCalc Sample Screens

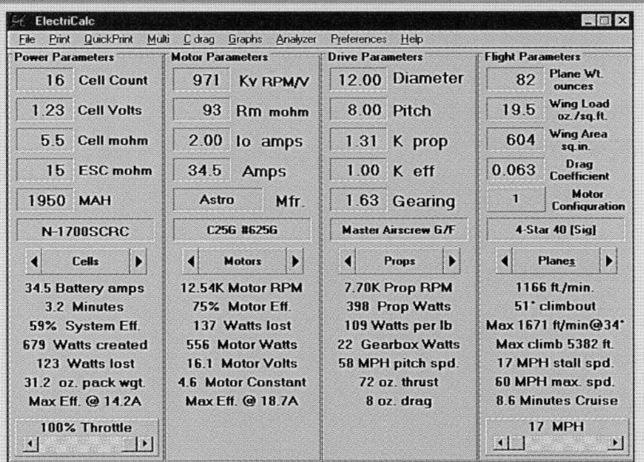

ElectriCalc's main screen logically groups and shows all data at once. This includes amps, volts, watts, rpm and much more.

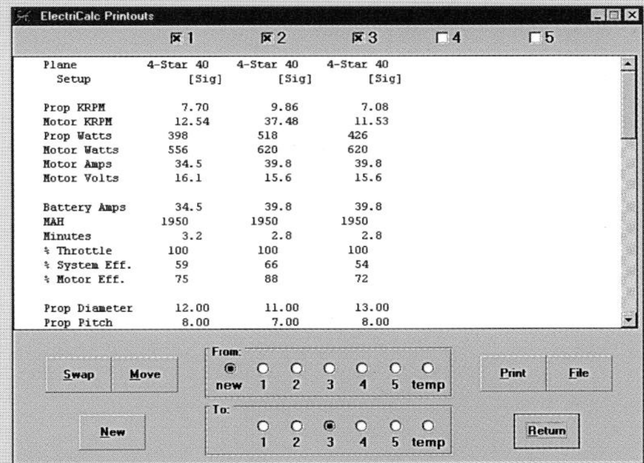

Electricalc's print screen allows comparison of up to five power-system configurations.

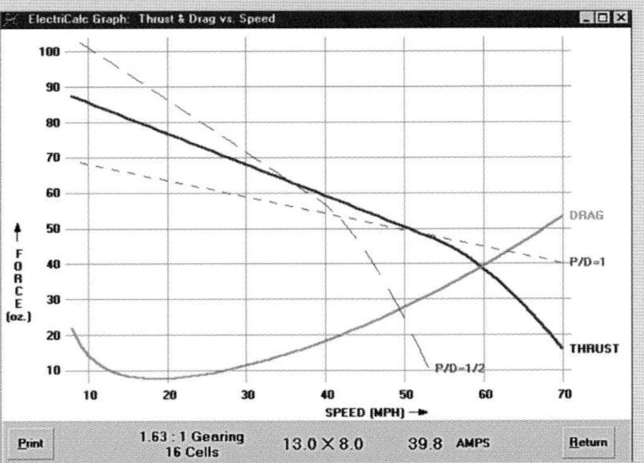

ElectriCalc's graphs help you understand electric flight dynamics.

MODEL WEIGHT & GUIDELINES

CATEGORY	WEIGHT (oz.)	WING AREA (sq. in.)	WING LOADING (oz./sq. ft.)	MOTOR
ULTRA-MICRO	UP TO 2	50-100	UP TO 5	
Micro Lite Flyer	1.6	68	3.4	Kenway KR-1 geared 4.2:1
Blu-Bug	1.23	68	2.75	KP-00 geared 2.7:1
Punkin-II	1.7	80	3.0	N-20 geared 4.2:1 low-V wind
SUB-MICRO	2-3	75-125	UP TO 5	
Pixie	2.6	80	4.7	DC-5.24 geared 4.2:1
Pepper	2.64	86	4.4	DC-5.24 geared 4.2:1
DJ Aerotech Roadkill series	2.8	80	5.0	Mabuchi N-20 geared 4.2:1 high V-wind
MICRO	3-8	125-300	UP TO 5	
GWS Pico Stick	7.7	238	4.7	GWS IPS-A DX geared 5.86:1
Flitter-B	5.0	176	4.1	GWS IPS-A DX geared 5.86:1
Tiny	4.5	220	3.0	D1717 geared 11.8:1
PF-5	4.2	195	3.1	DC-5.24 geared 8.3:1
GymFlyer	4.8	264	2.6	D1717 geared 11.8:1
Starlight	3.7	216	2.5	DC-5.24 geared 8.3:1
PARKING LOT & BACKYARD	8-14	300-600	UP TO 8	
Merlin	17	511	4.9	Speed 380 geared 5.6:1
Scooter	10	450	3.2	Speed 280 geared 4:1
Miss Bohemia	14	325	6.2	Speed 280 geared
Johnny Bee II	8.7	330	3.7	Twin Johnson 100 geared
Piper Cub	9.0	165	7.9	Titanic Speed 280 geared 3:1 or Astro .010 brushless (direct)
Miss Stik	9.0	212	6.1	Speed 280 Direct
SPEED 400	14 AND UP	300 AND UP	8-10	
Impress	26	310	12	Speed 400 geared 1.7:1 (7.2V)
Miss-2	29	390	10.8	Speed 400 geared 2.3:1 (6V)

*See 11/01 *RC MicroFlight* at www.rcmicroflight.com **See 1/00 *RC MicroFlight* ***See 3/00 *RC MicroFlight* at www.rcmicroflight.com

can approximate the weight of a model if you know the wing area and wish to have it work out to the target wing loading figure (expressed in ounces per square foot).

MOTOR THRUST AND CURRENT CONSIDERATIONS

Another guideline involves the use of motor thrust. Over a period of time, electric-power experts have come up with an important rule of thumb for small models; it indicates that the model total weight can be approximately four times the rated motor thrust, expressed in either ounces or grams. If you have a motor specification that indicates that a particular motor/

PROP (in.)	**BATTERY**	**REMARKS**
Kenway Blue 12cm	4x50mAh Ni-Cd	IMA Belgian kit
Union 3.15	3x120mAh NiMH	Don Srull plan
Peck 6	4x50mAh Ni-Cd	Dave Robelen design*
5x3.75	7x50mAh Ni-Cd	Dave Robelen design**
Gunther 5x4	7x50mAh Ni-Cd	Dave Robelen design***
Gunther 5x4	7x120mAh NiMH	Profile kits include Mustang Spitfire, Corsair, etc.
GWS 10x4.7	6x110mAh Ni-Cd 7x270mAh NiMH	ARF kit, stick or fuselage versions available
GWS 10x4.7	8x150mAh	Greg Sutter kit
Braun 10x5 carbon	8x50mAh Ni-Cd	Todd Long design
WES-Technik carbon 9x5	8x50mAh Ni-Cd	Dave's Aircraft Works kit
Arc-1 9.5-in. diameter	Ray-O-Vac 9V NiMH Tadiran lithium	Carl Martin design; Anything RC kit
WES-Technik carbon 23x12mm	7x50mAh Ni-Cd	Tom Herr design, Sig kit
11.5-in. diameter	7-cell 600mAh NiMH	Complete RTF kit with radio, charger, battery
	7x110mAh Ni-Cd	Aerocraft kit distributed by Hobby Lobby
9-in. diameter	7x270mAh NiMH	Hobby Lobby kit
	8x110mAh Ni-Cd	Northeast Sailplanes kit
Gunther 7x6 (Titanic)	7x270mAh NiMH	House of Balsa kit
Gunther 5x4	7x350mAh Ni-Cd	Tom Hunt design; Modelair-Tech kit
7¾x6	8x800mAh NiMH	Global Hobby kit
Slim 8x4	8x1100mAh NiMH	Hobby Lobby kit

gearbox, propellers and battery will produce 2 ounces of thrust, then the model can weigh up to 8 ounces (4x2). However, obtaining motor thrust data can be difficult.

Selecting a motor for a specific electric-powered model aircraft is further complicated by the fact that some electric motors are run on direct drive (with the propeller attached directly to the motor shaft), while others use a gear-reduction drive. The gear-reduction drive is usually the better way to go for most applications because you can obtain more thrust using less motor current. You will, however, end up using a larger diameter prop with a gear drive, which might be a problem with short landing gears on some model designs.

Some of the tradeoffs in electric-powered flight can be subtle. Finding the exact reduction ratio and prop size requires a lot of patience because, while you go through your motor/prop experimentation to find the right choice, you need to keep in mind that each electric motor has a maximum current rating. When you purchase a motor, ask about that rating (maximum motor current). If your dealer doesn't know, look on the shipping box or in the supplied instructions. Always measure your motor current using an AstroFlight digital meter when changing gear-reduction ratios, prop diameter and/or pitch, or the number of battery cells in your pack.

MODEL WEIGHT AND GUIDELINES CHART

To give a little more meaning to all of these words, I've come up with a chart that is broken down into the five basic categories mentioned in the introduction to this book see pages 10 and 11. Within each category I've provided some guides as to model size, weight and target power systems. In addition, I've provided some typical models that fit each of these categories to provide some realistic application information. Is this the final word on motor selection? Probably not, but it will help get you started toward making that first successful flight. After that, it is strictly a matter of perfecting the system to obtain the very best results.

TECH TIP

MOTOR CHARACTERIZATION CHARTS ON THE WEB

The Motor Characterization Charts provided by Dick Miller of Wernerville, PA, are an excellent source of information on motor parameters. As mentioned in Chapter 3 (Propellers), Dick maintains his own website for the benefit of electric-powered modelers at http://home.ptd.net/~rcm65/. This website provides a very important tool for electric-powered fliers, especially those interested in parking-lot and indoor RC flying.

RC Systems

9

Basic components of the RC system include the radio control transmitter, receiver and servos. Several RC systems are relatively inexpensive, rugged and well suited for use with park flyers and smaller aircraft. Specialized, ultra-miniature RC systems for the tiniest models are also available. In this chapter, the author reviews the best systems for novice pilots and offers pointers on some more advanced RC systems.

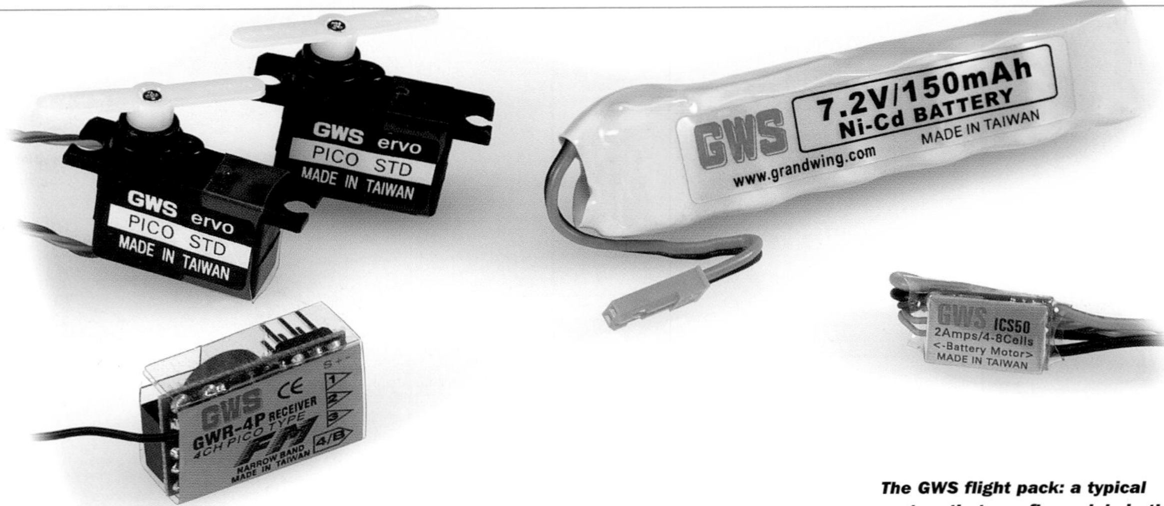

The GWS flight pack: a typical system that can fly models in the 6- to 8-ounce range.

By this point, you should have a good handle on power systems for small model aircraft. The next step is to discuss the equally important radio control (RC) system, which allows you to maneuver the aircraft while in flight. As with any RC system, the pilot holds a transmitter that broadcasts a radio frequency signal from the ground up to the model. A receiver inside the model picks up this signal, processes it and then feeds it to the actuators (servos) that move the control surfaces (rudder, elevator and, in some cases, ailerons). The receiver also sends a signal to the motor speed control to adjust the throttle.

Over the years, RC systems have become quite reliable and very inexpensive. With the current popularity of micro RC model aircraft, the hobby industry has met the challenge by producing some micro and lightweight RC system components. These can be purchased at very affordable prices.

Within the past two years, we have seen a group of new micro-size RC receivers come to market. One in particular, the GWS R-4P, weighs 6 grams (0.21 ounces) and costs only $28. Similar small servos are now available at approximately 0.2 ounces each and cost less than $30. Additionally, small, lightweight ESCs and battery packs are contributing to the ability to fly micro-size model aircraft. In this chapter, I will provide a crash course on micro RC systems so that you will be able to select the most practical and cost-effective equipment for your specific application.

The Grand Wing Servo (GWS) R-4P single conversion micro receiver that weighs about 0.2 ounce and, best of all, sells for only $28 with the crystal.

SINGLE STICK TRANSMITTERS

The easiest and least expensive way to operate a parking-lot or indoor flyer is with a simple 3-channel, single-stick RC system like the Hitec Focus-III SS or the Futaba Skysport SS-3 (Model 3FR). These operate on FM in the 72 to 73MHz RC aircraft band. Both of these systems come with single (2-axis) control sticks. This is very important because, with either of these transmitters, you rock the single control stick side to side to control rudder or aileron turning, while you move the same control stick fore and aft to operate the elevator (to make the model pitch its nose up or down).

Inexpensive single-stick RC transmitters, such as the Hitec

Left: the Hitec RCD Focus-III SS FM transmitter has 3-channel control using a 2-axis single stick to operate rudder and elevator, with a third or auxiliary channel to work the motor throttle.

Futaba's SkySport SS3 single-stick radio. The throttle switch on this 3-channel transmitter is a near the thumb grip.

An entry-level transmitter with two 2-axis sticks is the JR Quattro. Double-stick, 4-channel radios offer aileron, elevator, rudder and throttle control.

Less expensive than the Eclipse transmitter, but still employing microprocessor control, is the Hitec RCD Flash 5 System X.

Focus or Futaba Skysport, also have a third channel control, usually a lever, from which you can operate the motor speed control or motor throttle. They also have a built-in electronic mixing circuit that allows you to fly a delta-wing model or one with a V-tail. This is a good feature to have for these special-purpose models. Servo-reversing switches that allow you to reverse the direction of the servo rotation are another interesting feature.

Some of these transmitters will come with rechargeable Ni-Cd battery packs and a charger, or they can be added later on. A beginner could get away with using 8 AA alkaline non-rechargeable battery cells the first time around. But if the hobby holds your interest, you should switch to the rechargeable Ni-Cd batteries.

DUAL-STICK TRANSMITTERS

There are also a variety of dual-stick transmitters designed for beginners. On these, the right stick will typically control rudder and elevator, and the left stick will control throttle. On more advanced airplanes that use ailerons, the right stick will con-

"PROGRAMMABLE" TRANSMITTERS

THE NEXT STEP up from inexpensive RC transmitters are those with a built-in microprocessor. One of my favorites is the new Hitec Eclipse transmitter. It has up to seven channel functions, so you can easily fly a model with aileron, rudder, elevator and throttle control and still have three extra channel functions for flaps, spoilers and retractable landing gear.

Another nice feature of the Hitec Eclipse is that it can be electronically switched between high and low FM deviation or "shift." Over the years, the RC systems manufactured by Futaba and Hitec have employed FM deviation on what we call the "low" side, while systems provided by Airtronics and JR use "high" side FM deviation. Normally, you would have to purchase a receiver of the same deviation as the transmitter to make the system work properly. With the Hitec Eclipse transmitter, all you have to do is select the deviation you want; any receiver will work with the Eclipse transmitter as long as both are on the same channel.

The Eclipse transmitter can be purchased with a Spectra synthesized RF module that will allow you to dial up any of the 50 aircraft RC channels assigned to the 72 to 73MHz model aircraft band, so you never really have to worry about your receiver's channel of operation.

There are many more features associated with the Eclipse transmitter, including its ability to store control sequences for up to seven different models. This means that seven different model aircraft, with seven different receivers, can selectively be operated from one Eclipse transmitter.

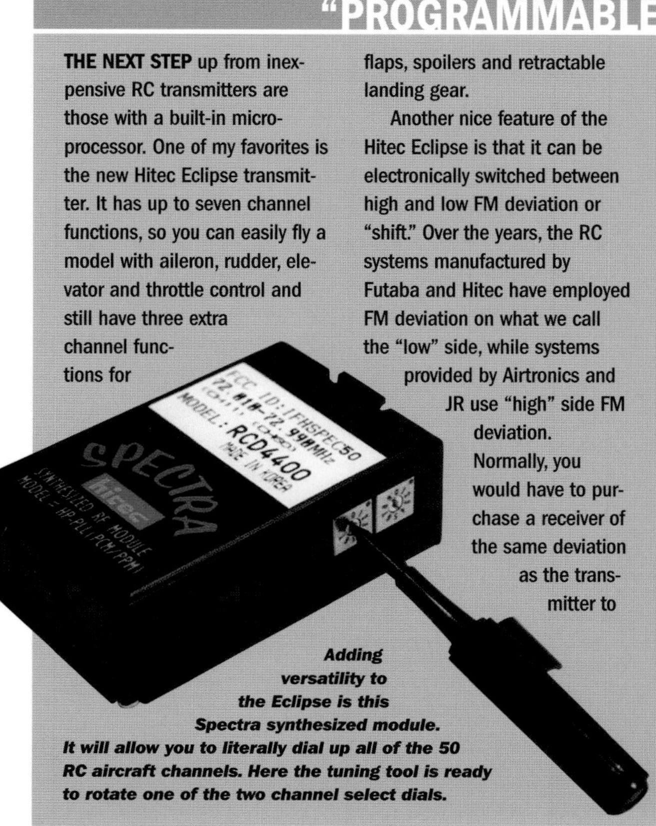

Adding versatility to the Eclipse is this Spectra synthesized module. It will allow you to literally dial up all of the 50 RC aircraft channels. Here the tuning tool is ready to rotate one of the two channel select dials.

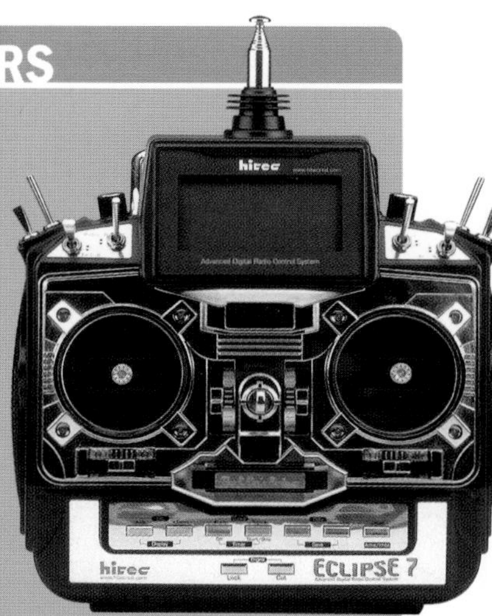

This is the new Hitec RCD Eclipse transmitter. The Eclipse features microprocessor control. It has seven memory position and can operate on upper or lower FM deviation, as explained in the text.

trol aileron and elevator, and the left stick will control throttle and rudder—but you need not worry about this if you are just starting out.

Some very inexpensive two-stick RC transmitters use separate sticks for the rudder and elevator controls (i.e., the left stick only moves up and down, and the right stick only moves side to side). Although such systems have sometimes been bundled with some of the least expensive RC airplanes, they are intended more for surface vehicle operation (cars and boats) than for model aircraft. Rule number one for model aircraft is to always use a transmitter with a control stick that offers "2-axes" control.

If you are a beginner, a simple 3-channel RC transmitter is the best way to start, and you will find use for it even after you have "bought up" to the more elaborate transmitter. Once you gain experience, you will appreciate the features of selecting FM deviation, channel number and model memory positions on the more sophisticated unit.

Before making your purchasing decision, I suggest you look at all the popular RC transmitters

The smallest dual conversion FM receiver to date is the FMA Direct Extreme at 0.4 ounce. This is perfect for indoor flying in a crowded environment and also for parking-lot flying where better than average selectivity is necessary.

The FMA Direct Quantum 6 dual conversion receiver weighs just 0.5 ounce. Perfect for parking-lot and Speed 400 models, especially when flown at a crowded regular RC flying field.

now on the market. In addition to Hitec RCD and Futaba, there are Airtronics, Horizon/JR, Multiplex, Tower transmitters—and soon a new transmitter from FMA Direct—just to name a few. Request catalogs and brochures from all of these suppliers before making your final choice.

DUAL CONVERSION RECEIVERS

Over the years, RC receivers have been based on three kinds of basic circuits. The most popular today is a dual conversion circuit. As the name implies, it converts from broadcast signal to operating signal twice. A dual conversion RC receiver will always have two crystals and will generally provide more selectivity, so that you are not bothered by an adjacent channel RC signal (just 20kHz away). It is also more sensitive in that it can provide greater radio range than other circuits; but, unfortunately for micro applications, dual conversion receivers are somewhat larger and heavier. Currently, the lightest receiver in the dual conversion category is the FMA Direct Extreme micro receiver at 0.4 ounce. Also in that same category are the FMA Direct Quantum receiver at 0.5 ounce and the Hitec Model 555 at 0.6 ounce.

SINGLE CONVERSION RECEIVERS

The next lightest are single conversion receivers. Single conversion receivers may not always be as selective and sensitive as their dual conversion counterparts, but fewer parts are used, (i.e., a single crystal), and they are therefore smaller and lighter. Since parking-lot and indoor models are flown rather close-in, radio range isn't much of a problem. The Grand Wing Servo Co. (GWS) Model R-4P micro single conversion receiver, at 6 grams (0.21 ounce), is very popular and will work well with the RC transmitters already mentioned. Some extraordinarily small receivers have been produced by Sky Hooks & Rigging as well, one of which includes a speed control with a total weight of around 3.5 grams. I'm sure as technology improves and micro flying gets more popular we will see more progress in the area of reduced-weight RC receivers.

SUPER-REGENERATIVE RECEIVERS

The third type of receiver circuit is called the super-regenerative. It was the only way to fly about 50 years ago, but now it's almost obsolete. Selectivity is the real problem with a super-regen circuit, so much so that you must block out several adjacent

Abbott Lahti's RP-27 27MHz super-regen micro receiver. Weighs just 1.66 grams. This equipment is available from Cloud 9 RC.

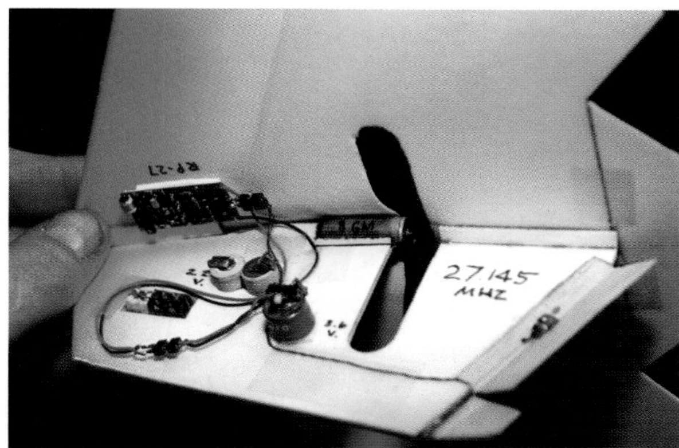

A close-up of the fuselage of John Delegrange's little "Stealth Bomber" model. The micro super-regen receiver is at the upper left. Mounted on the control surface are several battery cells, an ESC and a pulse decoder that controls the single magnetic actuator. This model is under 2-channel control and weighs only about 1 ounce.

channels on either side of your operating frequency to be able to fly safely. This fact alone makes it very unpopular, but, for some very special purposes, a super-regen micro receiver can offer the smallest size and lightest weight. For those interested in a super-regen RC system, I suggest you contact John Worth at Cloud 9 RC. John has available a system manufactured by Abbott Lahti of Cambridge, MA. Abbott's system operates on the 27MHz band where the channel spacing is a broader 50kHz. That does help the selectivity problem.

Several specialized RC systems are available that permit micro indoor flying of models at around 1-ounce total flying weight (ultra-micro class). Because these systems are so special they are also relatively expensive. One such system is manufactured by Clarence Hurd of Dynamics Unlimited; the other is manufactured in the Netherlands by Rick Ruijsink. Rick's MicroMag RC equipment is available in the U.S. from both David Lewis and Bob Selman. Although these special systems are presently offered only on 27MHz channels, a new 72MHz version of the MicroMag system will soon be manufactured under license by FMA Direct in the U.S.

MICROSERVOS

The next component of the RC system we must talk about is the proportional control servos and actuators that move the control surfaces. The typical proportional control servo consists of a motor with a gear drive and an amplifier that have been scaled down for micro applications. An entire group of these tiny servos is now available at about 0.2 ounce; they cost approximately $30 each.

A popular sub-microservo in this category is the

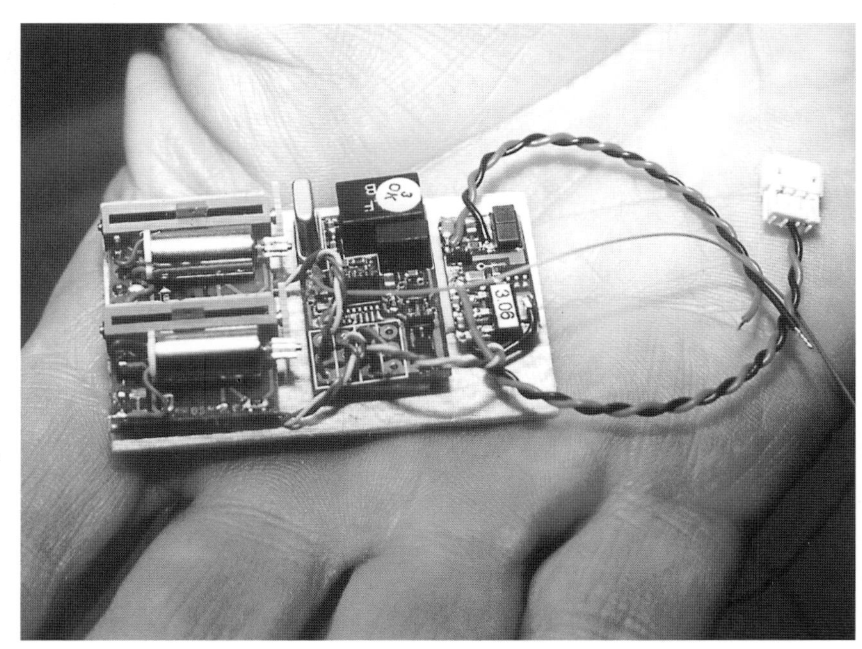

Innovative scale modeler Stew Meyers of Washington, DC, built this 3-channel RC "brick" for his model. It contains a GWS receiver, two WES-Technik LS-2.4 servos and a tiny ESC. Much of this equipment was stripped down to reduce weight further. Total weight of the brick was 11 grams or 0.39 ounce!

SAMPLE MICROSERVOS

JR-241

JR's sub-microservo (0.28 ounce) is lightweight and has a fast transit time. Its cable length is a generous 6 inches, and it's a perfect companion for the new JR micro receiver.

FMA Direct S-60

Currently, this is FMA Direct's smallest servo; it weighs 0.21 ounce and has an output of 10 oz.-in. and a cable length of 4½ inches. Five other microservos are available through FMA, including the S-100 at 0.49 ounce and 25 oz.-in. output.

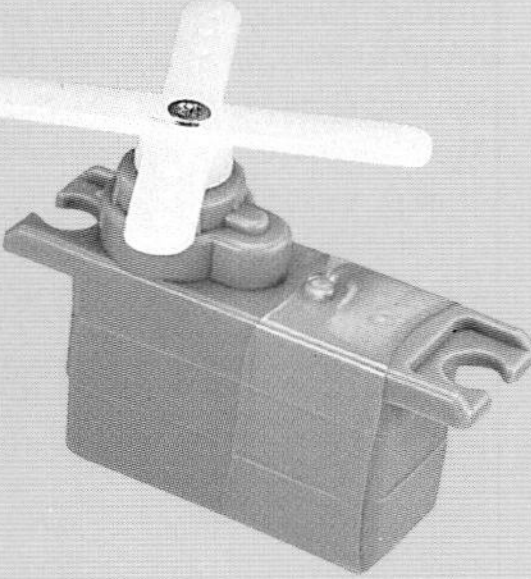

Cirrus CS-10 BB

This ball-bearing microservo weighs in at 0.21-ounce. Output is rated at 7 oz.-in., and this makes it better suited to indoor RC flying. At 4½ inches, its cable length is short, but Cirrus has four other microservos that range up to a ½ ounce unit with a 25 oz.-in. output (very strong!). All five of these servos have ball-bearing-supported output shafts.

WES-Technik LS-2.4

This servo is intended for the sub-micro class models at 2 to 3 ounces total weight. The LS-2.4 weighs less than 3 grams (0.1 ounce), but it is more costly!

Hitec RCD HS-50

The very popular Hitec RCD HS-50 sub-microservo. This is about the smallest and lightest of the conventional rotary servos. Weight is around 0.2 ounce. Cost is under $30.

Maxx Products (MPI) MX-30

With a very nominal weight of 0.21 ounce, the MX-30 BB has a ball-bearing-supported output shaft, but the cable is only 4 inches long. Both the MX-30 and MX-32 are available with a JST (European) connector. The MX-50 servo comes with or without ball bearings.

GWS BP-101

This is actually a GWS (Grand Wing Servo) Pico BB. This servo will also soon be sold by Sky Hooks & Rigging under a different model number. Also one of the lightest conventional servos at 0.21 ounce, it has a cable that's only 4½ inches long, but a good selection of output arms is provided. Three other microservos are available from Balsa Products, all weighing less than ½ ounce.

Futaba S3103

This servo has an output of 17.3 oz.-in. and weighs 0.28 ounce (8 grams). This is a strong servo that is also light, and it's well-suited to anything from indoor to the larger parking-lot-size models.

Dymond Modelsports D60

For the parking-lot and Speed 400 flyer is this new Dymond Modelsports D60 sub-microservo. It weighs 0.28 ounces, has a very thin profile and an output thrust of 24 oz.-in.

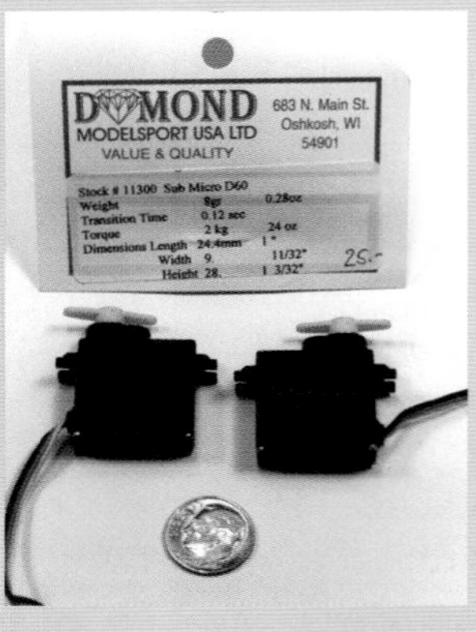

Fritz Mueller's Super B.I.R.D. magnetic actuators that permit proportional control of the smallest models. These actuators are mounted directly on the control surface and are powered by a special digital pulse converter circuit. Weight is 1.5 grams each.

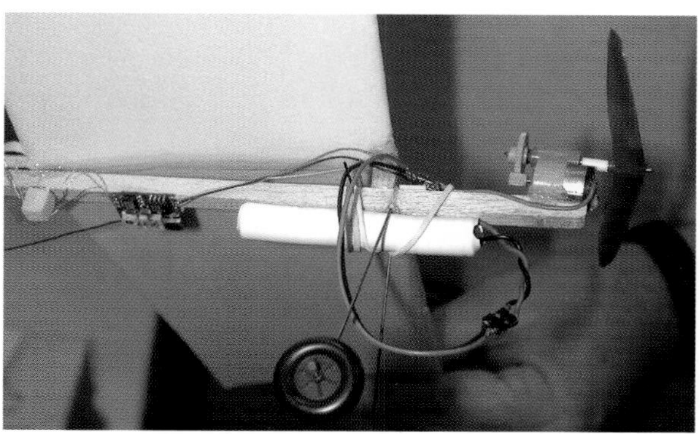

Far left: Rick Ruijsink's (of the Netherlands) MicroMag RC system. The model is Bob Selman's Micro Lite Flyer built from an IMA (Belgium) kit. Total model weight, ready-to-fly is 44 grams (1.6 ounces). This is true ultra-micro class.

Left: rudder actuator example.

Hitec HS-50. These servos use standard RC connectors and are plugged into mating connector blocks on the micro RC receivers. The BEC circuit of an ESC also plugs into this same connector block, thus providing power to the receiver and servos from the same shared motor battery pack. This means only one battery is necessary to operate the motor and the RC system.

A step down from the traditional rotary servo is a special linear output servo, the WES-Technik LS-2.4, which weighs just 3 grams (0.1 ounce). This servo is perfect for the 2- to 3-ounce sub-micro category indoor models; however, it is considerably more expensive than the rotary servos.

Recently, I heard of two new servos, each weighing approximately 3 grams, which may be introduced during 2002 by Mr. Houng Wen Lin of GWS and Dr. Mike Gross of MTM Intl. The prices are said to be "attractive."

ACTUATORS

Still smaller are the magnetic actuators similar to the Built Into Rudder Devices (BIRD) designed and manufactured by Fritz Mueller of Columbus, GA. The BIRD actuator, which weighs just 1 gram, is mounted directly onto the control surface and is basically a magnet with a coil of wire. A decoding device attached to the receiver feeds the necessary signal to this magnetic actuator. Control movement will still be proportional and smooth (the controls won't flap back and forth). Magnetic actuators are supplied with both the Dynamics Unlimited system and Rick's MicroMag system. Again, this is what is needed at the present time to fly a model in the 1-ounce weight class (ultra-micro).

PARKING-LOT AND SPEED 400 MODELS

It is safe to say that models from 8 ounces on up can employ more conventional RC equipment. This would include a dual conversion receiver and micro-size traditional rotary output servos. I think it is obvious that we shouldn't consider the smallest micro RC components for this size

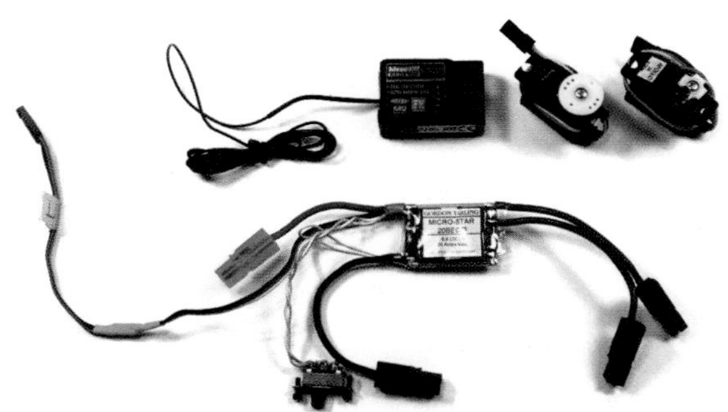

This is a typical RC system intended for heavier parking-lot and Speed 400 flyers. At the top center is a Hitec RCD 555 mini dual conversion receiver. In the foreground is a Gordon Tarling Micro-Star-20 BEC ESC. These miniature servos weigh about 0.5 ounce each.

model. Many of the parking-lot models will also be flown at regular RC flying sites and, as such, the RC equipment employed needs to co-exist with the regular RC models flown at the field. Keep all of this in mind when selecting and purchasing your RC equipment.

IR RC EQUIPMENT

So far, all references to RC equipment have assumed the use of radio frequency broadcast signals. There is another way to achieve remote control of a model aircraft; it involves the use of an infrared (IR) or optical signal. This is similar to the remotes used today to control TV sets, VCRs, etc.

Sergio Zigras has produced an IR RC system. Still another IR control system is offered by Clarence Hurd of Dynamics Unlimited (see the Source Guide at the end of this book for addresses). They are operated from what looks like a standard RC transmitter except that they have no antenna, as they only transmit a light source. These IR systems are primarily intended for indoor flying in lower light levels. Their range is somewhat limited, and usually only one system can be flown at a time. The advantage is very light airborne weight. These systems are not very expensive, which is something to consider if you want to fly in the ultra-micro class.

CHECKING YOUR RADIO'S RANGE

Regardless of which RC system you decide to purchase, you must be prepared to check the radio range before making your first flight and periodically thereafter. The best way to do this is to collapse the transmitter antenna or, if you are using a shortened antenna ("Rubber Ducky"), remove it entirely. By doing this, you cut back considerably on the transmitter's radiated power, which makes a range check an easier chore. With the transmitter antenna collapsed or removed, have a friend walk away from you while you continuously operate one of the control surfaces on the model. While doing this, you might also turn the electric motor on and off a few times to make sure that electrical noise isn't getting into your receiver.

Most RC manufacturers will give you a reference distance in which the system should still work. With the transmitter antenna collapsed or

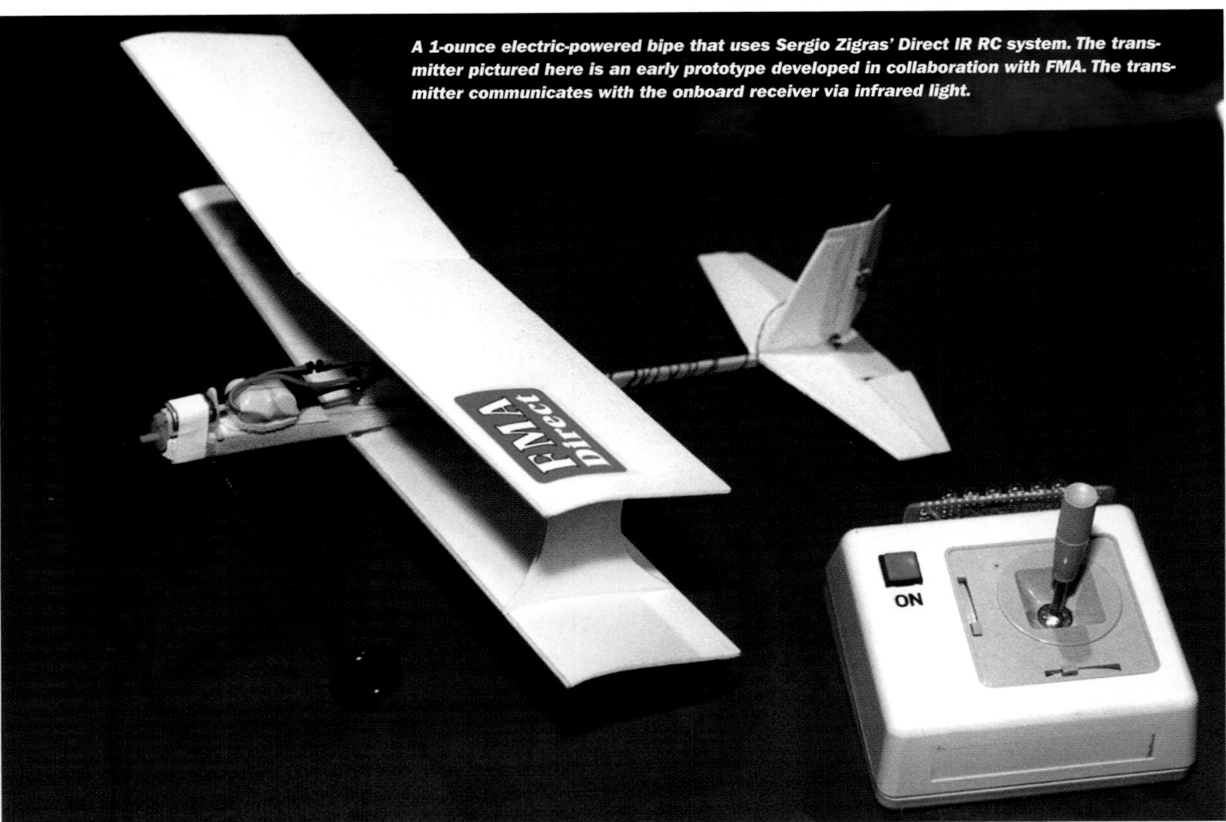

A 1-ounce electric-powered bipe that uses Sergio Zigras' Direct IR RC system. The transmitter pictured here is an early prototype developed in collaboration with FMA. The transmitter communicates with the onboard receiver via infrared light.

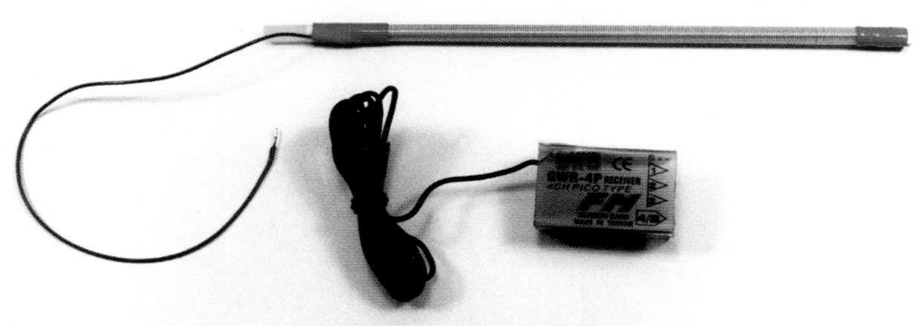

Long receiver antenna wires can be replaced by these short antenna coils developed by Azarr at Eclectic Electric Necessities. The short receiver antenna coil, at top, is shown with a GWS R-4P micro receiver. The short RC receiver coil replaces the heavy 40-inch antenna attached to the GWS receiver. Reception is reduced by only 15 percent when using this 0.6-gram antenna. It can be placed inside the fuselage. As we went to press, the short RC antenna coil cost $10 plus shipping.

removed, this distance is usually approximately 50 to 100 feet. If your range is significantly less than that, your system may have a problem. For example, the receiver might be out of tune with the transmitter; it is also a known fact that the location of certain RC components within the aircraft can also reduce radio range. Before you seek help from your manufacturer, try relocating some of the components, i.e., move the ESC away from the receiver, or locate the receiver antenna so that it isn't in close proximity to the servos. Remember, the servos contain tiny electric motors, which can also be noise generators.

SHORT RECEIVER ANTENNAS

Most micro RC receivers have rather long antenna wires; in many cases, they can be almost 40 inches long. Certainly a wire that long can be cumbersome when you consider the size of a micro indoor model, and these long wire antennas add undesirable weight. Recently, Azarr of Eclectic Electric Necessities developed a shortened receiver antenna (Model M72-6) that consists of a fine wire coil wrapped around a plastic tube measuring only 5 to 6 inches long. It weighs just 0.6 gram and costs approximately $10.

All you need to do is cut off your existing long wire antenna about an inch from the receiver case and solder the short antenna coil lead wire (about 6 inches long) to the "stub." The antenna coil is usually placed inside the fuselage of the model aircraft. Tests have shown that the radio range is reduced by only 10 to 15 percent, which is negligible for our purposes; however, this short antenna is only intended for indoor and parking-lot flyers. With Speed 400 power, it is best to use a full-length antenna.

RC SYSTEM CONNECTOR POLARITY

When discussing electric connectors in Chapter 6, we concentrated on connectors used for the motor batteries, chargers, etc. However, RC systems also employ connectors of a different type. Until several years ago, there was no real convention on RC system connector polarity. The majority of proprietary connectors had the center wire (of three) as battery positive (+), with one outside pin being the negative battery (-) and the remaining pin for the signal or amplifier contact.

With this type of arrangement, if you accidentally plugged the connector in backwards, the receiver and/or servos wouldn't work and nothing would burn out. The older-style Sanwa connectors used on the Airtronics' radios had the positive battery lead on the outside. If you inserted this connector in the reverse direction you would instantly cook the circuits. These older-style Sanwa connectors have been replaced in recent times with a new Z connector with the positive pin in the center. Although most of these connectors have alignment keys to maintain the proper polarity, some can still be plugged in in either direction. To be on the safe side, read the instructions supplied with your RC system components, and be sure you have the correct connector pin orientation before applying the power for the first time.

10

RC System Installation Control & Hookups

The ground rules for installing the RC system, system batteries, motor and other airborne components are covered in this section. You will also learn tips on how to install control rods, hinges and more.

Once you have selected and purchased your RC system, you must decide how to install it in your model aircraft and how to connect the control surfaces to the equipment. Several parking-lot flyers are currently being sold as ready-to-fly (RTF) with the radio, motor and battery already installed in the model. If you have purchased one of those, you can skip this chapter for now (if you elect to replace any of the internal systems in an RTF model, be sure to read this chapter).

The majority of models intended for parking-lot flying will be in the almost-ready-to-fly (ARF) category. Some final assembly will be required with these models. For example, the motor and radio must be installed and the various controls, such as the rudder and elevator, will need to be hooked up. Generally speaking, most of these ARF models will come with detailed instructions that explain how to complete the assembly. If you purchase a full construction kit with no prefabrication, then everything must be built up and then covered. The manufacturers of these kits will include suitable RC system installation instructions in the package.

PLACEMENT OF ONBOARD COMPONENTS

The key to RC installation is to locate the equipment so that the aircraft's center of gravity (CG), or balance point, is not compromised. Aerodynamically, this is the key element to successful flight. The motor, in most instances, will be located in the nose of the aircraft. It's advisable to position the ESC or motor controller directly behind the motor. You could leave some of these components hanging inside the fuselage by their own wires or cables. I personally choose to anchor my RC equipment to the fuselage sides or bulkheads using either double-sided tape or hook-and-loop fastener tape.

ELECTRONIC SPEED CONTROL (ESC)

Since both the motor and the ESC can get warm with normal operation, do not place them directly one on top of the other. Instead, leave an inch or two between them. Also, consider that two wires will run from the ESC to the motor and two more wires will run from the ESC to the motor battery. It is important that you plan ahead for your battery location so that the model is balanced properly and that you still have enough wire to reach it.

The third cable exiting from the ESC is a servo pigtail connection. This cable must be routed to the receiver, where it plugs into the throttle port (connector). Again, plan ahead so that this cable can reach the receiver location.

MICRO RECEIVER

Next, attach the micro receiver to the fuselage side, floor, or bulkhead using tape or hook-and-loop fastener material. At the receiver, you will need to

The top half of this molded Styrofoam fuselage has been removed to show a typical RC system installation. At the right is the electric motor mounted on the front or nose of the model. Not visible in this photo, but pasted to the right fuselage side near the battery pack, is the ESC. The 8-cell 120mAh NiMH battery pack is affixed to the fuselage floor with hook-and-loop fastener tape. On the left fuselage side, by the end of the battery, is the GWS R-4P micro receiver. On either side of the fuselage, toward the aft portion, are the two Hitec RCD HS-50 sub-microservos. Both servos are attached to the fuselage side with double-sided servo tape. The control rods lead from the servos out to the rudder and elevator. Also exiting out the rear is the receiver antenna wire.

identify the channel functions to ensure that the elevator servo is plugged into the elevator port and the rudder servo to the rudder port. The RC system instructions should clarify the connector identification. If in doubt, power up the RC system and move the transmitter control sticks to verify the correct servo hook up. Side to side motion of the control stick should operate your rudder, while a fore and aft motion should move the elevator.

TECH TIP

SEPARATE COMPONENTS TO AVOID NOISE

It is generally a good idea to get some separation between the electric motor/ESC and the receiver, as well as between the receiver and the servos. Electric motors are noise generators. When something is in the wrong location you may notice the control surfaces "wiggling" or the electric motor "burping" (turning on and off quickly).

OVERALL LAYOUT

As you work your way back from the nose of the aircraft to the rear of the model, the ESC will usually be located forward of the wing leading edge. The receiver is installed next and may be just aft of the wing leading edge. The battery pack will often be near the CG position, since it has the most mass. A small shift in the battery position can greatly affect the balance point of a model. Generally, the CG position is approximately 25 percent of the wing chord (width) measuring rearward from the leading edge.

INSTALLING SERVOS

The last items to be installed are the servos, which traditionally are located closer to the wing's trailing edge. This places the servos in a better position to reach the control surfaces that they must operate; generally speaking, short control rods connecting servo arms to control surfaces are better than longer control rods (there's less potential for slop in the mechanics).

On a training or sport model, there will be two servos: one for rudder and the other for elevator. They are generally mounted side by side using hardwood bearers and screws or, better yet, simply attached with double-sided tape. Keep in mind that the ESC provides the on/off and throttle control of the motor and actually takes the place of a third servo, which would normally be used on an engine-powered model to operate the carburetor.

As previously mentioned, we try to keep micro models as light as possible, and we normally don't use any switches to turn the power on and off. When the battery is plugged in, the airborne RC system is turned on and the motor is armed. When installing your RC system, always make sure you remove the propeller from the motor. Although most modern ESCs have built-in circuits that prevent accidental motor start-up, it is always better to use safety precautions.

CONTROL RODS

One of the last steps in the installation process is to attach the control links or control rods that go from the servo output arm to the control surfaces on the models. A good way to do this is to use a small diameter wire (i.e., .015 to .020 inch), which can be found at most hobby shops.

Tail surfaces of a typical model. In this case, a semi-scale Cessna Skyhawk that weighs a total of 4.8 ounces, ready-to-fly. Handmade plywood control horns are employed. A .020-inch-diameter wire is fed inside the yellow plastic tubing from the servo back to the control surface.

In addition, you will need thin-wall tubing through which the control wire is slipped. This tubing supports the wire that connects the servo arm to the control surface horn. My personal preference is the Sullivan Products No. 508 (the yellow outer tubing) or House of Balsa NEC-04 CA micro tubing. Micro tubing is normally sold for use as a spout on CA cement bottles, but it is excellent for control rod needs; just be sure the wire fits loosely inside the tubing so that it doesn't bind in any way, as that could stall the servo motor.

CONTROL WIRES AND Z-BENDS

The basic idea is to first attach the wire first to the servo output arm (the outermost hole first); then run the wire and tubing aft to the control horn, which is attached to the control surface. A small Z-bend at the end of the wire will allow it to slip into the hole on the servo output arm. At the other end of the wire, a second Z-bend will allow the connection to the control horn. Next, I power up the RC system and make sure the servo is in the neutral position. Then, with double-sided tape on the servo, I move the servo fore and aft until the control surface is also in the neutral position. At that point, I press the servo to the fuselage side; finally, I cement the support tubing every couple of inches as it leads from the servo to the control horn. When you operate the servo, be sure that the control wire does not bind and

TECH TIP

MAKING Z-BENDS

If you're wondering how to make Z-bends in the wire, you'll be interested to know that several hobby suppliers sell Z-bend pliers. An excellent one is offered by Great Planes (Part No. GPMR8025); another comes from a private source, Mr. J. C. Smith of Delta, OH. A simple Z-bend can also be made using a pair of small pliers. You make one 90-degree bend, then rotate and make a second 90-degree bend. Finally, straighten the end and you have a Z. Take a look at the illustration of this process.

Above: making Z-bends is important, since it is a way to attach the control wires to either the servo output arm or the control horn. Pictured here is a Z-bender sold by Great Planes Model Manufacturing Co. (top) and a custom-made Z-bender by Mr. J. C. Smith of Delta, OH. Note the Z-bend on the piece of wire in the foreground.

The Smith Z-bender in action. One squeeze and you have a perfect Z-bend.

MAKING Z-BENDS WITH NEEDLE-NOSE PLIERS

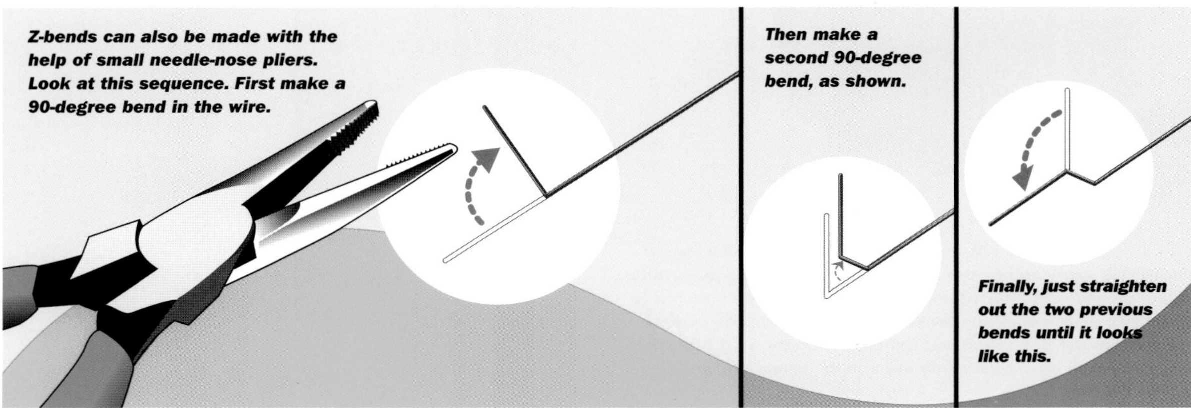

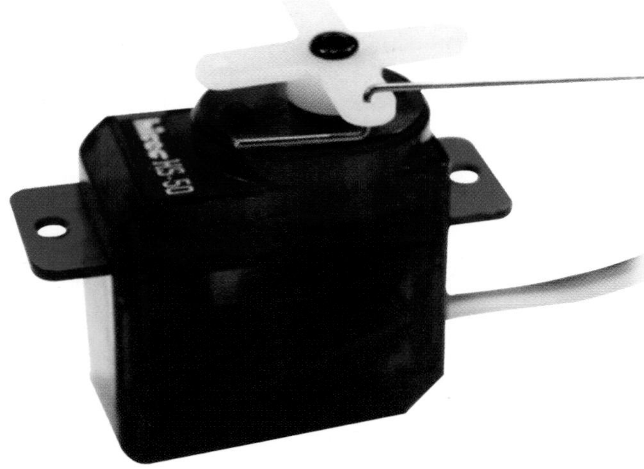

This is typically how a Z-bend wire end hooks into a servo output arm. Shown here is a Hitec RCD HS-50 sub-microservo.

that the support tubing does not buckle in any way.

E-Z CONNECTORS

The Dymond Modelsports company recently introduced a scaled-down version of the popular E-Z connector. It is their Easy Pushrod Connector (catalog no. 50358). The connector is first inserted into the servo output arm hole or the control horn hole. Next, the small diameter control wire is passed through the connector. A tiny

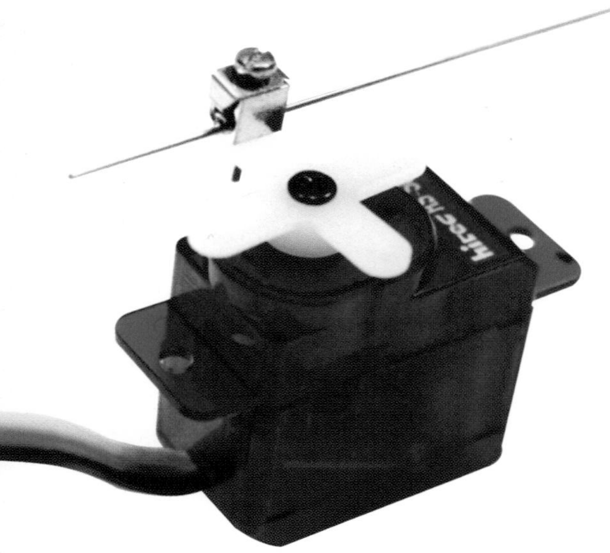

This excellent E-Z type connector has been scaled down for our micro-flying applications. Our hats off to Dymond Modelsports for coming up with this catalog no. 50358 connector. You attach it to the servo output arm. Open the top screw and pass the control wire through the hole; then just tighten the screw so it grips the wire. From then on, adjustments are simple. Something you can't do with Z-bends.

screw holds the wire firmly in place. The best part of using this connector is the ability to make easy control movement adjustments, which you can't do with Z-bends.

Just as this book was going to press, we learned that the Du-Bro Company, the originator of the E-Z connector, had just produced a new mini version, which it has identified as their P/N 845. Du-Bro claims it weighs 0.25 grams, will hold up to .047-inch-diameter wire and uses a 2-56 machine screw to secure the control wire in place. So now two choices of this popular product are available for micro fliers.

CONTROL SURFACE HINGES

Most of the ARF models come with the control surfaces pre-hinged at the factory, which is convenient, but in some cases you will need to install the hinging. For parking-lot and larger models the Lite Hinge offered by many companies, including Sig Manufacturing and Sonic-Tronics, will make the job easy. Simply make a slit in the control surface and the mating half, insert the Lite Hinge and add a few drops of CA cement, which will quickly penetrate the hinge joint. This hinge material will stay flexible for years.

On the micro indoor models, using iron-on covering material to make the hinge is easier, and the resulting hinges are lighter in weight. Apply strips of the covering between the flying surface and the control surface (some pieces of masking tape can be used temporarily to hold the surfaces together); then, using your iron, heat the material until it adheres to the already covered surfaces.

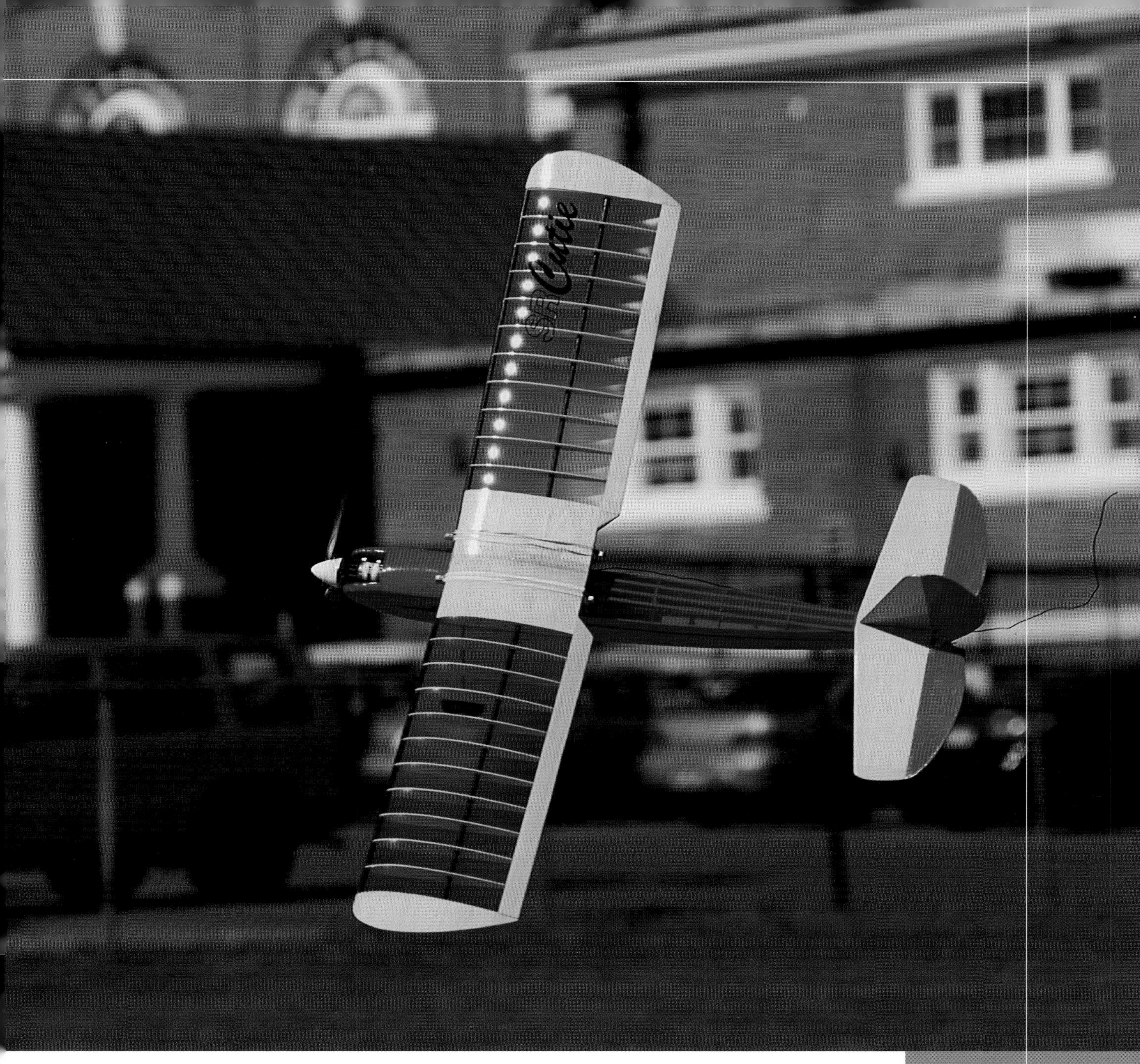

Choosing Your Aircraft

11

A wide variety of aircraft types, styles and platforms exist; moreover, the materials of which they are made and the level of fabrication "out of the box" is highly variable. The author offers advice that will help you make the right choice.

We now have a good understanding of the electric power system and the RC system, so the next logical step is to talk about the kinds of model aircraft available. Years ago, model aviation was considered strictly a hobby. The hobby included first building the model and then flying it. In the early days, the primary interest was in free flight and control line models. By the early '50s we began to see the introduction of radio control (RC) models.

As the years passed we saw breakthroughs in construction materials with the development of iron-on coverings and cyanoacrylate (CA) adhesives and cements that cure in a matter of seconds. These advances made building and finishing a model aircraft easier and less time consuming.

ARF AND RTF MODELS

These and other innovations in model-building technology led to the current popularity of the almost-ready-to-fly (ARF) and ready-to-fly (RTF) models. Today, it is possible to buy a model that is not only fully assembled, but has both the motor system and the RC systems installed and ready to go. All you need to do is to charge the battery and fly.

Today's model aviation hobby offers many possibilities. You can choose to build a model from a kit or, perhaps, scratch-build an entire model from plans. You can finish the assembly of an ARF model, or, if you are not interested in building, you can buy an RTF model and simply fly, which is what we call the "sport" aspect of model aviation.

Left: my 2½-year-old grandson, Hayden Parkes, holds my replica Profile Powerhouse, an 80-square-inch free-flight design from the '50s. I converted it to indoor electric flying. The article appears in the January 2001 issue of RC MicroFlight.

Right: on the very light side of things is this ultra-micro model built by noted Canadian scale modeler, Jack McGillivray. It is a 920 Moto-Aviette Farman, weighing just 1.2 ounce ready-to-fly. It has an 88-square-inch wing area and is powered by 3 50mAh Ni-Cd cells.

IF YOU ARE A NOVICE

Which is best for you? If you a beginner getting involved with model aviation for the very first time, my suggestion is to first experience the thrill of flying. Don't let yourself get sidetracked by trying to learn basic model-building skills. Get an ARF or RTF model and get out to the flying field as soon as possible. I also recommend that you try a parking-lot model (the 8- to 14-ounce category) for that first model. There are many ARF kits now offered in this category, and models of this size are good training planes. Micro indoor-type models should be put off until you learn the basics of flight.

Lil Hornet designed by Merril Brady at MM Glider Tech and sold through David Thacker at Radical R/C Inc. The model has a 232-square-inch wing and weighs 9 to 10 ounces, putting it in the parking-lot category. Battery is a 7-cell 720mAh NiMH.

IF YOU ARE AN EXPERIENCED RC PILOT

So far I have addressed the needs of the beginner. But what if you are an experienced glow-fuel pilot who wants to enter the world of micro flight? Since you likely have the necessary building skills, you might want to consider building a kit or building from published plans. You still will have to learn some of the tricks of electric-powered flight (e.g., battery charging), but that will come with time. Basic flying skills gained from fuel models can easily be converted to skills used with micro electric-powered planes.

Regardless of your modeling background, you

Fred Marks, President of FMA Direct, with an Aeronca C-3 look-alike design. This model weighs 6 ounces. Motor is a GWS operating on a 7-cell 250mAh Ni-Cd battery. Area is 260 sq. in. with a wing loading of only 3.3 oz. /sq. ft. Included in the 6 ounces is one of Fred's new Quantum-6 dual conversion micro receivers.

Another popular indoor and parking-lot flyer (in calm wind conditions) is Dan Kreigh's MINI-IFO. It weighs only 4 ounces, with 320 sq. in. of area and a wing loading of only 1.8 oz./sq. ft. Powered by a D-1717 geared 1.8:1 on 10 50mAh Ni-Cd cells. A very agile performer, it can literally turn on a dime. A great, fun plane—perfect for the backyard as well.

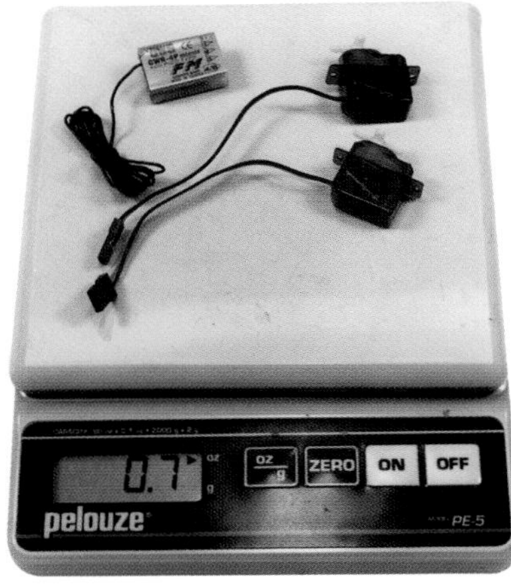

Knowing the weight of your models and the individual components is absolutely essential to micro flying. This Pelouze digital scale, purchased at Staples for about $80, does a good job. It is capable of measuring weights of up to 80 ounces with an accuracy of within 0.1 ounce. It will also read up to 2,000 grams with an accuracy of within 2 grams. In this example, the scale is weighing a GWS R-4P micro receiver and two Hitec RCD HS-50 sub-microservos. Total weight is 0.7 ounce.

will need to keep certain things in mind when building and flying small electric-powered models. Weight is of primary importance, as is wing loading. If you have the wing loading too high, the model is not going to get off the ground. Since weight is so important, it is a good idea to buy an accurate digital readout scale at the onset. Several good scales are available for less than $100 from major stationery suppliers, such as Staples, OfficeMax and Office Depot. The scale should be used often and will be very useful in determining the correct choice of materials and components.

ADHESIVES & COVERINGS

When constructing or assembling your models, be sure to use the proper cement for the application. Basic CA cement in thick and thin viscosities is used for wood framework assembly. High-stress areas (e.g., wing-panel joining, motor and landing-gear mounting) need a 5-minute epoxy. Caution should be taken with models constructed of foam material, since many CA cements will melt the foam. Always test for that possibility using scrap pieces of foam.

Lightweight iron-on covering material in either opaque or transparent colors

For those who like to build from plans is this 2.6-ounce model, the Pepper, designed by Dave Robelen. This is in the sub-micro category. It uses a DC 5-2.4 coreless motor on 4.2:1 gearing and a 7-cell 50mAh Ni-Cd battery. Servos are the WES-Technik LS-2.4 linear types. Also a marvelous indoor or backyard flyer.

Falcon/RCS Technik scale SE5a, built by Stew Meyers of Washington, DC. Model weighs only 3.1 ounces ready-to-fly. Wing area is 160 sq. in., and the wing loading is 2.8 oz./sq. ft. Photo taken by Bob Aberle while attending the Indoor Fly at the National Building Museum in Washington, DC.

Hitec's Sky Scooter is a 2- or 3-channel aileron/elevator model for outdoor flying. The 32-inch span plane weighs 16.8 or 18.5 ounces depending on whether you are flying the lighter 2-channel version (300mAh Ni-Cd battery) or Pro 3-channel version (600mAh Ni-Cd pack) with throttle. It comes with transmitter and the receiver and servos are factory-installed. Wing loading for the Pro version is 9.65 oz. per sq. ft.

The Dumas Aircraft Kestral weighs only 5.5 ounces with a 34-inch wingspan.

is used primarily for the parking-lot flyers. Lightweight tissue covering such as Litespan is preferred for the micro indoor models. The exact techniques for covering small models can be found in several how-to articles. See, for example, Dave Robelen's article in the February 2001 issue of *Model Airplane News*, pages 80 to 82. Also, several of the large mail-order houses offer videos concerning all aspects of model-building techniques. I refer you to the websites for Tower Hobbies, Horizon Hobby Inc., Hobby People, Hobby Lobby Intl. and Northeast Sailplane Products (see the source guide for further information).

TECH TIP

CHOOSING AN AIRFOIL

Airfoil choices are also important. Parking-lot or micro indoor flyers perform better with higher-chambered airfoils that permit slower flying speeds. Most of the airfoils will have been pre-selected for you by the kit designer, but you should learn which airfoils will offer the best slow-flying performance.

The website, http://digilander.iol.it/neon1/profili.html, developed by Stefano Duranti of Italy called Profili, will give you good information, and offers free airfoil-drawing software that will run on Windows 95 and later Windows operating systems. Some excellent high-chamber airfoils can be found at this website (e.g., Benedek BE6356B, used successfully by micro flier, Dave Robelen). This website will be very helpful if you decide to design your own models.

The GYMFLYR was designed by Carl Martin (the prop man!) and is being sold through Anything R/C. It has a 264-square-inch wing area, weighs 4.8 ounces, and the wing loading is 2.6 ounces per square foot. The motor is a D1717 geared 11.8:1 using a 9.5-inch diameter ARC-1 prop running on a Rayovac 9V NiMH battery. The deep under-chambered airfoil makes this a true slow flyer, perfect for indoor flying or outdoor flying in dead calm conditions.

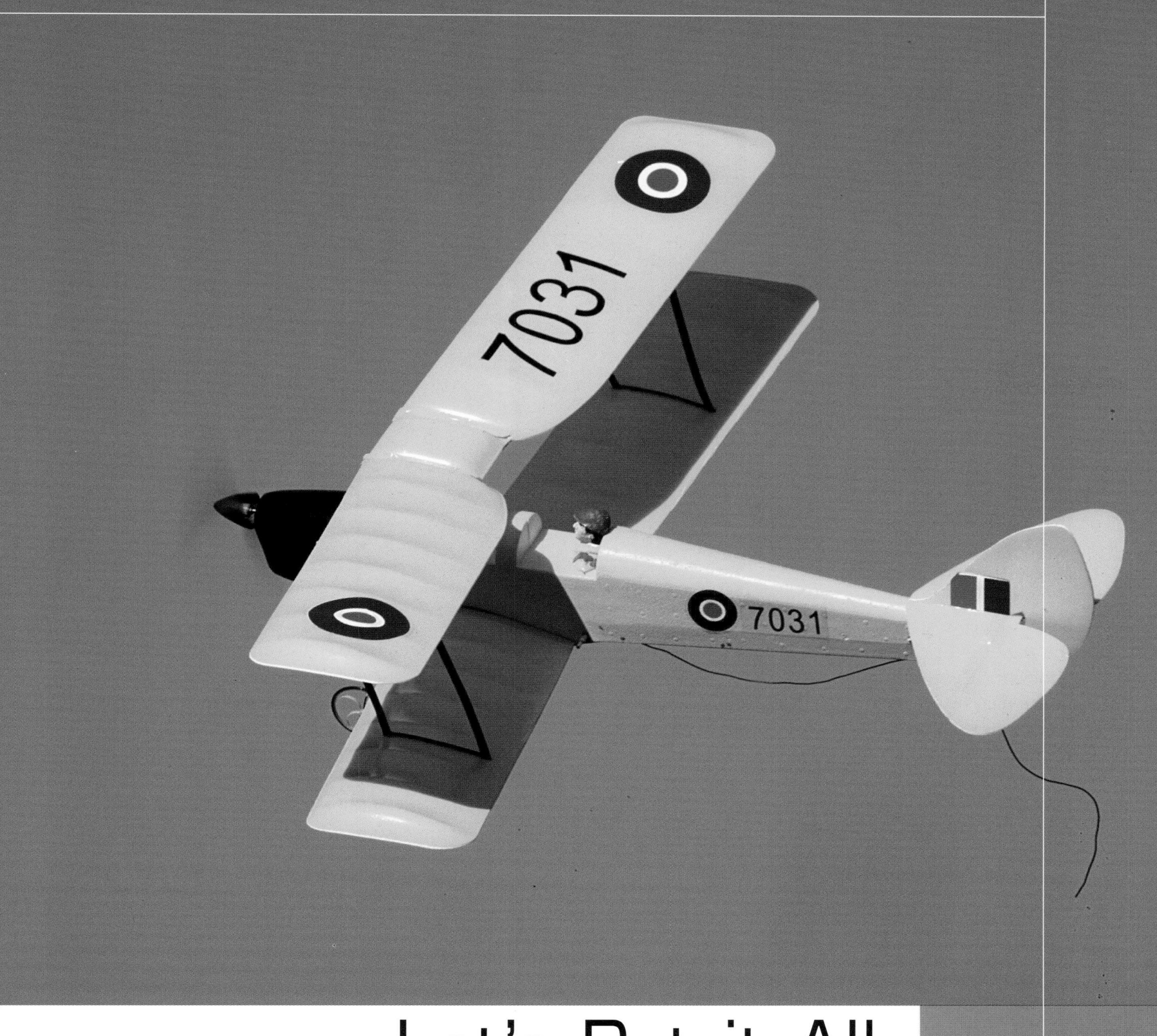

Let's Put it All Together

12

Here, the author assembles, flies and offers comments on three representative micro electric airplanes that illustrate what you can do today. He continues with a description of how he improved the performance of two other airplanes by experimenting with different props and batteries. This chapter puts together all the knowledge contained in previous portions of this book and offers valuable insights that can help you choose your next micro airplane.

Now it is time to apply what we have learned in the previous chapters and put a model aircraft together and then head out to the flying field or indoor flying facility. In the last part of this chapter, we will look at how you can enhance your model's performance by judiciously experimenting with different props, motors and batteries.

Please note that the products mentioned as ready-to-fly (RTF) or almost-ready-to-fly (ARF) models are not endorsements of any particular product but are simply some examples of what is available at this writing.

Here I'm posing with all three example models. I'm holding the the blue Miss Bohemia and the red WattAge Lite Stik. In front is the Merlin.

Because most of the ARF and RTF models to date have been in the parking-lot category, I have used those as my choice for these examples. However, I suspect that in the near future we will begin to see ARF and RTF models in the micro indoor size as well, which will be a welcome addition to the hobby.

EXAMPLE ARF AND RTF MODELS

An example of an RTF model, the Merlin Ultra Lite R/C manufactured by Megatech, Inc., weighs almost 17 ounces, which is slightly heavier than my 14-ounce limit for parking-lot flying. However, it has 511 square inches of wing area, which equates to a wing loading of 4.9 oz./sq. ft., putting it within a workable limit. The motor supplied is a geared Speed 380. This model flies at extremely slow speeds which makes it a perfect candidate for parking-lot flying.

The next model, Miss Bohemia, available from Hobby Lobby, is in the ARF category and has been available for some time. This particular design has a 325 square inch wing, employs conventional RC equipment, and, at 14 ounces, is at my recommended upper limit for a parking-lot flyer. The resulting wing loading is 6.2 oz./sq. ft., which is actually a little more than my recommended 5 oz./sq. ft.. However, with lighter RC equipment, that weight can be reduced somewhat. The Miss Bohemia comes close to a Speed 400-type model and, as such, is an interesting example. Despite its slightly heavier weight, it is also an excellent slow-speed flyer, making it perfect for parking lots.

Another popular ARF is the WattAge Lite Stik. The wing area of this little plane is 238 square inches, and the model weight can be 6 to 7 ounces, yielding a wing loading of around 4 oz./sq. ft. Literally thousands of these models have been sold because they are easy to assemble, light in weight, and just about the perfect size for parking-lot flying. They are capable of indoor flying and, best of all, are remarkably inexpensive.

STUDY THE MODEL'S SPECIFICATIONS

Before buying any model kit, ARF or RTF, you should study the published specifications. Unfortunately, many manufacturers and distributors do not offer as much detail in the published specifications as I would like. I'd like to see more data on wing loading, total model weight, wing area, wingspan, recommended motor, gear reduction ratio (if applicable), prop size, estimated motor current, suggested battery (type, capacity and number of cells) and the type of RC equipment intended for this specific application. Alternatively, let's hope the magazine reviewers can supply the necessary data because you need this information to make an intelligent choice.

Following are my impressions of all three of these example models, which I assembled and flew.

MERLIN

This is essentially a RTF model that comes with "everything." It is a fully constructed model that requires only a few steps of final assembly. The radio system—even the control rods—are all in place. Included with the Merlin is the motor, prop, ESC with BEC, battery, battery charger, complete RC system (including the receiver and servos) and an RC transmitter. The only thing you must purchase is a set of eight AA alkaline batteries to power the RC transmitter.

This is the Megatech Merlin, a parking-lot-size, ready-to-fly (RTF) model. It comes almost completely assembled and includes the motor, battery charger and the complete RC system already installed in the model.

ASSEMBLY

The Merlin's wing and tail surfaces are made from sheet foam and a carbon stick fuselage. The RC system is already enclosed in a molded-plastic box that is attached to the stick fuselage. Exiting out the rear of the RC box are the two control wires that attach to the rudder and elevator flying surfaces.

You simply slide the motor assembly onto the front end of the fuselage stick and add a drop of CA to hold it in place. The tail surfaces (vertical and horizontal tailpieces) are snapped into position at the aft end of the fuselage stick. An under-carriage assembly is formed between the wheel axle and a lower fuselage tray, which provides room for a pilot figure if you care to add one. The molded-plastic brackets that hold the axle and the supporting carbon rods are a little tricky to orient. Some clearer sketches are in order for this assembly step. All of these carbon rod/molded-plastic part joints will need a few drops of thin CA to hold them in place.

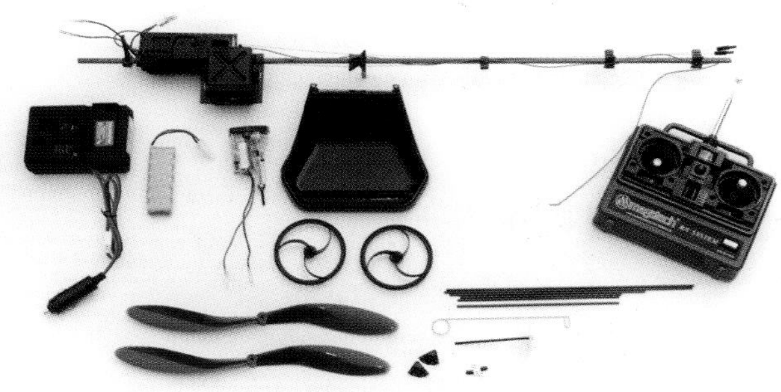

Some of the components supplied with the Merlin. The assembled fuselage is at the top. The entire radio system and ESC are contained in the molded-plastic box that is already joined to the carbon-fiber fuselage. Control rods are installed at the factory; you only have to connect them to the control surfaces. At left is the charger.

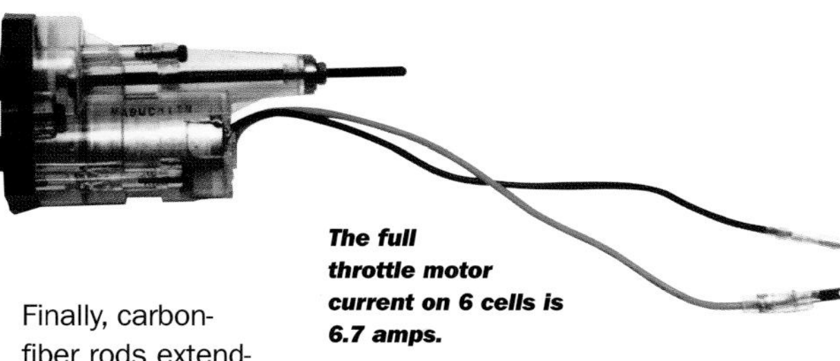

The full throttle motor current on 6 cells is 6.7 amps.

Servos, ESC and receiver are pre-installed in these plastic housings.

Finally, carbon-fiber rods extending from the wing panels are inserted in special receptacles on either side of the boom, and they simply snap into place. Total assembly time is less than an hour. So it is possible to open this kit box one morning and be flying before lunch.

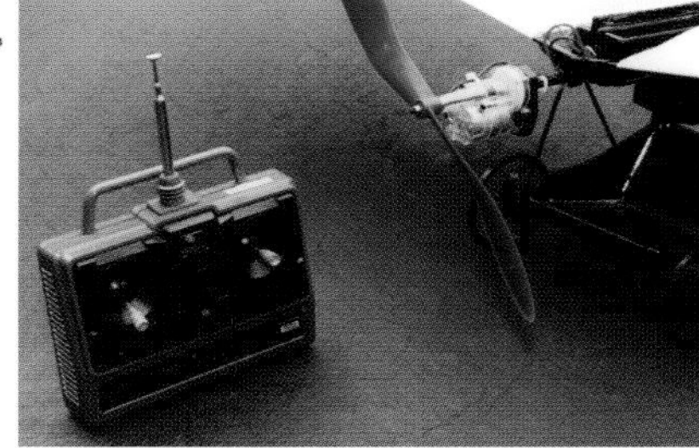

A close-up view of the Merlin's nose. The geared Speed 380 motor is supplied, as is the plastic prop (plus a spare prop). Transmitter at left is provided by Megatech.

MERLIN SPECIFICATIONS

MODEL: Merlin

DISTRIBUTED BY: Megatech, Inc.

TYPE: a ready-to-fly (RTF) electric-powered parking-lot category RC model that comes complete with everything necessary to fly.

WINGSPAN: 49 in.

WING AREA: 511 sq. in.

WEIGHT (WITH BATTERY): 17 oz.

WING LOADING: 4.9 oz./sq. ft.

MOTOR: geared Speed 380 with 5.6:1 reduction ratio

PROP: 11½ in. diameter—plastic as supplied

MOTOR CURRENT: 6.7 amps

FLIGHT DURATION: 5 to 7 minutes, depending on throttle settings

BATTERY: 6- or 7-cell 600mAh NiMH

RC EQUIPMENT: 72MHz AM receiver and transmitter provided, along with two servos and an ESC with a BEC. Equipment is already installed and sealed, so the origin is unknown.

FLYING EXPERIENCE

The Merlin literally flew right out of my hands on the first flight. Control throws were not critical nor was any trim necessary. It flies ever so slowly. I could walk under the model to take photos while a friend flew the Merlin for me. I was able to maintain a regular walking pace. Flight performance is majestic. There are no bad traits; it is just fun to fly.

The only unusual characteristic was that the very flexible sheet-foam wings acquired considerably more dihedral in flight. They almost look like they might snap from the extra stress. Because of my concern for this condition, I added a bracing cord (actually monofilament fishing line) from the lower tip on one wing panel through a hole drilled in the "pilot's seat bottom" and on out to the underside of the other wingtip. This line was pulled just tight enough to maintain a reasonable dihedral angle with the model at rest. It was a simple, worthwhile fix to restrict the amount of "acquired" dihedral.

The Merlin in flight, with Tom Hunt at the controls and Bob Aberle on the camera. The photo was taken at the Grumman Wing Nuts Field at Calverton, on the eastern end of Long Island, NY.

COMMENTS

What is particularly nice about this model for the beginner is that everything is set up with connectors. Nothing needs be soldered during the equipment assembly. It is strictly what we call "plug and play."

The Merlin 3-channel transmitter requires you to purchase a set of 8 AA alkaline batteries.

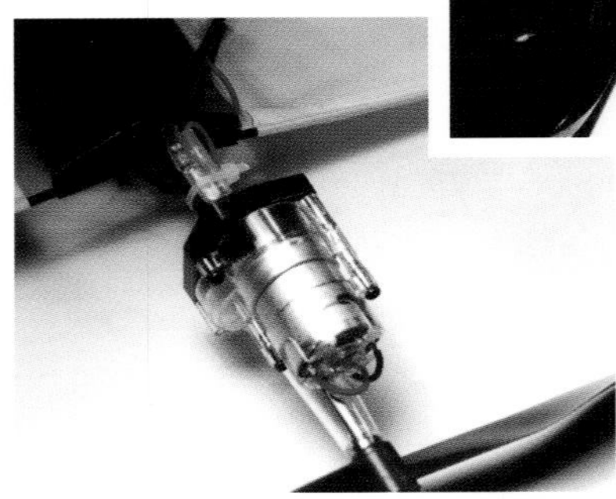

This molded-plastic part (one on each side of the "gondola" pilot seat) accepts three different carbon-fiber rods. The molded fitting must be oriented in this manner. Also, be advised to add a drop of thin CA cement on each rod joint.

The geared motor is just slipped over the end of the carbon stick fuselage and held in place with a few drops of thin CA.

The horizontal stabilizer (constructed of thin foam sheet material) snaps into place and then is retained by a long carbon-fiber rod that runs underneath. No CA is necessary.

The vertical tail with a pre-hinged rudder also snaps into place. A small amount of clear silicone sealer (such as bathtub caulk) on each bracket will hold the vertical tail even more securely in place.

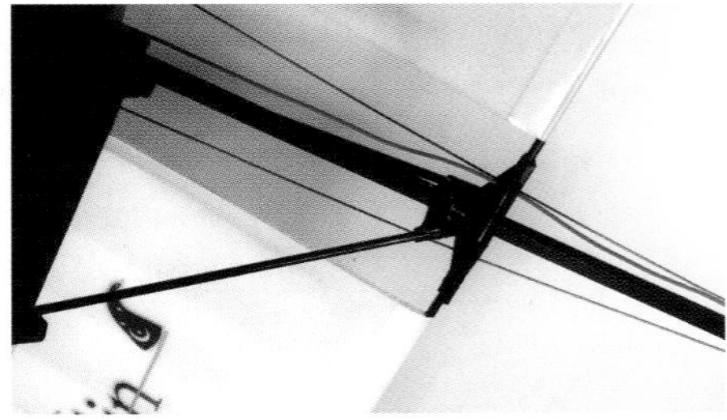

Another molded fitting is located by the wing trailing edge. It accepts the two longest carbon rods. Again, add a few drops of thin CA to hold these rods in place.

MISS BOHEMIA

This is an ARF model. It is constructed of standard model material, e.g., balsa, spruce, plywood and iron-on covering material. A geared Speed 280 electric motor is supplied, which is suitable to fly this model. You must, however, purchase the full RC system, the ESC, battery and battery charger. You must also install the RC system, motor and all the controls, so a little more work is required than for an RTF model, but it should take only about a day to complete the model and get out to the flying field.

Our second example aircraft is the Hobby Lobby Intl. Miss Bohemia, another parking-lot category, almost-ready-to-fly (ARF) model. The plane is available in several different colors. The basic structure is already built up and covered. You get to cement the wing halves together, attach the tailpieces, and install the motor, radio system and control rods. The geared RE-280 motor is supplied. You must purchase the radio system, ESC, battery and charger. Pictured here is my Airtronics Radiant R/C transmitter.

ASSEMBLY

Since the entire model is constructed and covered, the final assembly is very simple. First the two wing halves are joined with 5-minute epoxy cement. Next the tail surfaces are epoxied in place. Both the rudder and elevator control surfaces are pre-hinged, which is a real convenience.

You must first assemble the gearbox to the motor and then mount it on the nose of the model. Next comes the radio/ESC installation. There are two control wires that pass through plastic rods and run from the rudder and elevator servo back to the control surfaces. These rods run along the outside of the fuselage on both sides because the model comes already assembled and covered. These rods translate servo rotation into control surface movement. When you master this concept, you are on your way to being an RC expert! At the servo end, a Du-Bro E-Z connector is installed on each output arm. On the control surface end is a control horn. One end of the control wire will have a Z-bend (as noted in Chapter 10). That Z-bend is inserted into one of the holes in the control horn. The other end of the wire is passed through the E-Z connector on the servo output arm. With the RC system turned on and the controls set at neutral trim, position the rudder or elevator at the neutral flight position and then tighten the E-Z-connector screw. That's all there is to it!

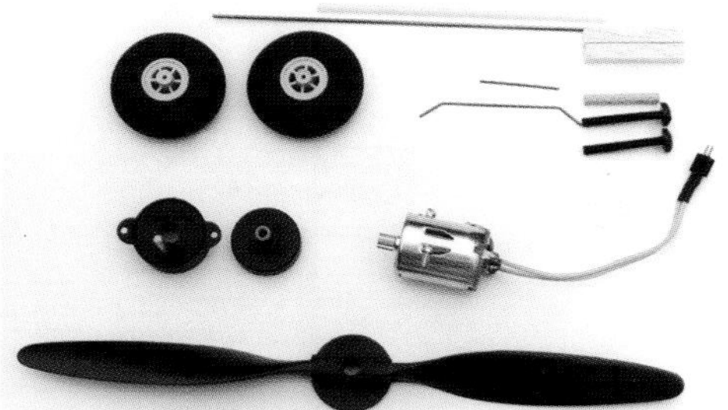

This is how the Miss Bohemia arrives in the kit box. All the covering and hinging is already completed for you.

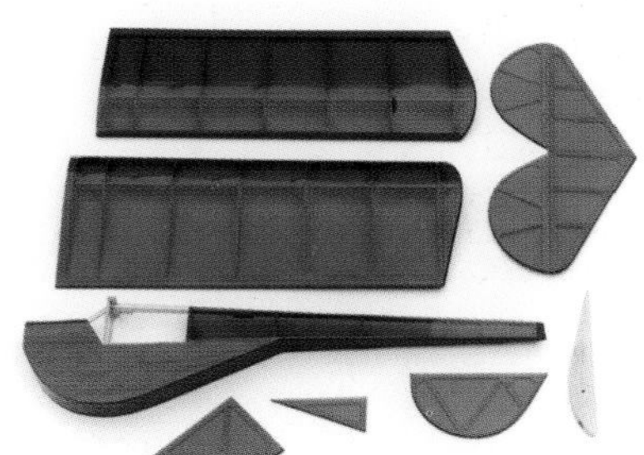

Motor assembly involves only a few parts. Wheels and landing-gear wire are supplied.

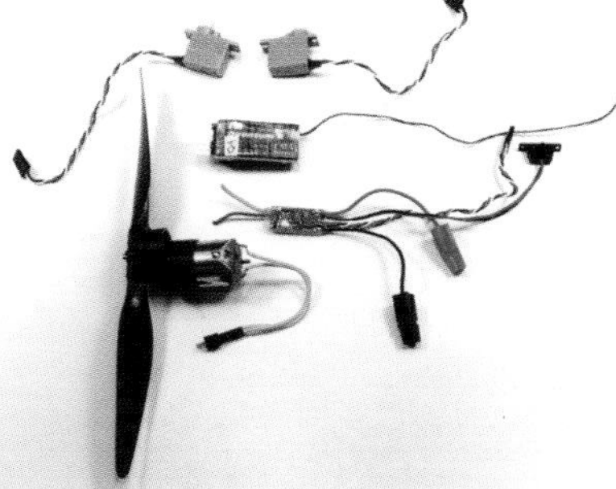

This is what goes inside the Miss Bohemia. The Speed 280 motor, gear drive and prop are provided in the kit. You must buy two servos (shown here, FMA Direct S-80s), a receiver (shown here, an FMA Direct Quantum-6 dual conversion) and an ESC with a BEC (shown here, an FMA Direct Mini-20).

MISS BOHEMIA SPECIFICATIONS

MANUFACTURED: in the Czech Republic

DISTRIBUTED BY: Hobby Lobby Intl.

TYPE: almost ready-to-fly (ARF) electric-powered parking-lot category

WINGSPAN: 41 in.

WING AREA: 325 sq. in.

WEIGHT (WITH BATTERY): 14 oz.

WING LOADING: 6.2 oz./sq. ft.

MOTOR: geared Speed 280 with 4:1 reduction ratio

PROP: 9-in. diameter

MOTOR CURRENT: 3.2 amps

FLIGHT DURATION: 5 to 7 minutes depending on throttle settings

BATTERY: 7-cell 270mAh NiMH

RC EQUIPMENT: my choice—FMA Quantum dual conversion receiver, two FMA S-80 servos and an FMA-20 ESC with BEC

The second example, the Miss Bohemia from Hobby Lobby Intl., in flight. Another excellent parking-lot flyer at 14 ounces with a geared Speed 280 motor, it will fly at very low speeds and maintain perfect control.

FLYING EXPERIENCE

The Miss Bohemia also flew right out of my hands. It was reasonably fast at full throttle, but could be slowed down considerably and still be quite maneuverable. I did notice a tendency for the model to yaw when going through a turn. My feeling is that the wing could use more dihedral. It tends to be too flat as originally designed. A new variation of the Miss Bohemia is now being offered. This new design, Bloody Mary, has a wing with polyhedral in both tip panels; otherwise the rest of the model (fuselage and tail surfaces) is identical to the Miss Bohemia. At any rate, the Miss Bohemia has sufficiently rugged construction to last a long time even in the hands of a beginner. It is easy to fly at various speeds and is another fun airplane!

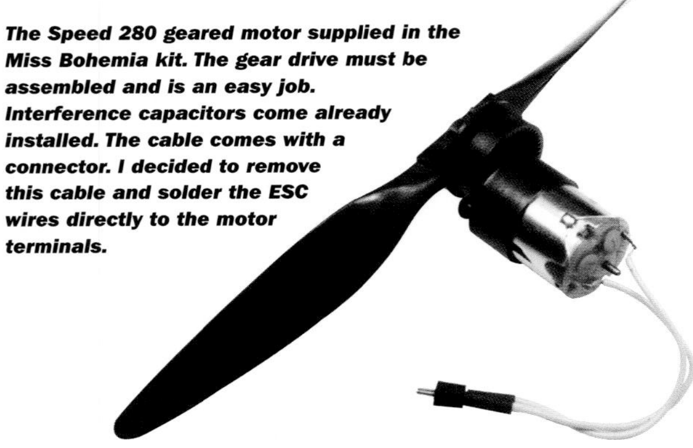

The Speed 280 geared motor supplied in the Miss Bohemia kit. The gear drive must be assembled and is an easy job. Interference capacitors come already installed. The cable comes with a connector. I decided to remove this cable and solder the ESC wires directly to the motor terminals.

The deep forward fuselage is reminiscent of the Aeronca C-3 of the '30s. The motor is easily mounted to the plywood firewall with two small sheet-metal screws.

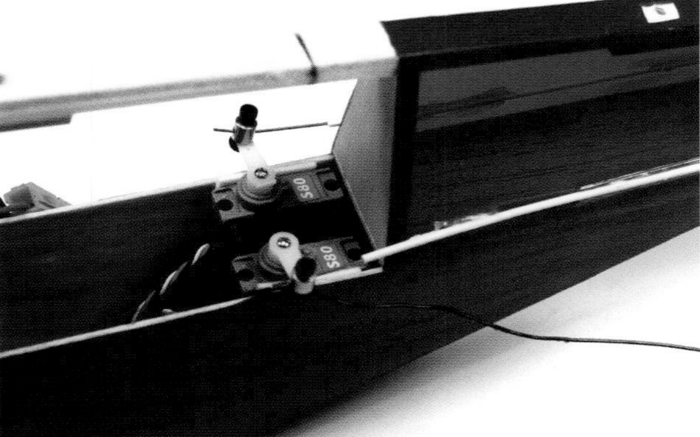

The two FMA Direct S-80 servos are held in place with double-sided tape. Du-Bro E-Z connectors are attached to each servo output arm. This makes for easy adjustment of the controls. Since the fuselage comes already covered, you must run the control rods along the outside of the fuselage to the rear control surfaces. This takes a little of the beauty away from the model, but it is practical.

WATTAGE LITE STIK

The WattAge Lite Stik (also marketed as the GWS Pico Stick) is also an ARF model. It is smaller and lighter, and it requires a little more assembly time than the other two examples. The Pico Stick has become a standard for parking-lot flyers and lends itself well to both indoor and outdoor flying. It sells for less than $30, including the geared motor and prop.

The wing and tail are made of a lightweight molded foam sheet material. It looks similar to the type used at fast food restaurants to enclose hamburgers. The fuselage is simply a hardwood stick. Everything "hangs off" this stick, including the RC equipment, the motor, battery and the landing gear. Total assembly time will be only a couple of hours. Aside from the kit, you will need to purchase a full RC system (transmitter, micro receiver and two servos), an ESC, battery and battery charger.

Last in my series of three examples is the very popular WattAge Lite Stik, of which literally thousands have been sold to date. This plane can be flown indoors (just keep the weight below 8 ounces) and is also well suited to outdoor backyard fun (it qualifies also as a parking-lot flyer). It has 238 sq. in of wing area, and this particular version weighs 7.7 ounces. It is an almost-ready-to-fly (ARF) model that comes with a geared motor and prop. You must purchase the RC system, ESC, battery and charger. Pictured at the left is my Hitec RCD Eclipse RC transmitter.

ASSEMBLY

Note: a tube of special cement is supplied with the kit, which appears to behave like a rubber cement in the sense that it never completely dries. I chose to substitute regular modelers' 5-minute epoxy cement (mixed in two stages, A and B), which worked much better. Start the assembly process by cementing a long and short wooden dowel to each wing panel. This will eventually allow the wings to plug into a molded-plastic bracket mounted on the fuselage stick.

Next, mark off the location of the various molded-plastic parts that go along the fuselage. This will include the forward wing mount, landing-gear mount, battery mount, the rear wing mount and, finally, one of two guides for the wire control rods going to the tail. Next, slip all of these items into position, but don't cement any at this point.

The rudder and elevator control surfaces are pre-hinged but are rather stiff.

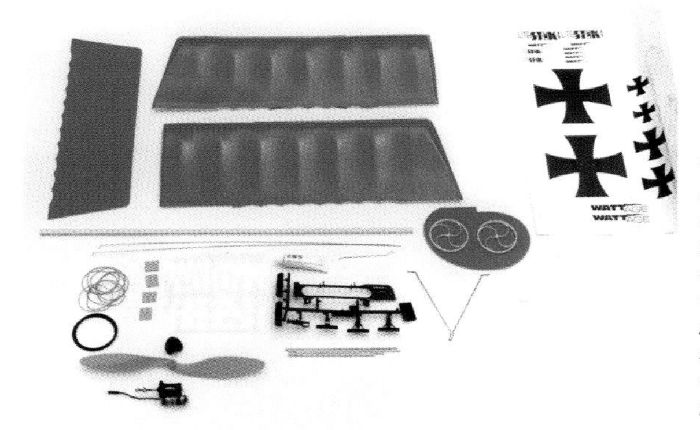

The Lite Stik kit contents. Most of the parts are molded plastic on two separate "trees." Assembly is very simple, requiring only a couple of hours work.

A close-up of the GWS geared motor. Keep in mind that the entire Lite Stik kit with this motor costs less than $30.

The supplied GWS-IPS "A" STD geared motor is approximately the size of an RS-180 motor. A GWS 10x4.7 prop is supplied; but be advised that going to a 9x7 prop might improve the performance, especially when flying outdoors.

WATTAGE LITE STIK SPECIFICATIONS

MODEL: WattAge Lite Stik/GWS Pico Stick

MANUFACTURER: Grand Wing Servo (GWS) in Taiwan

DISTRIBUTED BY: Global Hobby Distributors (WattAge label); Horizon Hobby, Inc. (GWS label)

TYPE: almost ready-to-fly (ARF) electric-powered parking-lot category

WINGSPAN: 38 in.

WING AREA: 238 sq. in.

WEIGHT (WITH BATTERY): 7.7 oz.

WING LOADING: 4.7 oz./sq. ft.

MOTOR: GWS-IPS "A" DX motor with 5.86:1 reduction ratio

PROP: GWS 10x4.7

MOTOR CURRENT: 1.9 amps

FLIGHT DURATION: 7 to 9 minutes, depending on throttle settings

BATTERY: 7-cell 270mAh NiMH

RC EQUIPMENT: my choice—GWS R-4P micro receiver, two Hitec HS-50 sub-microservos and an Airwise Intl. SMM-08 ESC.

The instructions recommend that you run a ballpoint pen over the hinge lines to "free up" the control surface movement. After doing this, cement both the vertical and horizontal tail surfaces to the aft the fuselage.

The motor is press-fit on the front of the stick fuselage. A drop of CA will hold it in place. After you have completed these steps, proceed with mounting the servos, receiver and ESC. I chose to fill in the battery compartment area with thin plywood and then used hook-and-loop fastener tape to hold the battery in position.

The final assembly step is to plug in the wing panels. Mark the center-of-gravity (CG) location and then slide the wing fore and aft until the correct balance is achieved. In a couple of hours the assembly is complete and you're heading for the field.

FLYING EXPERIENCE

Like the other two example models, the Lite Stik flew right out of my hands without the need for any trim. It can be slowed down to a very low flying speed and still maintain altitude. This slow-flying ability makes it perfect as an indoor flyer. For outdoor flying in wind of about 5mph, the Lite Stik still flew comfortably. Landings are always gentle because the model can be slowed down to practically a standstill without a tendency to stall.

Our third example, the WattAge Lite Stik, is a smaller and lighter model that is also capable of indoor flying. At 7.7 ounces and 238 square inches of wing area, it is very lightly loaded.

OVERALL COMMENTS

All three example models were easy to assemble, and took very little time to put together. Although the instructions initially looked thorough, I found as I proceeded with the assembly that the instructions could have offered a little more detail. I would encourage manufacturers of RTF or ARF models to consider offering a supplemental videotape that describes the assembly and initial flying instructions. Some manufacturers already provide such videos, but it is not yet a standard practice. Watching an assembly step in real-time can be more informative than words and illustrations alone, particularly for a beginner.

All three of my example models employed 3-channel control (i.e., rudder, elevator and motor throttle). A beginner would benefit to learn with this type of control, using a single-stick (dual axes) RC transmitter. This best prepares you for future models, as most of the really good performers are 3- or 4-channel aircraft. There are however, some very flyable RTF models that are flown with 2-channel control. See the RTF 2-Channel Alternatives sidebar.

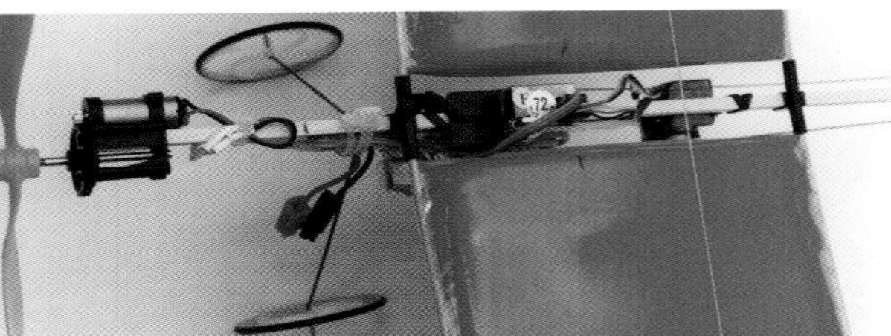

The nose of the Lite Stik looking down. The motor slips onto the nose and is held in place with a little CA. The receiver and servos can be seen between the two wing panels (which do not touch).

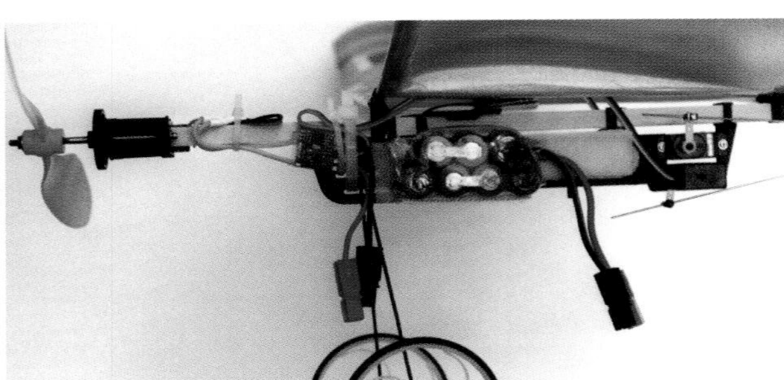

I filled in the battery space with a thin piece of plywood, then used hook-and-loop fastener tape to hold the battery in place. Note the two HS-50 servos toward the wing trailing edge. The ESC is taped in place just forward of the wing leading edge.

MORE STICK DESIGNS

In the process of writing this book, I learned that Horizon Hobby Inc. has introduced a new GWS Stick Series, known as the F Series. The F stands for fuselage. In these models, the stick fuselage structure has been replaced with a foam fuselage. This design adds strength to the wing-fuselage structure and imparts more of a scale-like model appearance. Two versions include the GWS Pico Stick F and a GWS Pico Cub F. A Zero has also been added to the line. From what I can gather, the prices are slightly higher than the basic Stick series—but they are still very reasonable.

Horizon Hobby Inc. has also released a Tiger Moth biplane in its F series that has won wide acclaim for its rugged but lightweight design and outstanding flight performance.

The GWS Pico Cub FD is the fuselage version of the popular stick model.

RTF 2-CHANNEL ALTERNATIVES

THE HOBBYZONE FIREBIRD

The HobbyZone Firebird II is currently available from Horizon Hobby Inc. It is interesting in several respects. It employs only 2-channel function control, basically rudder (through a V-tail) and motor throttle control (which is used to control altitude). It has proved to be a very good "first plane" for many enthusiasts.

The Firebird II comes with an already installed 27MHz RC system, a matching transmitter, battery pack and battery charger. This RC model sells complete for only $100. It has a 30-inch wingspan, 105 square inches of wing area, and 8 ounces total weight, so the resulting wing loading is a relatively high 11 ounces per square foot. The motor is a Speed 200 direct running on a 4-cell, 600mAh NiMH battery.

There is also a larger version of this airplane called the Firebird XL. Although both versions can soar on rising columns of air like a traditional sailplane, I've seen the Firebird XL perform very much like a traditional sailplane. Both models come with an instructional video. The video takes you through the nominal assembly process, tells you how to charge the battery, and then goes on to the basic flight training.

Although I'm not in favor of a student learning with 2-channel control, the Firebird II is a load of fun! It is perfect to introduce a child or grandchild to the world of RC model aviation; but remember, when flying on only two channels, control of altitude is achieved only by varying the motor speed. This can get tricky, especially for a beginner.

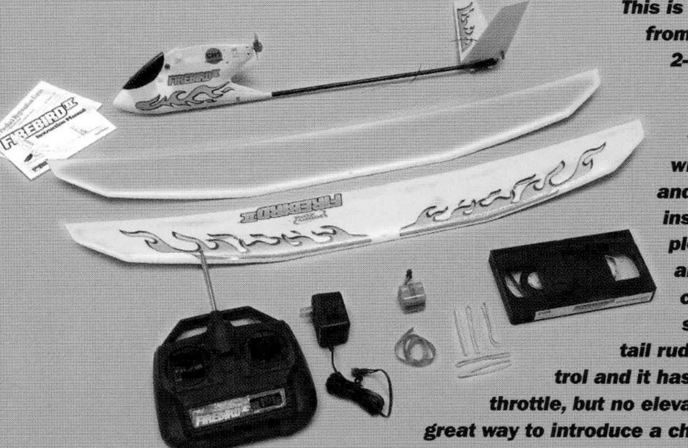

This is the Firebird II from HobbyZone, a 2-channel electric-powered RTF model that comes with the motor and radio already installed, a complete RC system and a battery charger. It steers with a V-tail rudder-type control and it has a motor throttle, but no elevator control. A great way to introduce a child or grandchild to the hobby.

THE HOBBICO SKY ZAP

The Hobbico Sky Zap is a 13.5 oz. 2-channel RTF that has a wing loading of 9.17 ounces per square foot. Two Speed 180s control this 42.5-inch-span aircraft. It has a fixed tail, and turning results from differential throttle that slows the left or right motor. A 6-cell, 600mAh NiMH battery powers the airplane. The $79.99 package comes with transmitter, charger, extra props, screwdriver and a video. Remember that, as in the case of the Firebird II, control of altitude is achieved only by varying the overall power delivered to the motors.

IMPROVING AIRCRAFT PERFORMANCE—TWO EXAMPLES

UPGRADING THE BEBE JODEL ARF

The two major challenges modelers are confronted with in electric-powered flight are: "How can I get the aircraft to go faster?" and "How can I make it fly longer?" Many popular ARF and kit models come supplied with good sport-type power systems, but as you become more experienced, you want livelier performances from your model. And any pilot, regardless of experience, can benefit from longer flight duration. By improving these two facets of your model's performance, you can make your plane more fun to fly and have more time to enjoy it.

Making the necessary improvements in almost any electric-powered model aircraft involves selecting the right motor, gearing, prop and battery. To demonstrate the types of improvements that are possible with an electric-power system, I chose the popular Hobby Lobby/Hacker Bebe Jodel ARF. This model has 163 square inches of wing area and weighs 9 ounces. I originally reviewed the Jodel in the June 2001 issue of *Model Airplane News*, and I liked its stock configuration—a direct-drive Speed 280 motor running on a Gunther 5x4 plastic prop. My choice of battery pack was a Sanyo 7-cell, 270mAh NiMH pack that weighs 2.3 ounces. With this setup, the motor current was 3.6 amps running at 23 watts, so the watts per ounce worked out to 2.53. The Jodel flew well but wasn't fast, and it did have some trouble gaining appreciable altitude. All I could get out of the system was about 4 minutes of flight. I felt I could do better—with a little work!

As you follow this series of "experiments," it's best to use an ammeter/voltmeter/wattmeter; I recommend AstroFlight's micro-digital unit. It is essential that you know motor current, and this meter will tell you that all-important e-power parameter. My first step was to go to a geared drive. I chose the popular Titanic Airlines Speed 280, geared 3:1. You can also purchase a gear set from Dymond Modelsports (see *RC MicroFlight*'s October 2001 issue for more on this gear set) and add it to your direct-drive Speed 280 motor. I usually prefer a Gunther 7x6 prop on this motor, but I recommend experimenting with APC "Slo-Flyer" or "Thin Electric" props of similar size as well. I also decided to go up one cell (from 7 to 8) using the new Balsa Products 280mAh NiMH cells (weight: 2.4 ounces). By substituting the geared motor, a larger prop and a slightly larger battery pack, my total weight went up to 9.8 ounces. Motor current was measured at 3 amps (0.6 amp less) at 22 watts (almost the same power), and the watts per ounce went down slightly to 2.2. This combination produced flights of 6 minutes—an improvement, despite the fact that the flight performance was more aggressive!

At this point, I decided to try a more premium motor; in this case, the MTM Intl. Lil Bee S-200 geared 4:1. This is actually a Kyosho DMC-20BB (ball-bearing) motor with a Maxon planetary gearbox. It weighs roughly the same as the geared Speed 280 (total model weight is 9.9 ounces), and I used the same Balsa Products 8-cell, 280mAh NiMH battery pack. A Graupner Cam 7½x4 foldable prop is recommended. I measured 2.2A motor

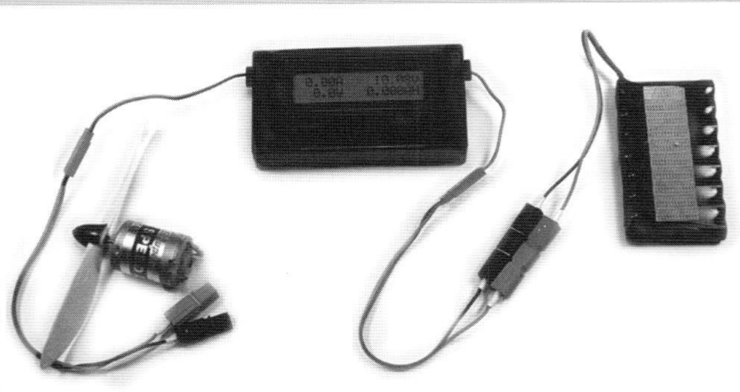

Here's AstroFlight's micro-digital ammeter/voltmeter/wattmeter. Connect a battery to the right side and let the meter light up. Then connect the left side output (load) to the motor terminals. Use an adapter cable to get from the Sermos connector to a pair of alligator clips to attach to the motor terminals.

At right is the original Speed 280 direct-drive motor. Its performance was OK, but its flight duration was only about 4 minutes. At left is the Titanic Airlines 280 motor geared 3:1 with a Gunther 7x6 prop. This motor produced better performance and about a 6-minute flight duration. In the center is the MTM Intl. Lil Bee S-200 motor, which is smaller than a Speed 280 and provides 8- to 10-minute run times.

The MTM Intl. Lil Bee S-200 shown in the front of the Jodel; again, note the use of rubber bands to hold the motor in place—simple and effective.

A closer view of the Speed 280 direct-drive motor, held in place by two rubber bands, with the Gunther 5x4 prop running direct.

current at 20 watts. The watts per ounce went down to 2. As expected, this was a step in the wrong direction, and the model could barely support flight; it didn't even fly long enough to get a good handle on flight duration. I was about to give up on this motor, recognizing that it is physically smaller than the geared 280. But MTM Intl. owner Mike Gross recommended that I try an APC 7x5E thin electric prop. The motor current stayed at 2.2 amps, the measured power was 22 watts (just slightly more), but the watts per ounce went back to 2.2. Flight performance with this APC prop was excellent; I quickly gained several hundred feet in altitude. Total flight duration (all at full throttle) was close to 8 minutes. Since the motor current, power and battery

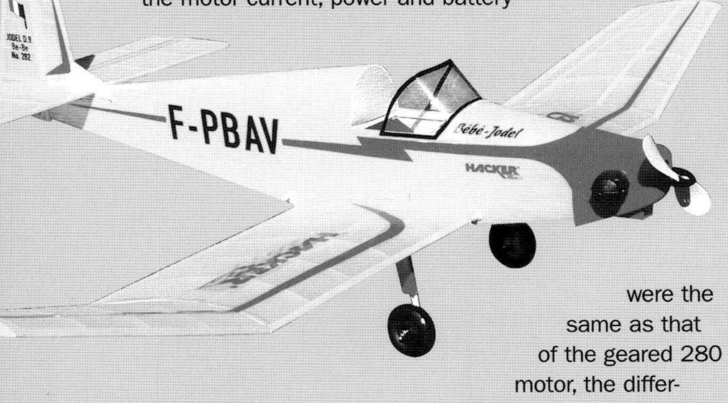

were the same as that of the geared 280 motor, the difference, obviously, was the choice of prop. The APC 7x5E appeared to be the perfect choice, and with the normal unloading in the air, the current went down and the duration went up.

My last experiment involved going to a new Balsa Products 8-cell, 600mAh NiMH battery weighing 4.1 ounces. This brought the Jodel up to a seemingly heavy 11.8 ounces. Because of the higher capacity, the initial readings were a little higher: 3.1A motor current, 29 watts of power and 2.5 watts per ounce. Flight performance was about the same as with the 280 battery, but because of the extra weight (almost 2 ounces more), the Jodel was definitely not as comfortable to fly. The duration at full throttle, however, increased to 12 minutes, 38 seconds.

If I was looking for sprightly (and comfortable) performance, I would stick with the 8-cell, 280mAh NiMH battery. If duration was my priority, I would choose the 600mAh NiMH pack. Either way, the improvement is notable; from 4- to up to 12-minute flights and with faster flying speeds than was possible with direct drive. The gear drive, the right prop and the right battery pack made the difference.

Those who want to experiment further might try the APC 7x5E prop on the geared Speed 280 motor (in place of the Gunther 7x6). You might also try the new Radical RC Sanyo 8-cell, 720mAh NiMH battery, which weighs about the same as the 600 cells. This could conceivably get you close to a 15-minute flight time!

I recommend that duration tests be performed with the model in the air because in flight, the model's prop unwinds (unloads), and this results in a slight reduction in motor current. This, in turn, will result in a slightly longer duration than is indicated by tests performed on the ground. Also, running an electric motor in still air—particularly indoors—for 10 or 12 minutes can easily cook it because of the lack of cooling airflow. You should check the temperature of the motor and battery pack after every flight; if you can't touch them comfortably with your fingers, they are getting too hot, and that can easily reduce the life of these components.

I hope that this example will allow you to apply the "lessons learned" to other models of similar size and weight. A perfect example is Tom Herr's Prowler, which appeared in the October 2001 issue of *RC MicroFlight*. This test data could easily apply to the Prowler, with its little more than 200 square inches of wing area and its 9-ounce weight.

Here are the battery packs used in this experiment. At left is the original 7-cell, 270mAh Sanyo NiMH pack obtained from Batteries America. In the center is the 8-cell, 280mAh NiMH pack from Balsa Products, and at right is a new, 8-cell, 600mAh NiMH pack from Balsa Products.

UPGRADING THE HAL DEBOLT R/C KITTEN

Continuing our discussion of improving aircraft performance, the subject this time involves a model originally powered by a geared Speed 400 motor. The model is an exact replica of the Hal deBolt R/C Kitten from the '50s. The Kitten has a 34-inch wingspan, 217 square inches of wing area and, with a new electric power system, a total weight of 20.5 ounces that yields a wing loading of 13.7 ounces per square foot. This puts it in the "Speed 400" category (a weight of more than 14 ounces and more than 8 ounces per square foot of wing loading).

For my initial electric flights, I used a Speed 400 6V motor with a 1.8:1 gear drive and a Rev Up 8x4 prop. I used a 7-cell, 500mAh AR Ni-Cd battery that weighed 4.9 ounces. How did I originally arrive at this e-power system? At approximately 20 ounces planned total weight, I knew I was in the Speed 400 range. I hoped to take the Kitten off the ground and wanted the necessary prop clearance. I chose a low gear ratio (1.8:1) so that I could use an 8-inch-diameter prop. This combination had a motor current of 6.5 amps at 7 volts, 49 watts and 7,200rpm (2.4 watts per ounce). Flight times with the 500mAh battery were only about 4 minutes. Performance in flight was moderately sluggish; the plane tended to hang on the prop and gained little altitude throughout the short flight.

A replica of the 1950s-era Hal deBolt R/C Kitten that was originally flown in 1957 with a McCoy .049 diesel engine. It weighs 18 ounces with single-channel rudder control. The model has a 34-inch wingspan and 217 square inches of wing area.

The solution to this problem was not what you might think. Yes, I did go to a higher reduction ratio; I also went to a larger-diameter prop. But I was also able to employ a smaller motor along with a lighter, higher-capacity battery pack. Sound confusing? Read on!

With the MTM Intl. WASP S-380 (280 size) 5:1 geared motor and APC 10x7 Slo-Fly prop, duration and performance dramatically improved.

The replica Kitten was originally powered by this Speed 400, 6V motor and a 1.8:1 gearbox. The prop was a Rev Up 8x4. The power was marginal, and the flight duration was quite short.

Mike Gross of MTM Intl. once again came to my rescue with one of his fine motors—in this case, his WASP S-380, which is actually a Speed 280-size motor (Multiplex Permax 280BB, 7.2 volts) employing a ball-bearing-supported 5:1 gear drive. As a starting point, Mike suggested several props, one of which was larger than my original choice of an 8-inch-diameter prop. So I wouldn't need to worry about prop clearance, I decided that in the future, I would exclusively hand-launch the Kitten. Mike went on to suggest that I try an 8-cell battery with either a Graupner 9x6 or 8x6 Slim prop. The 9x6 didn't fly the model very well, but with the 8x6, I measured the motor current on the WASP S-380 at 4.5 amps, 9.5 volts, 44 watts and 4,600rpm at the prop. Watts per ounce were 2.1. As expected, all of these figures were down somewhat from those recorded for the Speed 400 motor, since the WASP S-380 is smaller, but the flight performance improved. I was able to gain more altitude, and the flight time was up to 6 minutes. Total model weight was still essentially the same at 20.7 ounces (the motor was lighter, but the battery was heavier!). I could have left it at that and been satisfied with the initial improvement gained, but with Mike's encouragement, I went to a prop of a larger diameter: the APC 10x7 Slo-Fly. Clearly, I now had a "big" prop on this small plane; would it be worth it? Using the same 8-cell, 500mAh AR Ni-Cd battery that weighed 5.7 ounces, the motor current was 6.5 amps, 8.5 volts, 55 watts and 3,400rpm at the prop. Watts per ounce were 2.65 with the model weight still 20.7 ounces. Admittedly, these parameters were close to what I had started with using the Speed 400 motor, and the flight duration was again down to approximately 4 minutes.

Give up at this point? Not quite! I kept the APC 10x7 prop on the Kitten and changed over to a Radical RC 8-cell, 720mAh NiMH battery pack at 3.8 ounces. With this pack, the Kitten now weighed just 18.8 ounces, and wing loading was down to 12.5 ounces per square foot. Keeping in mind that the NiMH batteries have a lower characteristic voltage, these were my new measured parameters: 5.3 amps motor current, 7.4 volts and 39 watts at 3,100rpm. Watts per ounce were down to 2.1. Although these values were all down, interestingly enough, the flight performance was just about the best I had ever experienced. I was able to gain some very high altitude (almost out of sight) in less than a minute of flying. I was even able to do many maneuvers, most of which I could never have attempted before. But, best of all, at full throttle for the entire flight, I landed at 9:52—almost a 10-minute flight.

The MTM WASP S-380 fits easily into the Kitten's nose with the help of a plywood tray and two nylon ties.

So the bottom line is that I went from a Speed 400 to a Speed 280-size motor. The gear reduction was increased from 1.8:1 to 5:1. The prop went from 8 to 10 inches in diameter. The battery increased from 7 to 8 cells; the capacity increased from 500 to 720mAh yet decreased in weight. Ultimately, the model's weight decreased from 20.5 to 18.8 ounces. Its flight speed was markedly improved, and best of all, the flight duration went from 4 to 10 minutes ... some very interesting things to consider!

To try one more experiment, I substituted an 8-cell, Hobby Lobby 1100mAh NiMH battery at 7.3 ounces. This brought the Kitten back up to 22.3 ounces total weight. The higher capacity of this battery tended to increase all of my basic parameters, so the motor current went back up to 6.3 amps at 8.3 volts, 52 watts and 3,400rpm. Watts per ounce were up to 2.33. The flight performance seemed to feel sluggish, probably due to the heavier weight. But I was disappointed that the flight time was only about 10 minutes. So in effect, I did just as well with a much lighter battery and lower total model weight. It is still a good indication of how battery weight, battery capacity and total model weight all play into the same electric-power "equation."

The whole idea behind articles such as this one is to get you to conduct your own experiments. A manufacturer or author/designer can get you in the right ball park. Then it is up to you to optimize the motor gearing, prop size and battery pack to obtain the very best performance possible.

If you are also an experimenter and have success stories to share, please let us know! You can email *RC MicroFlight* at rcmicroflight@airage.com, or write to the editors at 100 East Ridge, Ridgefield, CT 06877-4606 USA.

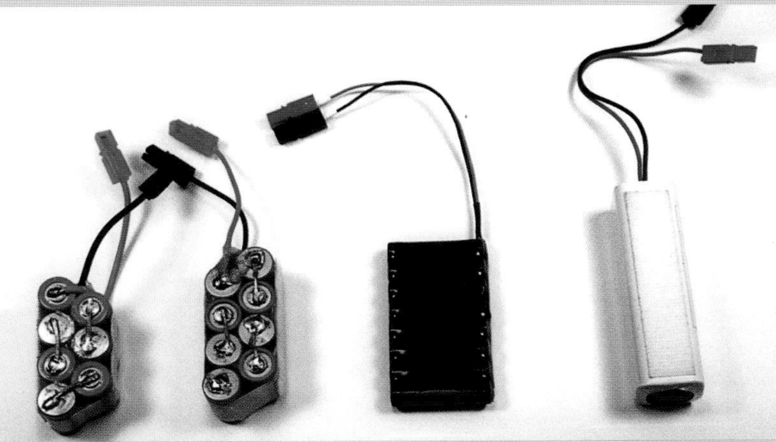

The "evolution" of battery packs used in this particular experiment; at left, the original 7-cell, 500mAh AR Ni-Cd pack. To its right are cells of the same type, with one more added for a total of 8. To the right of that is the Radical RC 8-cell Sanyo 720mAh NiMH pack that produced the 10-minute flights. At the far right is the Hobby Lobby 8-cell, 1100mAh NiMH battery that was just a little too heavy for this application.

13

Flying

Learning to fly an RC airplane safely can be greatly facilitated by seeking the help of enthusiasts who have already mastered RC flight. Standard procedures for preflighting your airplane are also key. Moreover, flying safely entails management of frequencies (two planes cannot be flown on the same frequency because interference will make them uncontrollable). The author offers important advice for any beginner on these and related issues. The chapter concludes with important tips on getting into the air and on flying techniques.

In this chapter I'd like to first address the problem of frequency control because it is important that the beginner understand this subject before heading out to the field for his or her first flight. Those of you who know the procedures, please be patient. I also will talk about the subject of "where to fly" and will include two articles reprinted from the *Backyard Flyer* magazine that offer tips on flying basics and technique.

The beginner (or any!) RC pilot must be aware of other model aircraft that may be operating in the same vicinity and, possibly, on the same channel. The primary band, 72 to 73MHz, as assigned by the FCC, provides us with 50 discrete channels or frequencies for flying RC model aircraft. Any number of models can fly at the same time, provided that they are each on a different RC channel. You cannot have two models flying on the same channel at the same time. If you attempt that, one model will interfere with the other, possibly resulting in a crash. Therefore, your first concern when flying RC is to be alert to other fliers at your location who may be operating on the same channel.

A good system of frequency control for a local flying field involves the use of a control board. On this board will be a total of 50 clothespins, one for each of the 50 channels (from Channel 11 to Channel 60). Each clothespin will be attached to a clip bearing the same channel number. The control scheme is simple: when you want to fly, go to the board and take the clothespin for your channel number and clip it to your transmitter's antenna. If that particular clothespin is not on the board, it means that someone else is using it at that time, and you must wait your turn. In the same regard, if you have the clothespin on your transmitter's antenna, another pilot must wait his or her turn until you are finished flying and return the pin to the board.

Until recently, frequency control was simple! All RC flying was done at local or regional flying fields, with many of these fields being operated by RC clubs; but now we have a new breed of model aircraft—parking-lot flyers that can be flown almost anywhere. The ability to fly anywhere can pose some problems. For instance, if you choose to fly at a local parking lot, you might operate in close proximity to a regular RC flying field. If you are within three miles, the parking-lot flyer might interfere with the regular RC flyer if you both attempt to fly on the same channel at the same time. This is a remote possibility, but it can happen!

The same is true for indoor flying at sports arenas or full-size aircraft hangars where regular RC flying is going on right outside these facilities. The radio signals can escape a wood or brick structure and broadcast a signal a few blocks away. So the solution at the local level is to identify where people fly

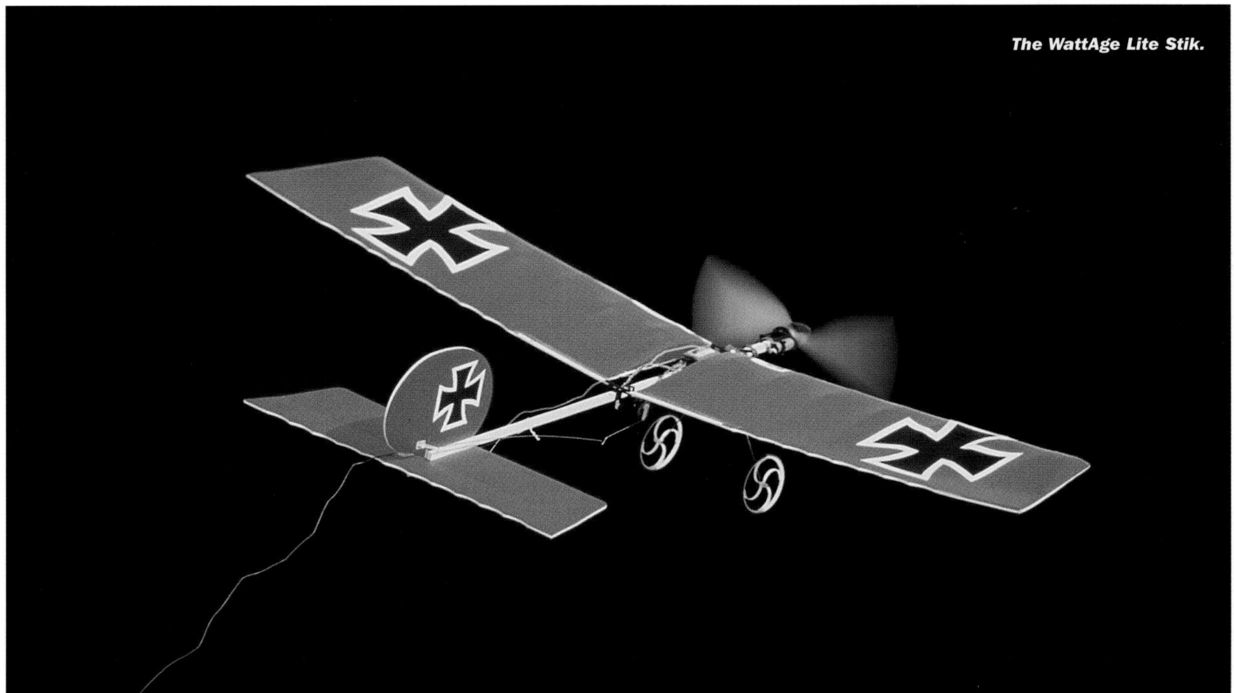

The WattAge Lite Stik.

Two Megatech Merlins in a dogfight.

and determine the best location to fly so as not to interfere with one another.

If you need help locating regular RC flying sites that are near parking-lot or indoor flying facilities, a good place to start is at your local hobby shop. Hobby shops should know about flying clubs and fields in their areas. Beyond that, the Academy of Model Aeronautics (AMA) has lists of club flying sites sorted by zip code and by global positioning system (GPS) data. In the near future, and with the cooperation of all RC fliers, it may be possible to obtain local flying-site information from a nationally maintained website. I urge you to keep pushing your local elected AMA officials to make this a reality.

If you are new to the RC hobby, you might ask your local hobby dealer or the AMA to help you locate a nearby club flying site. After you've found a location, it would be useful to visit the field and observe several flying sessions to see how things are done before you attempt your first flight. Once you have an idea of where to fly, you need to learn HOW TO FLY!

Although many have taught themselves to fly, this has traditionally been the exception, not the rule. The best way to learn to fly is to engage the help of an experienced RC pilot to get acquainted with flying procedures. Once you are acquainted with these procedures, try to find a person who is willing to spend some time helping you through your first series of flights. Learning to fly will take patience on your part, as well as on the part of your instructor. Fortunately, most RC pilots are willing to share their knowledge and experience with a rookie.

TRAINER CABLES

Several things can help in the learning process. One is the use of a trainer cable. This cable allows you to connect two RC transmitters by the same manufacturer to your plane. The student holds the "slave" transmitter, while the instructor pilot holds the "master" transmitter. During a training flight, if the student gets into any trouble, the instructor simply presses a button on the master transmitter and takes over the safe control of the model. This technique is an improvement over using a single RC transmitter. In that situation, if the student has a problem, the instructor must grab the transmitter to bring the model under control.

RC FLIGHT SIMULATORS

Other helpful training aids are the many model aircraft flight simulators now on the market. Three such simulators that come to mind are the Dave Brown Products Inc. R/C Flight Simulator Version 5, Great Planes Model Manufacturing Co. Real Flight R/C Simulator and the Cockpit Master Simulator distributed by Multiplex USA. These simulators use a home personal computer to which you attach a control box that resembles an RC transmitter. Control inputs can then be displayed on the computer monitor in real time. Most reports indicate that these simulators are quite responsive and accurate. They are not expensive, so you might want to try this as a supplement to your flight-training efforts.

PREFLIGHTING

My personal feeling is that a parking-lot model is the easiest model on which to learn. When you arrive at the flying field for that first flight session, let your instructor check over your entire model. This will involve pulling on the control surfaces to make sure that the hinges are cemented properly and making sure the prop is on tight and that the battery is anchored into position so it can't move around in flight. Your instructor will also check the center of gravity (CG) or balance point to make sure it is in the proper location. He or she will also turn on your RC system, check the radio range and check the amount of control-surface deflection

THE AUTO PILOT "TRAINING ASSIST"

RECENTLY, FMA DIRECT began marketing a new training product called the Co-Pilot. I recently had a chance to take a demo flight with this product, and I must tell you it works exactly as claimed. It involves the installation of a 1-ounce device at or near the model's center of gravity. Using a special proprietary sensor, the Co-Pilot will send correction control signals to the RC system servos, so that the model will tend to stay level in flight. When test-flying this new training device, I was able to put a fast-moving model into a forced dive and then remove my hand from the transmitter control stick. At that instant, the model literally jumped back to level flight. In theory, a student pilot could let go of the control stick when in trouble and the Co-Pilot would take over and level the model before it crashed. At 1 ounce, Co-Pilot would fit perfectly in a typical parking-lot flyer weighing between 8 and 14 ounces.

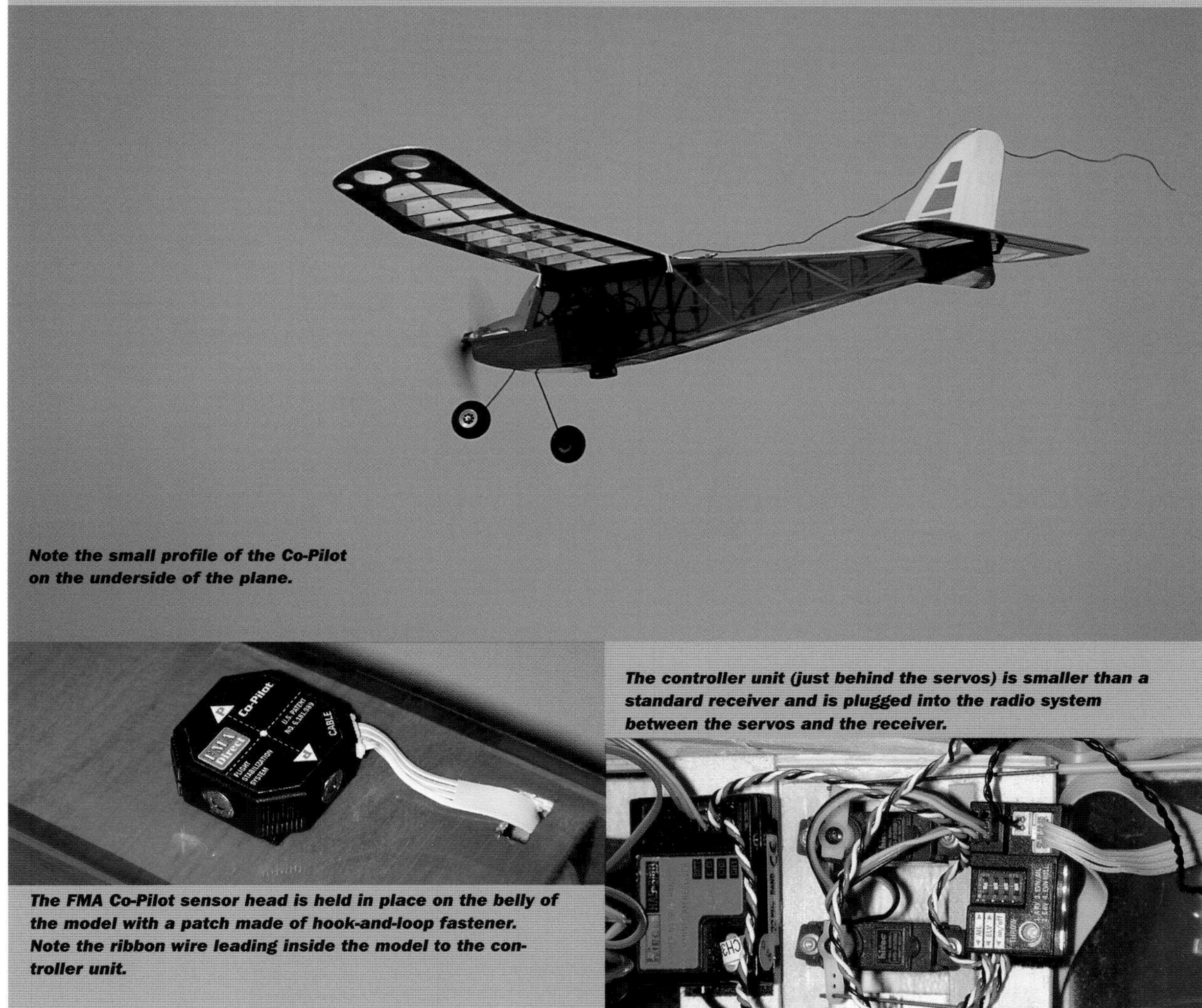

Note the small profile of the Co-Pilot on the underside of the plane.

The FMA Co-Pilot sensor head is held in place on the belly of the model with a patch made of hook-and-loop fastener. Note the ribbon wire leading inside the model to the controller unit.

The controller unit (just behind the servos) is smaller than a standard receiver and is plugged into the radio system between the servos and the receiver.

you have chosen. Too much control deflection could send you all over the sky, while too little control deflection can make you feel like you have no control at all. The direction of movement of the control surfaces must also be checked. Failure to check any of these important points could easily lead to a first-flight crash.

Most of these small models have landing gear that helps prevent the spinning prop from hitting the ground (that will spare you a number of broken props). The landing gear will also allow you to learn the techniques of taking off from the ground.

HAND-LAUNCHING

Most of the time, initial flights for a beginner are hand-launched. Hand-launching is especially appropriate if you are flying on a grass or rough dirt field. Most instructors will hand-launch and land your model for the first couple of flying sessions, or at least until you have shown that you are learning the basic skills.

DIRECTIONAL CONTROL OF AN ONCOMING MODEL

One of the most challenging aspects of learning to fly an RC model is managing directional control when a model is flying toward you. When your model is flying away from you, left is left and right is right. But when you turn the model around and it is heading back to you, the controls are reversed. As the plane approaches, if it should turn to the right, you need to apply left rudder to correct it. Think about that for a moment! With a full-size aircraft, the pilot doesn't have this kind of problem because, when sitting in the pilot's seat, left is always left and right is always right.

When learning to fly an RC model, this "control reversal" must be mastered early on before you can fly on your own. Your instructor will try several techniques to help this situation. The easiest way is to look over your shoulder while the model is coming back toward you. In this position, you can easily apply left and right commands without the "reversal effect" coming into play. But be careful that the model doesn't cross over to the other side, which would require you to quickly change positions. This technique does work for some pilots.

A better way to master this situation is to move the transmitter control stick to the side toward which the model turns (and the wing drops off). If the model was returning to your location and began turning to the right (i.e., the right wing began dropping off) you would move the control stick to that same side so that you would have applied opposite rudder without actually thinking about it. This may sound a little complicated, but with practice it can be mastered easily. You must learn this technique before you begin to land the model on your own.

LEARNING ON YOUR OWN

Beginners living in some remote locations may need to learn on their own, without the help of an experienced instructor. If you are located in a rural area, you probably couldn't damage anything in your attempt to learn to fly on your own. The worst case scenario is that you might crash on occasion, requiring some repair work as you go through the learning process—but no harm done. The FMA Direct Co-Pilot described in the sidebar might be the perfect learning accessory for the fly-alone beginner.

Even a pilot experienced with glow-fuel who attempts electric-powered parking-lot or indoor flying for the first time should seek help from an experienced micro flier as a point of introduction to this new category. There will be certain differences to learn, such as the routines for charging batteries and for recognizing when the charge is wearing down so that you know when it's time to land.

INDOOR FLYING

So far, the focus has been on parking-lot models, which I feel should be the starting point in micro flight before attempting to fly indoors. At some point in your quest for micro flight, however, you will probably want to try your skills at indoor flying.

Almost a half century ago (1953), I started flying RC models, and at age 64 I still fly in the AMA Electric

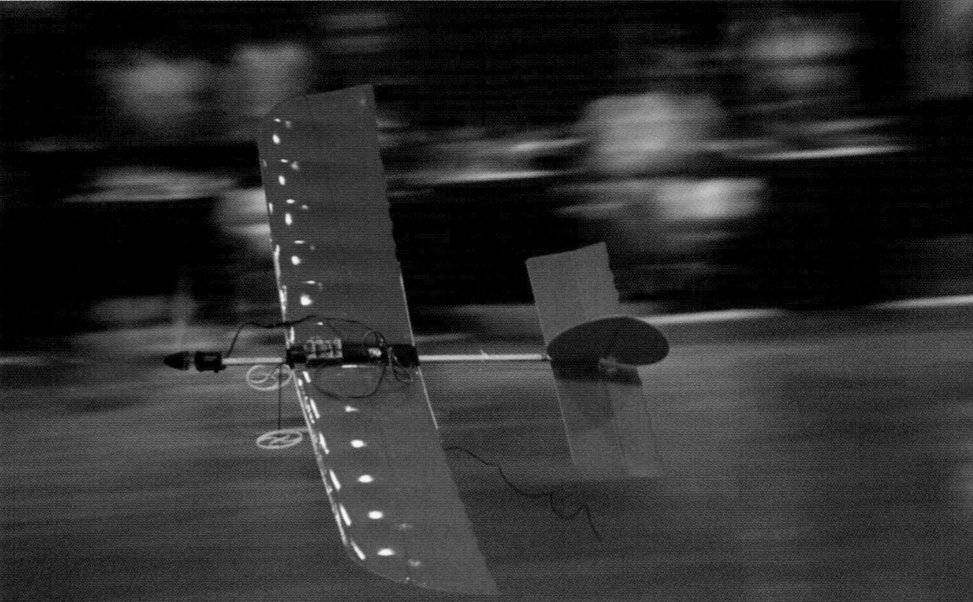

Chris Bowker modified this WattAge Lite Stik for indoor pylon racing at the Southwestern Aeromodeling Conference. He took 6 inches off the span, added dihedral, decreased wing incidence and increased the cell count by two. Photo by Tom Atwood.

National Competition held every year at the AMA Headquarters Flying Site in Muncie, IN. Even though the competition is tough, I've managed to win a place or two, or at least be in contention most years.

When I began flying indoor micro RC models, I was surprised to find that it was so challenging, even after all those years of experience. One of the main reasons is that the flying environment can be quite confining when compared to outdoor flying where you are not concerned with hitting walls or ceilings. Indoors, those walls and ceilings can come up rather quickly. The good news is that it doesn't take very long to master the new flying techniques and, before you know it, they become second nature. I still suggest, however, that you first learn on a parking-lot model before you attempt to fly indoors.

It is important when you fly indoors to keep the plane's weight down, which is why 8 ounces is the recommended model weight limit. The size or wing area of the model is also important. When combining the weight and area, we use a factor known as wing loading. It is expressed in ounces per square feet (oz./sq. ft.). The recommended maximum wing loading for most indoor and parking-lot flying is 5 ounces per square foot. The key to comfortable and safe indoor flying is to keep the model's flying speed as low as possible and still be able to support flight. As mentioned earlier in Chapter 11, the use of highly chambered airfoils are helpful in this respect.

Until you become familiar with RC indoor flying, choose a large site, such as a hall, sports arena, school gymnasium, indoor golf driving range, or indoor tennis court. These will give you the most room for a good flight. The facilities can be difficult to locate, however, and are usually rented collectively by a local club where everyone chips in to help defray the fee. In fact, some of the big annual hobby trade shows are now featuring indoor-flying activities at specially set-up local facilities. Most school basketball courts or small auditoriums are not recommended because they are very confining and force you to constantly turn the model to avoid hitting a wall or obstruction while at the same time trying to reduce power so that you don't hit the ceiling or a light fixture. You might look up a local or regional architectural society, since architects design the buildings and are aware of all the facilities in a given area.

The beauty of indoor flying is that it is not affected by weather problems such as rain, snow and cold. When flying indoors, you can even enjoy evening flight sessions. So RC flying need not be restricted to just weekends.

FLYING AT DUSK OR DAWN

There are other advantages to flying sub-micro models in the 2- to 3-ounce category. These small models can be easily flown at sunrise or at dusk when the wind conditions are very calm. Dead-air flying of these tiny RC models is very practical because the small electric motors do not make noise, so the neighbors are not disturbed. I have been making early-morning test flights at a local soccer field that I pass on my way to work. I usually bring several charged battery packs with me so that I can quickly get in a few flights without being concerned about charging time. One of the things that makes micro flying so appealing is the ability to fly close to your home at just about any time you want.

Depending on the size of your property, there is nothing to prevent you from flying an RC model on your own property; however, the safety aspect of flying an RC model should still be the main concern of every pilot. As previously mentioned, you must be aware of where other RC pilots are flying in the same area so that you don't interfere with them. Common sense will tell you that you must also be cautious of flying too close to a neighbor's property and, especially, too close to other people.

Note: the following articles, excerpted from the first two issues of Backyard Flyer *(published by Air Age Publishing), offer additional pointers that will be valuable to the novice learning to fly an RC airplane. The authors, Gerry Yarrish, senior technical editor for* Model Airplane News *and* Backyard Flyer, *and Thayer Syme, administrator of the SFRC slow flyer list serve sponsored by* Model Airplane News, *are both highly accomplished and respected modelers.*

Before Flight Training—
what you need to know before you make your first flight by Gerry Yarrish

If you have just built your first backyard flyer, the best way to learn how to fly is by asking an experienced friend to teach you. If, however, you want to learn to fly by yourself, here are some things to be aware of.

RADIO FREQUENCY

The radio that controls your model is on a specific frequency, and when you switch it on, it transmits a continuous signal. If someone else is using the same frequency as you are, the two radios will interfere with each other and cause both of you to lose control. Before you go out and fly, you should make sure you are at least three miles away from an established RC model flying field. You can ask the people at the local hobby shop whether there is a field nearby, or you can check with the Academy of Model Aeronautics (AMA) at www.modelairplane.org for a list of RC clubs in your state.

FLIGHT DIRECTION

Up and down are easy; no matter in which direction your model is heading, up will always be up and down will be down. Left and right are another matter. When you and your model are both facing in the same direction (i.e., the model is flying away from you), your left and right will be the model's left and right. If you move the stick to the right, your model will turn right and so on. But when the model is facing toward you (i.e., flying back toward you), its directions, relative to your stick command, will feel as though they have been reversed. When you push the stick to the right, the model will turn to its right, but that will be to your left! This is known as "returning control reversal," and if you are not prepared for this condition, it will claim your new model.

If we don't turn the model, it will soon be out of sight. To keep your model in the flying area, you have to think constantly about which way you want to turn your model. Holding the turn too long or turning in the wrong direction will cause it to spiral into the ground. When the model is coming toward you, pushing the stick toward the side with the lower wingtip will level the wings and prevent the turn from becoming so tight that you get confused.

If you have not flown a model before, you should ask someone who knows how to fly to teach you. It's safer to have help, your model will last a lot longer, and it will be more fun than learning alone.

WIND

The direction and strength of the wind have a great effect on your model. It's best to fly early in the morning and late in the afternoon when the sun is low and the wind is generally at its calmest, and this gentle air is good for beginners. Look at the trees around your flying area and note how much the wind causes the leaves and branches to sway. Is there a flagpole nearby? How much is the flag waving in the breeze? In a heavy wind, you may find you have no control at all over the model and it may be carried away by the wind. For your first few flights, the less wind, the better.

LAUNCH

Always launch the model into the wind. Face into the wind and hold the model above and slightly in front of you. Launch it by taking a few quick steps and lightly tossing it into the wind with its wings level. Release it with its nose pointing at the horizon or slightly below it. Don't throw it upward at a high angle; it will stall and lose lift.

LANDING

When flying, try to keep the model upwind from you. If you allow it to get too far downwind, at the end of its flight, it may not have enough power for you to bring it back to land. When it is time to land, keep the wings level and land straight into the wind. Throttle back and allow the model to descend gradually; don't dive toward the ground, or you'll increase the model's speed and make it difficult to land gently. Just as the model is about to touch down, gently apply up-elevator to keep its nose up slightly. Downwind and crosswind landings are difficult and may cause you to damage the model when it touches the ground. Whenever possible, land into the wind, not going with it. Landing upwind allows the model to settle onto the ground gently.

YOUR FLYING AREA

It may seem obvious, but you really need to evaluate the size and condition of the area in which you want to fly your model. Do you want to fly it in your backyard or at a local park? Is there a school nearby with a wide-open soccer field that's calling your name? The size of your flying area will dictate the size of the model airplane that can be safely flown there. Here's why:

The size of your model and how much it weighs will affect how quickly or slowly it can fly. Its speed then affects how quickly you can turn it, and the turning radius determines the size of the airspace you need. Yes, I said airspace—not the size of the field. Models can fly great distances away from you, and you could fly it so far away that it would be difficult to see and to control. Look for a flying site that allows you to keep the model close without

Left: the size and weight of your model will determine how big your flying area must be. For very light and slow flying models such as this Gym Flyer from Anything R/C, you'll need an area that's only as big as a baseball diamond.

This FMA Direct Park Razor all-foam flying wing flies well but requires a fair amount of space to be flown safely. Remember that these models can easily fly so far away from you that you'll have difficulty seeing them. Keep your model close to you, stay upwind and make sure your flying area is clear of obstacles.

BEFORE YOU FLY

Well, you're almost there; you've built and prepared your model and you've found a great place to fly it close to home. Is there anything left to do before that first flight? Yes; you should be aware of a few details that can make the difference between your having a great flight and a bad one. Let's see what's left.

BALANCE. Did you balance your model? Did you check to see whether the model's center of gravity (CG) is in the proper location? Every airplane kit instruction booklet should explain where the balance point should be. For a straight wing, this point will usually fall somewhere between ¼ and ⅓ of the chord back from the leading edge (LE). With a sweptback wing, the CG will be farther rearward; again, check the instructions.

To check the model's balance point, install the receiver (RX) and the battery pack and attach the wing to the fuselage. Support the wing with your fingertips—near the fuselage sides—and test the model's balance; move the receiver and battery until it balances level or slightly nose down. This is the balance point, and it should match that specified on the instructions. If it doesn't, try moving the RX and battery again; if that doesn't work, add a little weight to the nose or the tail until the model balances where it should. This is vital. A nose-heavy model will probably fly satisfactorily, but a tail-heavy one might not be controllable.

Control direction. One of the most common causes of a first-flight crash is that a model has its controls hooked up backward. Test your controls to make sure that they don't bind and that they move the control surfaces (rudder, ailerons, etc.) in the proper directions. Turn the transmitter (TX) on first and then turn on your model's RX. Make sure the TX's trim levers are centered, and check the control surfaces to make sure that they are straight and in their neutral positions. While facing in the same direction as your model, move the control stick to the right; the rudder should also move to the right. If your plane has ailerons, when you move the stick to the right, the right aileron should move up and the left aileron should move down. When you pull the elevator stick back toward you, the elevator should move upward; it should move downward when you push the stick away from you.

This is also a good time to check the throttle and to make sure that the motor is turning in the correct direction. When the throttle is pulled all the way back, the prop should not move. As you push the throttle stick forward, the prop should respond proportionally and should blow air back over the model. If your airplane has only an arming switch (no throttle), make sure the prop spins in the right direction (counterclockwise when looked at from the nose of the plane).

WARPING. Having assembled the model, make sure that the wing panels are straight—no twisting or warping. Look at each wing panel from the tip to the root (toward the fuselage), and make sure their angles match. If one tip has more positive or negative angle than the other does, your model will try to turn in one direction or the other.

To fix a warped wing panel, gently twist it into the opposite position, and then have a helper use a heat gun or a high-wattage hair dryer to remove the wrinkles in the covering. When the covering has cooled and the wrinkles have disappeared, release the panel, and it should be straight.

Check to make sure that the tail surfaces are also free of warps and that the wing and horizontal stabilizer are properly aligned.

That's about it. Make sure your RX and drive batteries are fully charged and that the TX batteries are also in peak condition. Check the little light indicator or the meter on the TX face and make sure your radio system is working properly. Have fun.

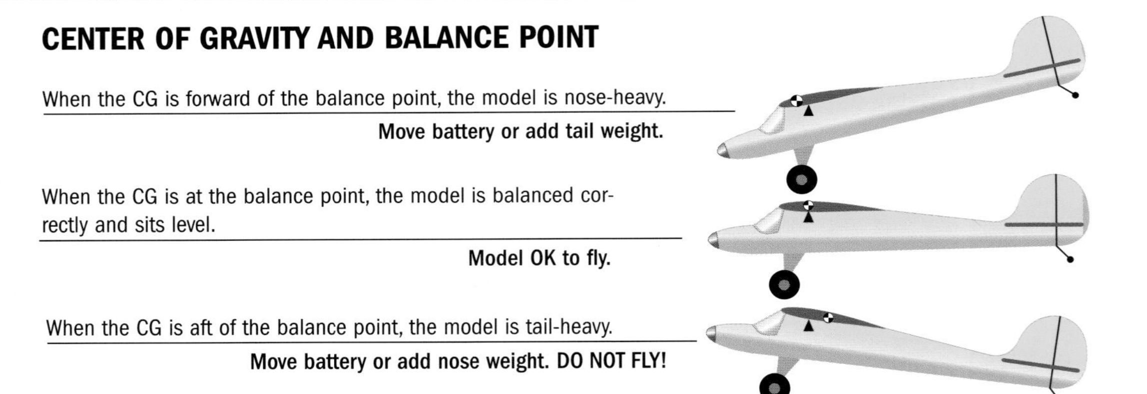

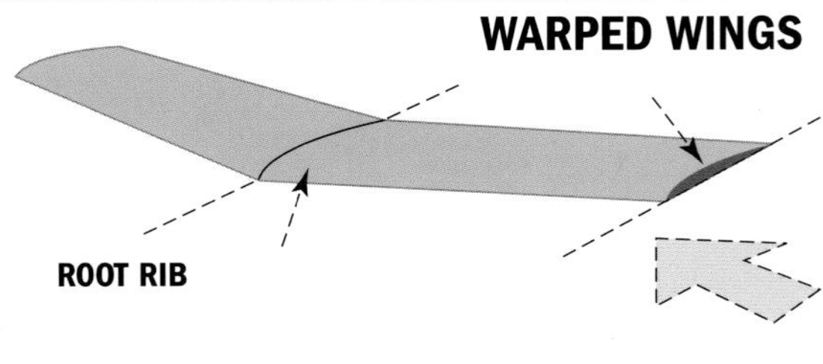

While looking at the wing from the tip, look at the bottom surface and compare the angles of the tip and root ribs. They should be the same. If the tip is at a different angle (twisted), the model will want to turn one way or the other.

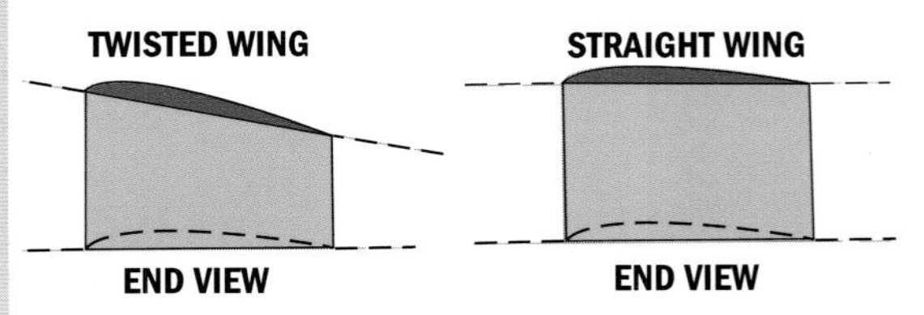

To fly straight, the two wingtips should be at the same angle and parallel with the root rib.

Most of the time, you'll have to hand-launch your model. Don't just throw it with everything you've got; take a few quick steps and gently release it.

your running it into trees or buildings. And for safety reasons, don't fly it over a road with traffic.

Most backyard flyers have small landing gear and wheels, so they can't taxi and take off from the ground. For this reason, you'll have to hand-launch the model (or have a friend hand-launch it for you). After the model has used up its battery charge, it's time to land. Small models can take off from hard, paved surfaces such as large parking lots, but remember that if you crash your model into a hard surface, it's more likely to be damaged. The safest areas to fly from are grass fields; tall grass is also great, especially if you're teaching yourself how to fly. Tall grass will cushion the model when it lands and could prevent it from being damaged in a hard return to earth.

ESTABLISH A "FLIGHTLINE"

When flying in an open field, it's good practice to define an imaginary safety line that helps separate your model from the people who are watching you fly.

Don't fly the model in a circle around you; keep the model's flight path in front of you, and have observers stay behind you. This gives an added margin of safety for everyone.

SMALL, SLOW, LIGHTWEIGHT MODELS

These can easily be flown in an area that's roughly the size of a baseball diamond. This is the minimum area in which to fly a model safely. Compare your backyard or a nearby vacant lot to a Little League diamond, and ask yourself whether you can safely fly there. You should be able to hand-launch the model and fly a circular course or a figure-8 pattern. If your model is very light and agile, you will, in time, be able to fly it between trees and over fences, but in the beginning, make sure your flying area is clear of obstructions.

SLIGHTLY HEAVIER MODELS

Because they fly a little faster, these planes will need an area that's roughly the size of the baseball diamond and the outfield. Sporting complexes often have two diamonds in one field, and this is ideal. Of course, you'll have to wait for a time when the home team is not practicing or striking out the visitors. If you're lucky enough to have a backyard this big or you live near a vacant lot, you're all set. Please, don't fly your model over other people; it can be distracting and is definitely unsafe.

BIGGER AND FASTER MODELS

These models should be flown in a football field or a soccer field. Typically, you should stand on the 50-yard line so you have a lot of space all around you. Large local parks may have this much open area, but regardless of where you fly, before you throw your model into the air, ask someone whether or not you can do so. It's the polite thing to do. People who are walking dogs and kids who are playing nearby are all attracted to model airplanes, so be aware of what's going on around you. Let people know you're out there; be seen and have fun.

When the charge in your model's battery is close to being used up, the model won't be able to climb while under full power. This tells you it's time to land. When your model gets close to the ground, gently apply a little up-elevator to raise its nose slightly just before you land it. This is called "flaring," and it ensures a slow and gentle landing.

Add some style with easy aerobatics by Thayer Syme

Small, light models designed for flying in restricted places offer much potential for exploring the realm of low-power aerobatics. Some, like the Wild R/C IFO, Great Planes Laser Mini 3D and

Although models like the Radical R/C Edge 540 are perfectly suited to aggressive aerobatics, lower-powered planes can easily fly loops and rolls.

THE LOOP

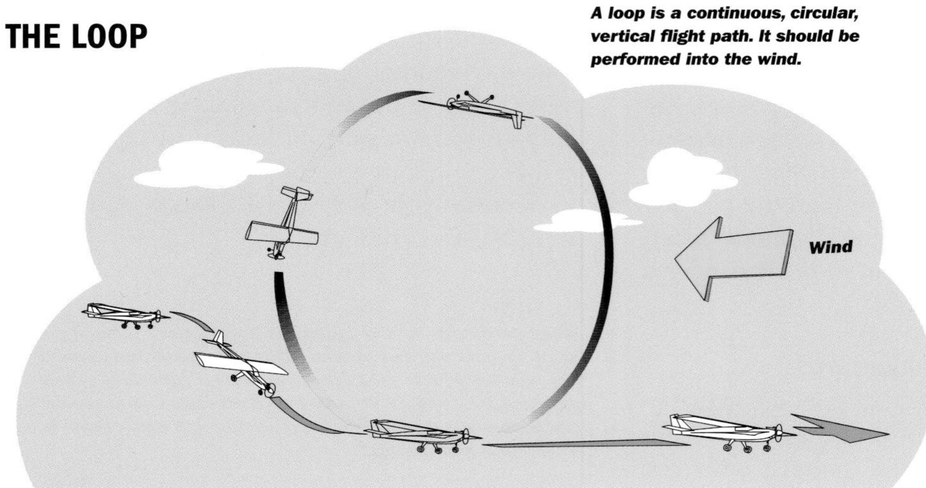

A loop is a continuous, circular, vertical flight path. It should be performed into the wind.

Radical R/C Edge 540, are intended for aggressive aerobatics, yet many more sedate scale and semi-scale sport designs are capable of very enjoyable aerobatic flight. Managing the available power and kinetic energy becomes much more important when there is a cap on your power budget. I've found this to be true in flying full-scale aircraft as well.

The basics of aerobatic flight are nothing more than the loop and the roll. Essentially, all familiar maneuvers are combinations and variations of these two steppingstones. For instance, a common turn for models consists of a ¼ roll to knife-edge, a ½ loop (albeit in the horizontal plane) and another ¼ roll back to straight and level flight. Though not as exciting as some, this maneuver will qualify as aerobatic. Other maneuvers, such as the Immelman and Split-S, are just bits and pieces of loops and rolls strung together.

FLYING A LOOP ...

An inside loop (the top of the wing is on the "inside") is perhaps the most common, safest and easiest first maneuver for a low-time RC pilot. (A similar but more advanced maneuver is the outside loop, where the top of the wing is on the outside.)

THE ROLL

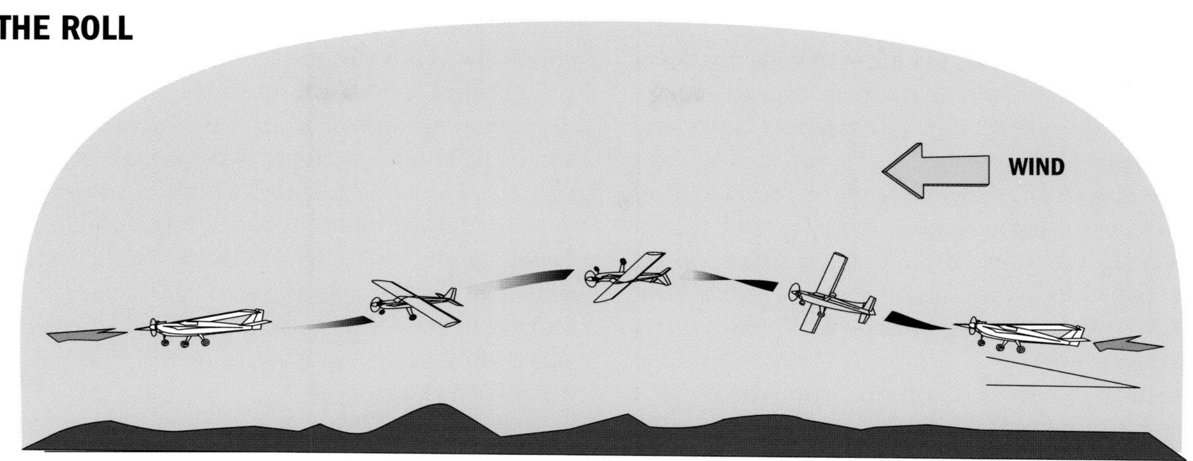

A roll is a 360-degree rotation about the aircraft's longitudinal axis.

With sufficient airspeed, you need only smoothly pull back on the elevator and wait for the model to complete the loop. Many full-scale aircraft, as well as lower-powered models, need a speed increase beyond normal full-throttle cruise, so the pilot lowers the plane's nose to gain speed; a bit of experimentation and practice with your model will help you determine the proper amount. Smoothly add elevator until you have achieved full deflection. Don't yank the stick back; such a rapid pitch change at high speed can cause a high-speed stall or cause the model to shed its wings. As the plane pitches up, the model will start to slow. Don't worry; as soon as it's inverted, the model will easily complete the loop. Full-scale pilots often reduce power when they're inverted to avoid engine damage or prevent the plane from over speeding in the second half of the loop, and I recommend the same for models, as the loop becomes more graceful and lasts longer. You will also be less likely to shed your model's wings in the last half of the loop. The model's nose will now be dropping toward the vertical, influenced by the lift of the wing pulling toward the ground, the up-elevator control you are still holding and gravity. The model will start to accelerate quickly as its nose is pointed at the ground. Continue to hold up-elevator until the nose rises and the airplane pulls out of the dive. Properly timed, you will have released all of the up-elevator just as the

THE SPLIT-S

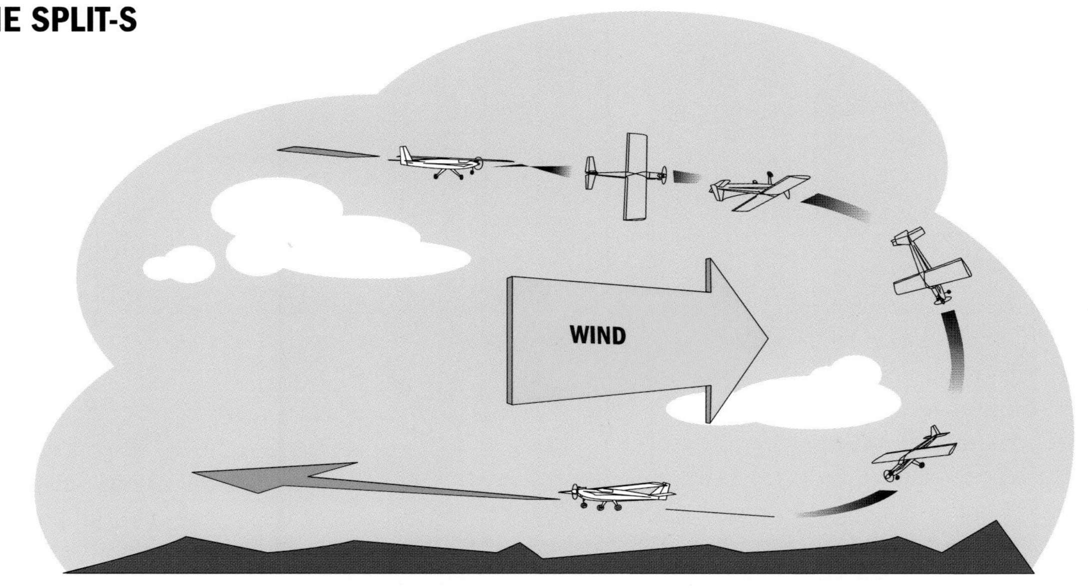

The Split-S is a descending maneuver comprising a half roll and a half loop.

model returns to level flight. Note that the model will have quite a bit of excess speed for level flight and may balloon dramatically. Be careful that you do not let the nose rise too far, or the model may stall.

The competition ideal of a perfect circular loop is not necessary for sport flying. Many lower-powered, full-scale aircraft trace more of an egg-shaped loop. The next time you watch "The Great Waldo Pepper," you will see Robert Redford's character loop his WW I vintage biplane in exactly this fashion during the movie's opening sequence. If you want to round out the loop a bit, ease off some of the up-elevator while the model is inverted.

... AND A ROLL

In a roll, the aircraft rotates about its longitudinal axis. Ailerons are necessary for a true axial roll, but don't despair if you are flying a model that has only rudder and elevator! You can still approximate an aileron roll and fly very nice barrel rolls. Begin the maneuver with plenty of altitude and full throttle. As with the loop, excess speed is often needed for a roll. Without this excess speed, the drag of the aileron deflection can slow the airplane to a point at which the controls become ineffective. Worse yet, the model could stall. If your model will not loop from straight and level flight, push the nose down 10 degrees or so and pick up a bit of extra speed. Once the model is flying fast enough to loop, pull the model back into a climb of at least 30 degrees. Release all of the up-elevator, and immediately apply full aileron. Hold the deflection until the model rolls through 360 degrees and returns to level flight. The model will likely be descending again, and the nose will need to be lifted with elevator.

What if your model doesn't have ailerons? You can probably still get it to roll, though the rotation will not be as smooth. As before, pick up a bit of speed, pitch the nose up, release the elevator and apply full rudder. A properly designed model should have enough rudder authority to roll.

When you've mastered the inside loop and a roll, try an Immelman turn (a climbing maneuver that combines a half loop and a roll) and a Split-S (a diving maneuver that starts with a roll followed by a half loop). These two relatively easy aerobatic maneuvers are the basis for many more complicated routines; when you've mastered them, you'll be well on your way to becoming a backyard ace.

THE IMMELMANN TURN

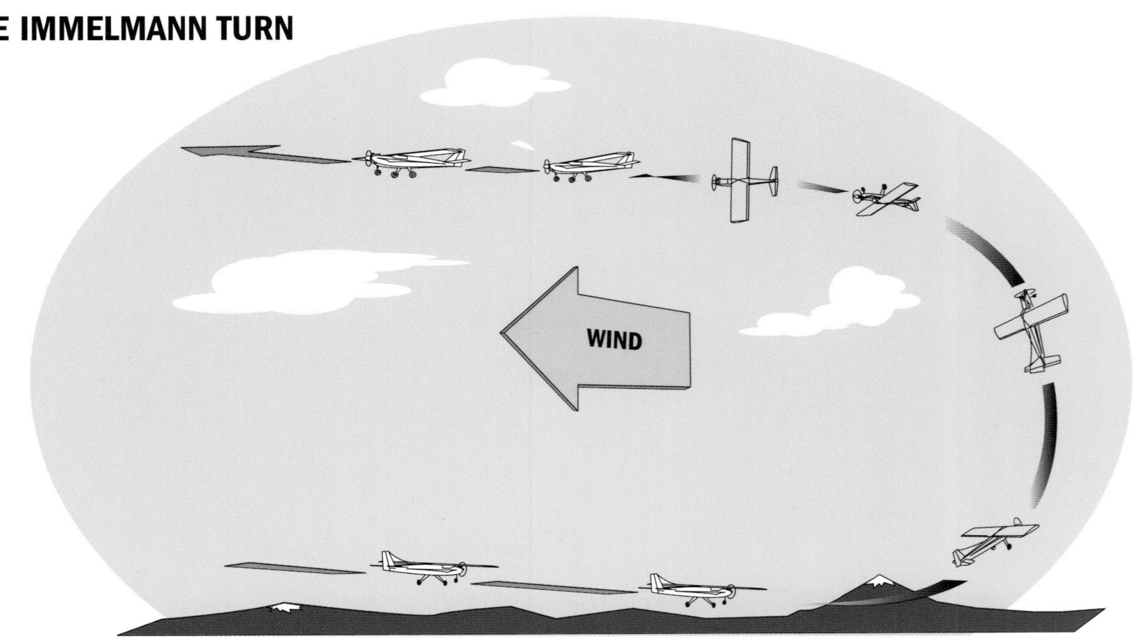

The Immelmann turn is a climbing maneuver comprising a half loop and a half roll.

Competition Flying

14

Many enthusiasts hunger for a little more excitement after they have mastered the challenge of flying in a park, parking lot or backyard. This chapter includes a brief review of competitive events for small electrics.

Thus far, we've talked about beginner-level flying, which allows you to get comfortable flying parking-lot and micro indoor models. Quite honestly, flying around in circles, sometimes alone, will eventually lead to boredom, and you will need something else to add to your enjoyment and to spur your enthusiasm. Competition flying could be the answer for you. Although competition isn't for everyone, sport and informal events can be a lot of fun.

A typical profile fuselage electric indoor pylon racer, as built by Bob Wilder of Colleyville, TX. This is Bob's "Buster" look alike. It weighs about 7 ounces and is powered by a geared DC 1524 motor. Indoor pylon racing is done with four planes in a heat. Provides a lot of fun and a few "bumps."

On June 30, 2001, Bob Wilder set a new official record with the plane he holds here at the Indoor R/C Electric Endurance AMA Record Trial held at the University of Texas at Arlington. His time was 4 hours, 14 minutes and 57 seconds. Note that Bob's original-design models rely heavily on microfilm-type indoor model construction.

Jerry Small, one of the founders of the indoor electric RC pylon racing activity. He is also from the Dallas/Fort Worth area of Texas. Jerry is holding a Travel Air Mystery racer (at left) and his Gee Bee R-1/R-2 (right), which appeared in RC MicroFlight.

Micro fliers have recently recommended that a series of new events be instituted to bring out the best in parking-lot and indoor RC fliers. So far the AMA Rule Book has only one official RC indoor event, No. 627, Indoor Electric Duration (Radio Control). An official record flight of 2 hours 34 minutes was set by Bob Wilder of Colleyville, TX, in May 1998. Later that same year, Bob unofficially made a 4-hour, 11-minute flight. Just as this book was going to press, I learned that Bob established another endurance record of 4 hours, 17 minutes and 57 seconds on June 30, 2001, while flying at an indoor facility at the University of Texas in Arlington, TX. For this record, his model had a 250 square-inch wing area and weighed 114 grams (4 ounces). The motor was a

Steve Davis's impressive 1910 British Valkyrie shows the exciting potential of micro-electric scale modeling. This beautiful ship won second place at the Indoor Fun Fly and Competition held in May 2001 at the Southwestern Aeromodeling Conference (Arlington Convention Center, Arlington, TX). The all-up weight of the 36-inch-span Valkyrie is only 6.5 ounces! A WES-Technik 1524 motor turns a WES-Technik 9x5 carbon-fiber prop via a handmade 4.5:1 gearbox. This setup pulls about 1.15 amps at 7 volts. Electronics include a Hitec Feather receiver, an FMA ESC and Cirrus CS-10 servos. The model is powered by a 7.2V 110mAh Sanyo Ni-Cd pack (TA120) that resembles a traditional 9V transistor radio battery. Photos by Tom Atwood.

WES-Technik D-1717 geared 11.8:1 with a 10-inch carbon prop. The battery consisted of three Varta 3V, 1300mAh lithium (CR-123A) cells.

While we are all amazed at the progress being made in endurance flying, the fact remains that long-duration flying can quickly become boring. It is also difficult to stage, since long flight times tend to limit flight opportunities, especially when modelers are operating on the same RC channels. In the next year or two, we are hoping to see a series of new events develop that will take us beyond endurance flying, such as: aerobatics; scale, load, or cargo carrying; glider towing; pylon racing; combat flying; and even postal-type events that could be staged all over the country. I didn't include electric helicopters in this book, but several small electric-powered helicopter kits are already on the market. Model RC helicopter flying offers many new and interesting possibilities for indoor competition.

The concepts for these new events will no doubt develop as experience and acceptance is gained. The idea is to eventually coordinate the parking-lot/indoor RC events into a more structured status so that they can be voted into the official AMA Rule Book. The ultimate goal is to stage an annual indoor RC national championship competition at a large, centrally located indoor facility.

15

Organizations

The Academy of Model Aeronautics (AMA) and National Indoor Remote-Control Aircraft Council (NIRAC) are two organizations that support micro RC endeavors. The author briefly describes their role in this chapter.

Any new movement, even within an existing hobby such as model aviation, can progress or advance if it has its own organization or representation. Model aviation, as a hobby, has been endorsed for years by an organization known as the Academy of Model Aeronautics (AMA), which was founded in 1936. The AMA is now an organization with between 100,000 and 200,000 members that is housed in a large national headquarters located in Muncie, IN. This facility includes a new executive office building, a wonderful and extensive model aviation museum and a tremendous outdoor championship model-flying facility that is almost the size of a full-scale airport. This flying facility hosts many model aircraft events each year, the most famous of which are the AMA National Model Airplane Competitions held primarily throughout the month of July. These events are known as the AMA "Nats."

Among the many benefits offered by the AMA is a high-value accident insurance policy, which is provided to every member. The cost of membership, which includes this insurance protection, is nominal. Most organized model aircraft clubs located throughout the country are chartered by the AMA and, as such, the members of these clubs agree to abide by all of the published AMA Safety Guidelines.

AMA membership is usually a prerequisite to becoming a local club member or to being allowed to fly at a local model aircraft site; therefore, as a beginner seeking aid or flying instructions, you must first show your AMA membership card to the local field representative before you will be allowed to fly.

The AMA can help you locate local clubs and flying fields, and can assist in finding and developing new flying fields and establishing new clubs in your area. For further information, log onto the AMA's website at www.modelaircraft.org.

NIRAC SPECIAL INTEREST GROUP

Over the years, second-tier organizations were formed in the model aviation hobby called Special Interest Groups (SIGs). In the year 2000, a SIG was established to help advance parking-lot and indoor RC fliers called the National Indoor Remote-Controlled Aircraft Council (NIRAC). This organization was founded by current Indoor RC National Endurance Champion, Bob Wilder, and is a good organization to join, in addition to the AMA.

NIRAC has a newly established website, www.nirac.org, and plans are being made to publish a newsletter on this site on a regular basis. The idea will be to share micro-flying technical information, to help establish a recognized set of safety guidelines for the purpose of flying parking-lot and indoor RC models, to develop new contest rules

Nationally famous cartoonist and popular electric RC flier Don Bousquet, from Narragansett, RI, was kind enough to design this logo for the new National Indoor Remote-Controlled Aircraft Council (NIRAC).

Founder and President of NIRAC, Mr. Bob Wilder of Colleyville, TX. Bob has traveled all over the country to set the stage for this new organization. One of its goals is to establish an Indoor National Championship, possibly in the Muncie, IN, area. Bob is shown here holding one of his GWS Pico Cub models, which he uses in indoor pylon racing competitions.

I thought enough of the new NIRAC organization to become a Charter Member back in June, 2000. I continue to be very positive about this organization, which is now recognized as the Special Interest Group (SIG) for the AMA on matters concerning indoor, parking-lot and backyard flyers.

Left: at the 2001 Toledo Weak Signals RC Show, indoor modelers were treated to a three-hour flying session at the Bowling Green University Field House (about 20 miles from Toledo). This tremendous indoor facility measures 187x360 feet with a 65-foot ceiling. This photo gives you a rough idea of the size. Four or five models flew at a time, all night long. We hope that more hobby trade shows will sponsor the same kind of indoor-flying sessions.

Below: this photo shows Gary Jones (foreground) and Ed Couch flying RC indoor combat. Note the large group of interested spectators. This indoor facility was inside the convention center at the 2001 Southwestern Aeromodeling Conference in Arlington,TX. The hobby trade show was going on at the same time.

and to coordinate these rules with official AMA rules in the future. NIRAC will also work with the AMA to help establish the National Indoor Model Aircraft Annual Championship I mentioned earlier. I hope this will be established at a centrally located facility so that every interested modeler in the country will have a chance to attend.

NIRAC is also hard at work locating and announcing large indoor flying facilities for the benefit of its members. As already pointed out, several of the large hobby trade shows are now featuring indoor flying sessions as well. At the Toledo Weak Signal RC Hobby Trade Show in April 2001, we were all treated to a three-hour flying session at the Bowling Green University Field House. This facility measures 180x300 feet with a 65-foot ceiling.

At the Southwestern Aeromodeling Conference (SAC) held in Arlington, TX, a portion of the large convention center is sectioned off expressly for indoor RC flying, so the trade show and indoor flying are under the same roof. I hope that in the near future other major trade shows (e.g., the WRAM show in New York and IMS in Pasadena, CA) will offer the same convenience.

If you enjoy micro flight and want to see it develop further, I urge you show your support by joining NIRAC.

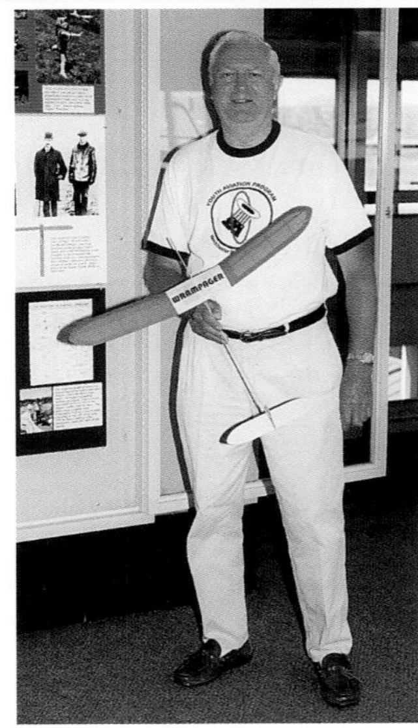

The Westchester Radio Aero Modelers (WRAM) club of White Plains, NY, has sponsored a big RC hobby trade show for more than 30 years. Hank Nielsen of the WRAM club helped developed a new Youth Aviation Program several years ago. The program's goal is to get young people interested in the world of model aviation. What better way to do this than with indoor and parking-lot flyers? Toward that end, the WRAM website (www.wram.org) offers a set of plans for a multi-purpose model they call the WRAMPAGER. It can be configured easily for indoor electric or CO_2 RC flying.

16

Publications, Internet & Electric Flys

Looking for more sources of information on the exciting world of park, backyard and indoor flyers? You will find them here.

To have a meaningful beginning in the hobby of RC micro flight, or to advance further into this wonderful new facet of model aviation, you must learn through an interchange of technical information. Being a member of a local club, especially one that either specializes in micro flying (parking-lot and indoor RC flying) or has a large number of members who share this enthusiasm, is an important first step.

RC MICROFLIGHT NEWSLETTER

In addition to club membership, other tools will enhance the learning process and help you have more fun while flying micro RC. In November 1999, Air Age Publishing, Inc., the publishers of *Model Airplane News*, took a bold step and started a new publication known as *RC MicroFlight* (RCMF). It is both a printed newsletter and an online "webzine" (see www.rcmicroflight.com).

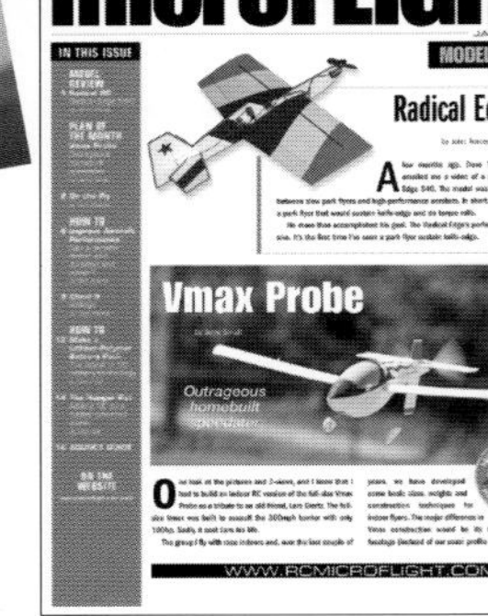

As of March 2002, 29 monthly editions of *RC MicroFlight* had been published. The newsletter consists of a 16-page hard copy publication, and, to date, there is no advertising. The 16 pages are crammed with technical information concerning parking-lot and indoor RC micro flying. The information includes editorials, construction articles with plans, product reviews, new product announcements, hobby trade show highlights and indoor RC contest reports from around the country and the world.

Very innovative, *RC MicroFlight* is distributed to subscribers not only in hard-copy format, but also on a secure website, which allows subscribers to view each issue on the Internet using a special access password. Even more useful is the complete index of all published material that is made available to subscribers. This allows you to look up, retrieve and print copies of any previously published *RC MicroFlight* article, and it means that, as a new subscriber, you immediately have access to everything that has already been published. What an incredible database to have at your disposal!

Another interesting feature of *RC MicroFlight* is that full-size plans for featured construction articles can be printed directly from the website. Subscribers can print copies as a mosaic and then paste together several pages to obtain a full-size set of plans; or they can take a more sophisticated approach by downloading plans and having them printed on a CAD-type machine or at a commercial facility (e.g., Kinkos) that offers wide-bed printers. With this feature, you can have all the full-size plans you want instantly, and, except for the local printing cost, the service is free to subscribers.

During the initial planning of *RC MicroFlight*, John Worth, retired AMA Executive Director, was invited to join the staff of *RC MicroFlight* and to bring with him his own newsletter entitled Cloud 9. John accepted the position of founding editor in November 1999, the first *RC MicroFlight* publication date. He now publishes Cloud 9 as a monthly feature technical column in the newsletter

I have had the privilege of being the *RC MicroFlight* editor-at-large since its inception. It is an excellent publication, and we would like to solicit your support by "earning" a new subscription from you. If you are interested, look us up at www.rcmicroflight.com, or call at (800)-243-6685.

***RC MicroFlight* founding editor, John Worth, at a recent NEAT Fair**

BACKYARD FLYER

By the end of 2001, Air Age had launched a new magazine called *Backyard Flyer*. This quarterly publication showcases the large variety of new products in the micro RC airplane market (see www.backyardflyer.com). It is a full-color magazine dedicated to RC micro flying.

FREE SLOW-FLIGHT LIST SERVE

Also supported by *Model Airplane News*, *Backyard Flyer* and *RC MicroFlight* is a valuable email forum called the "Small Flyers RC Net," the "slow flight list serve" or simply the "SFRC net." A "list serve" is a community of enthusiasts who are all members of an email forum group or list. Every member receives every email sent to the list. Free access is offered to this service, and once you sign on you can choose to receive one session (or batch) at a time, i.e., the emails containing the information exchanges are grouped and sent to members in batches each day. To sign up, go to www.rcmicroflight.com and click on the "email discussion group" option in the left navigation bar. Remember, this is a free service for modelers.

The SFRC net will allow you to monitor the release of new products and read comments on these products from various list-serve subscribers; you'll also learn about events of interest (e.g., trade shows, indoor fly ins). You can also ask questions of other modelers on the Net, making it possible for more experienced micro fliers to answer you in real time and without the need for letters or phone calls. Those of us involved in RC micro flying today would not let a day go by without "interrogating" the latest daily SFRC net output, so please sign up for this excellent service. Remember, it is totally free and is offered by Air Age to help you gain further knowledge of RC micro flying.

Air Age also sponsors the free online community at www.radiocontrolzone.com, which includes an online bulletin board community visited by thousands of modelers. Radiocontrolzone.com includes such forums as Indoor RC Microflight (moderated by NIRAC), Park and Backyard Flyers and Post Your Micro Flyer Photos. Click on the airplane section at the zone, and on the next page click on the bulletin board link.

TRADE SHOWS

As already mentioned, at least four or five major RC hobby trade shows are held throughout the country annually. Their locations (Ohio, New York, Texas, California, etc.) make it possible for almost any interested modeler to attend at least one show a year. These shows represent the entire RC hobby, from the smallest to the largest models. The variety is enormous, but keep in mind that you won't see only micro flyers. Attending at least one show per year is definitely worthwhile. The largest show is run by the Weak Signals RC Club of Toledo, OH, and it is traditionally held the first week in April of each year.

Several of these major hobby trade shows are now beginning to feature indoor RC flying at adjacent or nearby facilities, and one evening is usually set aside for indoor flying. This makes it possible for you to attend the RC hobby trade show during the day, have dinner and then fly indoor RC for several hours in the evening.

The annual Southwestern Aeromodeling Conference (SWAC) held in early May in the Arlington, TX, Convention Center features indoor RC flying over the entire two-day show period and within the same facility (as we went to press, SWAC 2002 had been cancelled but the show will be held again in May 2003 and thereafter). About one-third of the convention center facility is sectioned off for RC micro model flying, enabling you to visit RC

A scene from one of the several hobby trade shows where micro electric-powered RC airplanes are exhibited or sold.

hobby vendors at their booths and then watch the flying a short distance away. The organizers of this indoor session usually plan contests to keep spectators interested over the full two-day period. We hope that other show organizers will follow the lead of Dr. Sandy Frank and the modelers of the Dallas/Ft. Worth/Arlington areas of Texas.

ELECTRIC-POWERED RC MEETS

Historically, the largest electric-powered RC gathering in the world took place in Pennsylvania, first in Quakertown and then in Allentown. It was traditionally held on the third weekend in September and was staged by the Keystone RC club, known as the KRC. This show was an annual event for almost 20 years but, sadly, it was phased out in 1999.

Happily for e-powered modelers, the KRC concept was adopted for the new Northeast Electric Aircraft Technology Fair (NEAT), which was held for the first time in September 2000 and again in September 2001. The NEAT Fair is sponsored by the Silent Electric Flyers Club of Long Island (SEFLI), and the Event Director is e-power pioneer, Tom Hunt. The NEAT Fair is held in lower-central New York State, in the town of Downsville. For more information on the next NEAT Fair, please refer to their two websites, www.neatfair.org (event website) and www.peaceful-valley.com (host website). You may also email the event organizers at neatfair@optonline.net.

Several hundred pilots attend this three-day gathering; it is important, therefore, to make advance reservations at facilities in the area. Although the NEAT Fair covers all aspects of electric-powered flight, many micro fliers attend as well. Parking-lot/slow flyers and even some micro indoor RC models can easily be flown in the early morning and early evening hours, when the winds are likely to be calm. It is a great chance to visit and exchange technical information with friends who share the same interest in the model aviation hobby, and many e-power vendors set up booths to sell their products throughout the three days of the show. Many of these same vendors will walk you right out to the flight line and demonstrate their models first hand, which is a nice plus.

It is possible, as the RC micro-flying movement continues to advance, that the NIRAC organization may be able to establish a national indoor RC gathering at a large, centrally located facility. A three-day session of micro indoor RC flying might be the ultimate experience for this specialized portion of the model aviation hobby.

Tom Hunt and helper with Tom's Graupner Terry at the NEAT Fair.

17 What's Next?

In this chapter, the author takes a look at what the future holds in store for the exciting world of micro RC.

By now you have an understanding of RC micro flying for both parking-lot and indoor RC models, and we hope you have tried it or are planning to try it soon.

A question one might ask is: "how small can we expect or want to go?" Several special-purpose indoor RC models have been flown with a total flying weight of less than 1 ounce. These were both electric and CO_2 powered and used full 3-channel RC control. Flying at this minimum weight does require certain building skills, as well as special equipment. Currently, this equipment is quite expensive, but if you are willing to go to 2-ounces total flying weight you will be in an easier and less costly environment. Since the difference between 1-ounce and 2-ounce total flying weight is considerable, many of us are perfectly satisfied to keep our models at 2 ounces.

Above: Matthew Keenon of AeroVironment and his scratch-built electric-powered Thunderbolt P-47 micro flyer. Below: Bloom's Tomb weighs just 43 grams and is barely the length of a standard pencil. As technology continues to develop, will RC models as small as this be commonplace?

RADIOS

We do see improvements in RC miniaturization on the horizon. The new cell-phone technology is likely to influence RC development efforts. In the future, we may even see micro RC equipment designed to operate at frequencies above 900MHz. This would allow parking-lot and micro indoor fliers to operate on frequencies apart from other modelers operating on the regular RC model 72MHz band. This separation would eliminate, once and for all, the concerns of interaction and interference between frequencies used in both forms of flying.

Consider also that at 900MHz a quarter-wave antenna for both the transmitter and receiver might only be a few inches long. Both the selectivity and sensitivity of micro receivers might also be improved, allowing many pilots to fly safely at the same time.

A close-up of Phil Smith's breadboard 900MHz experimental RC receiver. Cell-phone technology contributes to this development work.

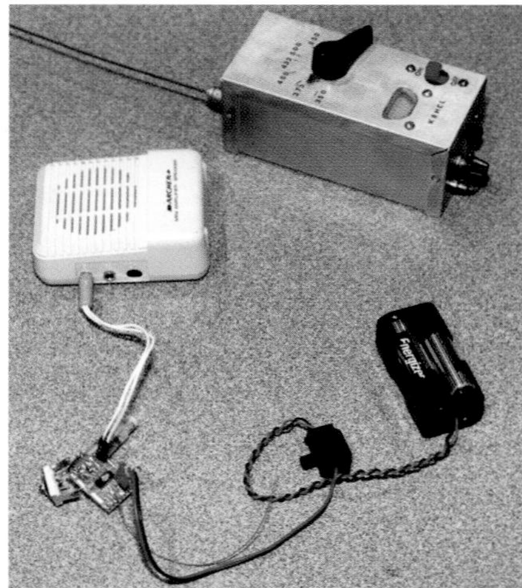

Experimental 900MHz RC system prototype as designed by Phil Smith of Adrian, MI. This is only proof of concept, but Phil reports strong signal reception at 900MHz.

Phil Smith while attending the AMA E-Nats in Muncie, IN. He is holding one of his very large yet lightly loaded parking-lot flyers. Phil experiments with both equipment and airframes.

SERVOS

I look forward to newer, lighter and less expensive proportional-control servo devices. Right now, our smallest micro models must use magnetic actuators and coils, along with special decoding devices, to make them operate in a reasonably smooth fashion. New concepts are needed in this area, yet we also need to keep an eye on cost. Modelers will pay $30 for a servo but tend to think twice when the price tag goes up to $90.

BATTERIES

New battery technology is surely on the horizon, which we hope will provide lighter cells of higher capacity and with very fast recharging capabilities. We may even see RC equipment and electric motors that will work from a single battery cell.

GOVERNMENT R&D

This is all possible in the not too distant future. As a matter of fact, in recent years, the Defense Department has spent considerable development money on unmanned aerial vehicles (UAVs). These are miniature RC models that weigh only a few ounces and are being developed for surveillance and reconnaissance missions. Sound far fetched? Maybe not! RC micro flight can only benefit from these developments, and we might even see some interchange of technology between our hobby efforts and those of the defense agencies. There are all kinds of possibilities for the future. Micro RC flying is a reality right now, and new developments in design will ensure an exciting future. We hope you will want to join us and be part of something new!

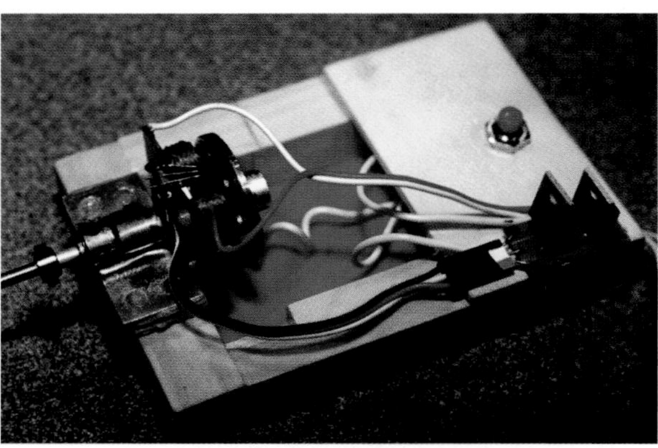

Prototype miniature brushless motor designed by Phil Smith. Phil is trying see how small he can construct a brushless motor for possible indoor RC applications. He is actually able to fly one of these motors.

MICRO ENGINES

Electric-powered micro RC without batteries!?!

Author's note: this brief look at miniature power systems now under development suggests how small electric airplanes of the future may be powered. Written by Matt Boyd, assistant editor for Backyard Flyer *magazine,* Model Airplane News *and other Air Age publications, it is excerpted from the "Current News" column of the spring 2002* Backyard Flyer *magazine.*

This tiny 4mm-diameter rotor is the centerpiece of an MIT-developed micro turbine.

It isn't here yet, but researchers at MIT, Columbia University and the University of California at Berkeley are hard at work developing micro engines that may well replace batteries as the preferred energy-storage device for electrical systems. These tiny powerplants (like all engines) turn chemical energy into thermal energy and then into motion, but the power they produce is only a means to a greater end. The idea is to couple these miniscule engines to micro motors and generators to convert the mechanical energy into electricity.

Berkeley has a working prototype of a Wankel rotary engine about the size of a penny, machined from steel. It is designed to run on butane or propane and at present produces about 2.5 watts, but it is being ramped up to produce more than ten times that output. Researchers are also attempting to create a smaller version that will be chemically etched from silicon.

A collaborative team from MIT and Columbia University is working on a silicon micro turbine. Its design sandwiches together several layers of silicon—each layer has various parts (the rotor, bearings, chambers, etc.) precision-etched into it before being bonded to the others. The construction process borrows much from the computer microchip industry. The engine burns hydrogen to spin the 4-millimeter-diameter rotor.

Why is a micro engine a better power storage device than a battery? It comes down to energy density: even the best NiMH and lithium batteries turn less than 1 percent of their stored chemical energy into usable electrical energy. Designers estimate that micro engines coupled to generators should be able to reach 5 percent fairly easily. The goal for the Berkeley project is 10 percent—an increase of nearly 20 times over conventional battery technology! The engines themselves are so small that almost all the available space in a given application could be devoted to fuel storage. That would mean unheard of durations for electric-powered devices before they needed to be refueled. And the fuel itself can be stored considerably longer before it starts to degrade, whereas a battery will "leak" away its charge even while not being used.

There are still some hurdles to overcome. Developers are struggling to maintain efficient combustion on a micro scale; the sizes of chemical components and their burn rates remain constant even though the size of the combustion chamber is radically smaller. There is also the issue of heat transfer—even at 10 percent efficiency, most of the energy released when the fuel is ignited will manifest as heat buildup. And as we all know, the delicate electronic devices these powerplants are likely to be used with don't respond well to heat. Even so, the potential gains in efficiency are so great that researchers aren't likely to give up searching for a way to make micro engines and generators the eventual replacement for batteries.

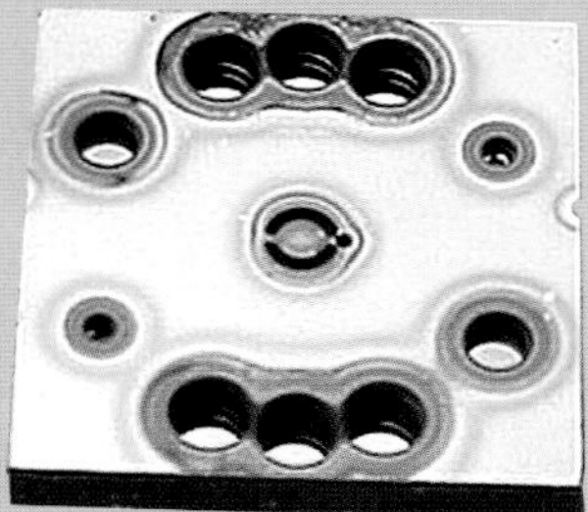

The development of this silicon-etched turbine micro engine (shown approximately actual size) borrows much from the computer microchip industry.

This Wankel rotary engine is machined from steel and is seen here roughly life-size. It is fully functional, and an even smaller silicon-etched version is in the works.

MODELING TERMINOLOGY

Here's a glossary of common RC airplane modeling terms and their definitions.

Aileron: roll control surface.

Airfoil: the shape of the wing's rib.

Angle of attack (AoA): the angle difference between the wing-chord line and the relative wind.

Auxiliary channel: any radio channel function other than the four basics (aileron, rudder, elevator and throttle).

BEC (battery eliminator circuit): a feature of some speed control units that permits both the motor and the receiver to be powered by the same battery.

Bulkhead: a vertical former inside a fuselage.

CA (cyanoacrylate): a modern hobby adhesive that cures very quickly.

Center of gravity (CG): the balance point of a model airplane.

Control linkage: any linkage that transmits servo movement to a control surface.

Control surface: a movable surface such as elevator, rudder and aileron.

Dihedral: the upward sweep (angle) of the wing panels; it provides stability.

Doubler: a second piece of balsa or plywood added to the fuselage side to enhance strength.

Drag: air resistance that slows the model.

Elevator: pitch-control surface.

ESC (electronic speed control): the unit that controls the rpm of the motor.

Flare: a gradual increase in pitch angle to bleed off excess airspeed just before landing.

Fuselage: the main body of the airplane.

Horizontal stabilizer: the flight surface that supports the elevator and also helps to stabilize the model in pitch.

Leading edge (LE): the foremost edge of an airfoil or propeller.

Lift: the aerodynamic force generated by air flowing around an airfoil that is equal to or greater than the weight of the aircraft and acts opposite to the force of gravity.

Moment (nose moment, tail moment): refers to a distance on a model forward or aft of the balance point.

Over-control: excessive control inputs that overcompensate for unwanted model movement.

Receiver: the part of the radio system that converts radio signals sent by the transmitter into electrical impulses.

Rib: the internal, vertical portion of the wing that gives it an airfoil-shaped contour.

Rudder: the vertical control surface that controls yaw.

Servo: an electromagnetic device that moves the control surfaces and is controlled by the electrical impulses from the receiver.

Stall: the point at which the wing experiences a loss of lift; the aircraft will tend to drop abruptly.

Trailing edge (TE): the aft-most edge of an airfoil or propeller.

Transmitter: the hand-held part of the radio system that sends the signal to the receiver.

Trim: the adjustment of a model's control surfaces to obtain a stable and balanced flight performance.

Vertical fin: a fixed, vertical stabilizer that reduces the model's tendency to yaw about the vertical axis.

Wing chord (chord): the distance measured horizontally between the wing's LE and TE.

Yaw: the left or right movement of an aircraft's nose about its vertical axis.

Z-bend: shaped like a "Z," it is the simplest way to connect a pushrod to a control horn or servo-output arm.

ACADEMY OF MODEL AERONAUTICS (AMA)
5161 East Memorial Dr., Muncie, IN 47302; (765) 287-1256; fax (765) 289-4248; www.modelaircraft.org.

ACE HOBBY DISTRIBUTORS
2682 Walnut Ave., Tustin, CA 92780; (714) 544-0633; www.acehobby.com.

AERO-MODEL INC.
2122 W. 5th Place, Tempe, AZ 85281; (480) 726-7519; fax (480) 963-5565; aeromodel@qwest.net; www.aero-model.com.

AEROVIRONMENT
825 S. Myrtle Dr., Monrovia, CA 91096; (626) 357-9933; www.aerovironment.com.

AIRPLANE PLANET INC.
14551 Judicial Rd., Ste. 140, Burnsville, MN 55306.

AIRTRONICS
1185 Stanford Ct., Anaheim, CA 92805; (714) 978-1895; fax (714) 978-1540; www.airtronics.net.

ANDERSON POWER PRODUCTS
(978) 422-3800; www.andersonpower.com.

ANYTHING R/C
Chris Hansen; 1822 E. 40th Ave., Spokane, WA 99203; (509) 747-2526; fax (509) 456-6430; chris@anythingr-c.com; info@anythingr-c.com.

APC PROPS
Distributed by Landing Products, 1222 Harter Ave., Woodland, CA 95776; (530) 661-0399; fax (530) 666-6661; www.apcprop.com.

ASTROFLIGHT INC.
13311 Beach Ave., Marina del Rey, CA 90292; (310) 821-6242; fax (310) 822-6637; www.astroflight.com.

AVEOX ELECTRIC FLIGHT SYSTEMS
31324 Via Colinas, #103, Westlake Village, CA 91362; (818) 597-8915; fax (818) 597-0617; www.aveox.com.

BACKYARD FLYER
AIR AGE PUBLISHING
100 East Ridge, Ridgefield, CT 06877-4606; to subscribe, call (800) 479-5849; www.backyardflyer.com.

BALSA PRODUCTS
122 Jansen Ave., Iselin, NJ 08830-2601; (732) 634-6131; www.balsapr.com.

BATTERIES AMERICA—E. H. YOST & CO.
2211 D Parview Rd., Middleton, WI 53562; (608) 831-3443; (800) 308-4805; ehyost@midplains.net; www.batteriesamerica.com.

BILL GRIGGS MODELS
3137 Whitelaw Rd., Canastota, NY 13032; (315) 697-8152; www.griggsmodels.com.

BMC MODEL PRODUCTS
10060 Maclura Ct., Fairfax, VA 22032; sales@bmcproducts.com; www.bmcproducts.com.

BOB SELMAN DESIGNS
9054 Gum Rd., Carthage, MO 64836; phone/fax (417) 358-9521; bselman@joplin.com; www.bsd.domainvalet.com.

BRAUN MODELLTECHNIK
Lagerhausstrasse 105 D-67061 Ludwigshafen, Germany; phone/fax (06 21) 56 71 52; braunmod@-online.de; www.braunmod.de.

B&T R/C PRODUCTS
508 Lake Winds Trail, Rougemont, NC 27572; (919) 471-2060.

CARL GOLDBERG MODELS
(UltraCote covering); 4734 W. Chicago Ave., Chicago, IL 60651; (773) 626-9550.

CARL MARTIN
2906 North 5th St., Coeur d'Alene, ID 83815; (208) 765-8826; cmartin@nidlink.com.

CASTLE CREATIONS
18773 W. 117 St., Olathe, KS 66061; (913) 438-6325; fax (913) 438-1394; pdelcast@air.net; www.castlerc.com.

CIRRUS VENTURES
115 Hunter Ave., Fanwood, NJ 07023-1030; (908) 322-7221.

CLOUD 9 RC
4326 Andes Dr., Fairfax, VA 22030; phone/fax (703) 273-0607; jwc9@mindspring.com; www.rcmicroflight.com/venders.

DAVE'S AIRCRAFT WORKS
34455 Camino El Molino, Capistrano Beach, CA 92624; (949) 248-2773; www.davesaircraftworks.com.

DAVE BROWN PRODUCTS INC.
4560 Layhigh Rd., Hamilton, OH 45013; (513) 738-1576; www.dbproducts.com.

DAVID LEWIS
3435 South Orange Ave., K205, Orlando, FL 32806; (407) 856-6245; dlewis@homefly.com; www.homefly.com.

DICK MILLER
rcm65@ptd.net; http://home.ptd.net/~rcm65.

DJ AEROTECH
719 Fisk St., Piqua, OH 45356; (937) 773-6772; fax (937) 773-9494; www.djaerotech.com.

DU-BRO PRODUCTS
P.O. Box 815, Wauconda, IL 60084; (800) 848-9411; fax (847) 526-1604; www.dubro.com.

DUMAS
909-A E. 17th St., Tucson, AZ 85719; (520) 623-3742; fax (520) 620-1329; for catalog: (800) 458-2828, ext. 600; dumas@azstarnet.com; www.dumasproducts.com.

DYMOND MODELSPORTS USA LTD.
683 N. Main St., Oshkosh, WI 54901; (888) 4FUN FLY; (920) 303-1100; fax (920) 303-2021; dymondrd@execpc.com; www.rc-dymond.com.

DYNAMICS UNLIMITED
2814 Cold Springs Rd., Baldwinsville, NY 13027; (315) 635-6290; du@tweny.rr.com; http://www.slowfly.com.

ECLECTIC ELECTRIC NECESSITIES/E CUBED R/C
1750 Lundgren Rd., New Carlisle, OH 45344; (937) 849-0418; info@ecubedrc.com; www.azarr.com.

ELECTRICALC/SLK ELECTRONICS
2906 Charolais Dr., Greensboro, NC 27406; www.slkelectronics.com/ecalc.

ELECTRIC JET FACTORY
8929 N. Ferber Ct., Tucson, AZ 85742; (520) 579-5609; fax (520) 579-5610; www.electricjetfactory.com.

FMA DIRECT
9607 Dr. Perry Rd., Unit 109, Ijamsville, MD 21754; (800) 343-2934; fax (301) 831-8987; www.fmadirect.com.

FRITZ MUELLER
4117 Searcy St., Columbus, GA 31907; (706) 561-3345.

FUTABA CORP. OF AMERICA
Distributed by Great Planes Model Mfg. Co., P.O. Box 9021; Champaign, IL 61826-9021; (800) 637-7660; www.futaba-rc.com.

GLOBAL HOBBY DISTRIBUTORS
18480 Bandilier Cir., Fountain Valley, CA 92708; (714) 963-0133; fax (714) 962-6452; www.globalhobby.com.

GRAND WING SERVOS (GWS)
Distributed by Balsa Products, Global Hobby Distributors, Horizon Hobby Inc. and Maxx Products Intl.; gws@grandwing.com; www.grandwing.com.tw; Mr. Houng Wen Lin, 4F, 183, Sec. 1,Ta-Tung Rd., Shi-Jr City, Taipei Hsien, Taiwan, R.O.C.; 886-2-2647-0057; fax 886-2-2643-0292.

GRAUPNER
Distributed by Hobby Lobby Intl.; www.graupner.com.

GREAT PLANES MODEL MFG. CO.
P.O. Box 9021, Champaign, IL 61826-9021; (800) 637-7660; www.greatplanes.com.

GUNTHER
Distributed by Hobby Lobby Intl. and Cloud 9 RC.

HERR ENGINEERING
Distributed by Sig Mfg. Co. Inc.; www.iflyherr.com.

HILINE INC.
P.O. Box 11558, Goldsboro, NC 27532; (919) 778-6653.

HITEC RCD INC.
12115 Paine St., Poway, CA 92064; (858) 748-6948; fax (858) 748-1767; www.hitecrcd.com.

HOBBY CLUB INC.
P. O. Box 6004, San Clemente, CA 92674; (949) 240-4626; fax (949) 240-5931; www.hobbyclub.com.

HOBBY LOBBY INTL.
5614 Franklin Pike Cir., Brentwood, TN 37027; (615) 373-1444; fax (615) 377-6948; www.hobby-lobby.com.

HOBBY PEOPLE
www.hobbypeople.net.

HORIZON HOBBY INC.
4105 Fieldstone Rd., Champaign, IL 61822; (800) 338-4639; fax (217) 355-1552; www.horizonhobby.com.

HOUSE OF BALSA
10101 Yucca Rd., Adelanto, CA 92301; (760) 246 6462; fax (760) 246-8769; www.houseofbalsa.com.

IMA OF BELGIUM
Kapelstraat 15B, B2387 Baarle-Hertog, Belgium; ++32 (0)14-699855; imamodels@skynet.be; www.rc-zeppelins.com.

J.C. SMITH
(Z-bend pliers); 2-3418-5, Delta, OH 43515.

JMP SOLUTIONS
Distributed by David Lewis; Jean-Marie Piednoir; jpiednoir@clubinternet.fr.

JOHNSON
www.johnsonmotor.com.

JR
Distributed by Horizon Hobby Inc.

JST CONNECTORS
Distributed by Balsa Products and Batteries America.

K&P (KNIGHT & PRIDHAM)
(Props); available from David Lewis, Hobby Club and Kenway Micro Flight.

KENWAY MICRO FLIGHT
P.O. Box 889, Hackettstown, NJ 07840; fax (908) 850-9571.

KONTRONIK
72108 Rottenburg-Hailfingen, Etzwiesenstr. 35/1 Germany; distributed by Northeast Sailplane Products.

KREIGH'S MODELS (IFO)
Distributed by Hobby Lobby Intl.

MAGELLAN TECHNOLOGIES INC.
10783 Northhampton Dr., Fischer, IN 46038; (317) 507-3038; www.magtechinc.net; weaverr@iquest.net.

MARK'S HOBBY SHOP
208 Maplewood Ave., Oakhurst, NJ 07755; (732) 539-8002; www.parkflyers.com.

MASTER AIRSCREW
Distributed by Windsor Propeller Co., P.O. Box 250, Rancho Cordova, CA 95741-0250; (916) 631-8385; fax (916) 631-8386; www.masterairscrew.com.

MAXX PRODUCTS INTL.
815 Oakwood Rd., Unit D, Lake Zurich, IL 60047; (847) 438-2233; fax (847) 438-2898; www.maxxprod.com.

MEGATECH INTL.
(201) 662-8500, ext. 115; www.megatech.com.

MICROMAG R/C SYSTEM
Rick Ruijsink; distributed by FMA Direct, Bob Selman Designs and David Lewis.

MICROX
P.O. Box 1063-A, Lorain, OH 44055; (440) 282-8354; microx@erinet.net.

MIKE DORFFLER
2418 Greenway Cir., Canon City, CO 81212; mkdorffler@earthlink.net.

MODEL AIRPLANE NEWS
AIR AGE PUBLISHING INC.
100 East Ridge, Ridgefield, CT 06877-4606; to subscribe, call (800) 827-0323; www.modelairplanenews.com.

MODELAIR-TECH
P.O. Box 1467, Lake Grove, NY 11755-0867; (631) 981-0372; Tomhunt@optonline.net; www.modelairtech.com.

MOTOCALC
Capable Computing Inc., RR3, Moorfield, Ontario, Canada N0G 2K0; (519) 638-5470; fax (519) 638-2812; www.motocalc.com.

MTM INTL.
Walkemuhlenweg 29, 37083 Gottingen, Germany; fax +49-551-770-7736; www.mtm-int.com.

NATIONAL INDOOR REMOTE-CONTROLLED AIRCRAFT COUNCIL (NIRAC)
Bob Wilder, president; 1005 Hidden Oaks Ct., Colleyville, TX 76034; (817) 498-6316; rjwmaw5@flash.net; www.nirac.org.

NEAT FAIR
Tom Hunt, event director; P.O. Box 1446, Lake Grove, NY 11755; (631) 981-0372; neatfair@optonline.net; www.neatfair.org.

NEW CREATIONS R/C
P.O. Box 496, Willis, TX 77378; phone/fax (936) 856-4630; kmassey14@cs.com.

NORTHEAST SAILPLANE PRODUCTS
948 Hercules Dr., Ste. 12, Colchester, VT 05446; (802) 655-7700; fax (802) 655-7755; www.nesail.com.

PEAK ELECTRONICS INC.
12520 Kirkham Ct. #8, Poway, CA 92064; (800) 532-0092; sales@siriuselectronics.com; www.siriuselectronics.com.

PECK-POLYMERS
P.O. Box 710399, Santee, CA 92072; (619) 448-1818; (619) 448-1833; www.peck-polymers.com.

PENN VALLEY HOBBY CENTER
837-A W. Main St., Lansdale, PA 19446; www.pennvalleyhobbycenter .com.

PROFILI
(Airfoil plotting software); Stefano Duranti; http://digilander.iol.it/neon1 /profili.html.

RADICAL RC
7046 Harshmanville Rd., Huber Hts., OH 45424; fax (937) 237-1521; davthacker@aol.com; www.radicalrc.com.

RC DIRECT
7750 Convoy Ct., San Diego, CA 92111; (619) 560-9695.

RC MICROFLIGHT
AIR AGE PUBLISHING
100 East Ridge, Ridgefield, CT 06877-4606; to subscribe, call (800) 243-6685; www.rcmicroflight.com.

RCS TECHNIK
22 Dartmouth Park Ave., London, England NW5 1JN; phone/fax 011-44-171-267-9049; rcstechnik@sesnet.net.

REV UP
Distributed by Peck-Polymers.

ROBBE MODEL SPORT
Distributed by Aveox Electric Flight Systems.

SERMOS R/C SNAP CONNECTORS INC.
Cedar Corners Station, Box 16787, Stamford, CT 06905; phone/fax (203) 322-6294.

SIG MFG. CO. INC.
P.O. Box 520, Montezuma, IA 50171; (800) 247-5008; (515) 623-5154; fax (515) 623-3922; mail@sigmfg.com; www.sigmfg.com.

SIRIUS
(Chargers); distributed by Peak Electronics.

SKY HOOKS & RIGGING
2206 Towne Blvd., Oakville, Ontario, Canada L6H 5H4; (905) 257-2101; fax (905) 257-0168; info@microrc.com; www.microrc.com.

SONIC-TRONICS
7865 Mill Rd., Elkins Park, PA, 19027-2796; (215) 635-6520; fax (215) 635-4951.

SOUTHWESTERN AEROMODELING CONFERENCE (SWAC)
Sandy Frank; 105 N. Brazos St., Weatherford, TX 76086-3207; (817) 599-7131; sfrank69@airmail.net; www.Dist-8.org.

SR BATTERIES INC.
Box 287, Bellport, NY 11713; (631) 286-0079; fax (631) 286-0901; www.srbatteries.com.

STAR FLIGHT
Alex Larionov; 1501 Woodbine Ave. #1417, Toronto, Ontario, Canada M4C 4H1; (416) 424-1607; www.jutstar.com.

SULLIVAN PRODUCTS
One North Haven St., Baltimore, MD 21224; (410) 732-3500; fax (410) 327-7443; www.sullivanproducts.com.

TADIRAN
Distributed by Magellan Technologies, David Lewis, Sky Hooks & Rigging and Todd's Models.

TITANIC AIRLINES
Distributed by Modelair-Tech.

TNC CUSTOM ELECTRONICS AND SOFTWARE
2 Whites Ln., Woodstock, NY 12498; (914) 679-8549; fax (914) 679-5542; tns@ulster.net; www.ulster.net/~tncweb.html.

TNR TECHNICAL
301 Central Park Dr., Sanford, FL 32771; (800) 346-0601; www.batterystore.com.

TODD'S MODELS
Todd Long; P.O. Box 827, Snoqualmie, WA 98065; (425) 888-8530; todd@toddsmodels.com; www.toddsmodels.com.

TOM NOTTI
(Prop adapters); 149 Porterfield Creek Dr., Cloverdale, CA 95425-5404; (707) 894-7336.

TOP FLITE
Distributed by Great Planes Model Mfg. Co.

TOWER HOBBIES
P.O. Box 9078, Champaign, IL 61826-9078; (800) 637-6050; fax (800) 637-7303; www.towerhobbies.com.

UNION MODEL CO.
(Propellers); distributed by Peck-Polymers.

VARTA
www.varta.com/eng.

VL PRODUCTS
2934½ Beverly Glen Cir., #255, Los Angeles, CA 90077; (310) 271-4805.

WATTAGE
Distributed by Global Hobby Distributors.

WEAK SIGNALS R/C TRADE SHOW (TOLEDO)
www.toledoshow.com.

WES-TECHNIK
Distributed by David Lewis, Todd's Models and Sky Hooks & Rigging.

WESTCHESTER RADIO AERO MODELERS (WRAM) HOBBY TRADE SHOW
www.wram.org.

W.S. DEANS CO.
7628 Jackson St., Paramount, CA 90723; (562) 634-9401; www.wsdeans.com.

Z TRON
Sergio Zigras; 171 Arundel Rd., Paramus, NJ 07652; http://home.att.net /~szigras.